Mad about Wildlife

Human–Animal Studies

Editor

Kenneth Shapiro

Society and Animals Forum

VOLUME 2

Mad about Wildlife

Looking at social conflict over wildlife

Edited by
Ann Herda-Rapp
and
Theresa L. Goedeke

BRILL
LEIDEN • BOSTON
2005

Cover: the photograph in the lower right corner is reproduced by kind permission of Rocky Mountain National Park.

This book is printed on acid-free paper.

Library of Congress Cataloging-in-Publication data

Mad about wildlife: looking at social conflict over wildlife/edited by Ann Herda-Rapp and Theresa L. Goedeke.
    p. cm. — (Human-animal studies, ISSN 1573-4226; v. 2)
  Includes bibliographical references and index.
  ISBN 90-04-14366-1 (pbk.: alk. paper)
    1. Animal rights. 2. Wildlife management. 3. Social conflict. 4. Human-animal relationships. I. Herda-Rapp, Ann. II. Goedeke, Theresa L. III. Series.

HV4708.M33 2005
179'.3—dc22   2005041988

ISSN 1573-4226
ISBN 90 04 14366 1

© Copyright 2005 by Koninklijke Brill NV, Leiden, The Netherlands. Koninklijke Brill NV incorporates the imprints Brill Academic Publishers, Martinus Nijhoff Publishers and VSP.

PRINTED IN THE NETHERLANDS

CONTENTS

PART THREE

DECONSTRUCTING AND RECONSTRUCTING
WILDLIFE POLICY APPROACHES

LIST OF ILLUSTRATIONS

Tables

Figures

Maps

ACKNOWLEDGEMENTS

Foremost, we want to acknowledge the extraordinary efforts and patience of our contributors throughout the editorial and publication process. It was easy to work industriously for folks who always stepped up to shoulder their share of the task. Some papers included in this volume were originally presented at the annual meetings of the Midwest Sociological Society (MSS) in sessions organized by the editors between 2000 and 2002. We offer our thanks to the MSS for facilitating the intellectual exploration and growth of sociologists interested in wildlife issues. We sincerely appreciate Brill Academic Publishers and the insight and assistance of Kenneth Shapiro and our Brill reviewers. Special thanks to Clinton Sanders, Joel Best, Sandy Rikoon and David O'Brien for their advice and encouragement along the way, and to our numerous reviewers who offered critiques and suggestions on earlier versions of the book prospectus. We would like to thank the Government of Canada, Fisheries and Oceans for giving permission to reprint copyrighted material. Thanks also to the Information Technology staff, Rose Brust and Scott Bouffleur, at the University of Wisconsin-Marathon County for their help in preparing graphics and maps, to UW-Marathon County reference librarian, Todd Roll, for his sleuthing, to Beth Bouffleur for translation assistance, and to the UW-Marathon County's Distinguised Faculty Society for its support of this project. Finally, on a more personal note, we both express our deep gratitude to our families who indulgently bore with our long hours of editing.

INTRODUCTION

Theresa L. Goedeke and Ann Herda-Rapp

Competition over habitat and natural resources, the core conflict between wildlife[1] and people, often gives rise to complex social issues. This is because there are essentially two dimensions to modern human-wildlife conflict, and they are closely related. The first dimension centers on conflict between people and wild animals. This friction may arise from the negative interactions that people have with wildlife, both individual animals (e.g., a raccoon in the chimney) and populations (e.g., flocks of geese on a golf course). The second dimension, and the focus of the present volume, encompasses conflicts among people, which frequently accompany instances of the former (e.g., public debate about if and how to decrease populations of Canada geese).

People can experience either positive or negative interactions with wildlife.[2] The competition between wildlife and agricultural producers, the encroachment of people into wildlife habitat and the ability of wild animals to adapt to human communities all pave the way for negative encounters. Farmers and ranchers have perpetually pitted themselves and their industry against wildlife, mostly to the detriment of the latter. Elk, prairie dogs and bison, for instance, are despised for browsing on row crops or grass earmarked for livestock. Some wildlife species, such as the American bison, potentially play host to diseases feared by ranchers or public health officials. Finally, ranchers still commonly advance the age-old complaint that predators, such as wolves and grizzly bears, pose a threat to domestic livestock and, consequently, profit margins.

However, the fate of the rural or agricultural way of life is in many ways similar to that of wildlife as both come up against the new environments that we craft for future generations and ourselves. As the human population continues to increase throughout much of the world, people move about the landscape aspiring to those lifestyle choices presently *en vogue*; they are in hot pursuit of economic progress and personal dreams. The last remnants of habitat, often disguised as agricultural lands, fall to concrete mixers just as prairies fell to plows in the late 1800s and early 1900s. In our effort to grow an economy and increase the standard of living, we are quickly reducing, altering or eliminating lands formerly used by wild animals.

Many creatures fare poorly when human-induced changes disrupt their surroundings and lives; these species frequently become rare or endangered. As this extirpation occurs, society must then decide whether or not to save such species, assuming we can figure out how to do that. Other wild animals make themselves at home in human communities, greatly benefiting from a human-dominated landscape or advantaged by their human stewards. Such animals have shifted in the human conscience from wildlife to nuisances or pests (Manning 2003). Urban crows and raccoons dine on the discarded food scraps dropped curbside (Ruben 2003), while deer nibble to nubs the prize plants of home gardeners (Singer 2004).

There are numerous native species, along with exotic animals, that exploit our changes to the natural world. These creatures, such as sea gulls, starlings, raccoons and rats, are frequently the focus of deep-seated loathing among people. Even species that people value for aesthetic and economic reasons, such as white-tail deer, Canada geese, beavers or rabbits, are viewed as nuisance wildlife if they are abundant and habitually frequent the wrong places at the wrong times.[3] In either case, government officials, property owners and sportspeople trap, shoot, poison and otherwise control such animals to alleviate the inconveniences and perils experienced by people and, often, other non-human species that might become endangered without such intervention.

As we usurp the habitat of wild creatures, encounters between animals and people at the urban and suburban interfaces with still-wild lands can turn injurious or deadly. Livestock and even pet animals are taken by predatory wildlife (General Accounting Office 2001). Moreover, people, to their surprise and horror, are not necessarily exempt from the harsh reality of the food chain. Predators have been known to attack, injure and, occasionally, kill people who venture, work or build into a predator's space (General Accounting Office 2001; Stange 2004). Fewer than five people die each year as a consequence of attacks from wild animals (General Accounting Office 2001); nevertheless, as we continue to alter more of the landscape our once distant, predatory neighbors may adjust their behavioral responses to fit into the new suburbia (Davis 1998).

The second dimension of human-wildlife conflict is spurred by the first. Unlike the encroachment of society into wild places, however, this dimension is purely social. In these cases, conflict over wildlife plays out between people. As society becomes more diversified and people hold more varied views about human domination over the environment, nature and wildlife, clashes between groups of people who understand human-wildlife conflict differently will grow in frequency and intensity.

While some social groups advocate for wildlife or habitat, others safeguard the interests of people; how each group acts depends upon how they understand the interests of ecology and society. Reasonable people disagree on what is to be done about issues like urban deer, flocks of crows and spotted owls. Moreover, wildlife often become surrogates for deeply embedded cultural discords within communities. Sociologists have increasingly examined the character, substance and deeper meanings of these social conflicts.

Nature, Environment and Social Problems

Surely, no one who has walked along a beach accompanied by only shorebirds or hiked along a mountain trail bursting with the color of spring wildflowers can deny the existence of nature. Even the most oblivious, anthropocentric of people cannot ignore the reality of a dust storm, tornado, hurricane or flood. Nature is real enough, as are the effects of natural processes and the consequences of human activity.

However, human perceptions of, understandings about and relationships with nature are in many respects more complicated than the reality of the shorebird, the wildflower or the flood. Further, to recover shorebirds, preserve wildflowers and live with floods, we, as a society, must understand the unique place each holds in human culture. Constructionist theory, the approach used in this volume, aids us in this task.

The contribution of a constructionist approach to studies of the environment is its analysis of the varied meanings of nature created by social groups. From this theoretical yet empirically-grounded perspective, nature is not *Nature* and this distinction is critical to understanding human relationships to the natural world. Nature, with an N, embodies the cultural meanings and connotations created by people within a society or social group to make sense of the natural and relate to natural things (Evernden 1992; Williams 1998). In other words, our perceptions of nature (i.e., the actual objects) are sifted through our cultural frameworks, experiences, training and expectations and what we end up with is our own peculiar version of Nature. We see shorebirds and floods (i.e., nature), but how we understand them as a part of Nature is a product of social interactions and our own cultural milieu. Gary Alan Fine (1997:70, emphasis original) explains it this way: "While individual trees and birds exist, nature as a *concept* derives from human cognition, cultural activity, and social organization."

Our personal experiences are important as we organize our impressions of Nature, but those impressions are culturally embedded. In other words, we understand our personal interactions with places, plants and non-human animals in light of cultural values and beliefs, and in relation to the shared experiences we have within that context. For example, people raised in a community valuing hunting will most likely understand – socially construct – deer differently than those who grew up watching suburban "Bambi's" from the kitchen window. Individual experiences and interactions with nature then mediate these cultural preferences. Thus, individual perceptions of Nature, termed *naturework* by Fine (1997, 1998), are framed by the broader social processes of making meanings of deer.

Comprehending human relationships with nature in this manner is helpful because it enables us to detect and recognize different versions of Nature. Differences may occur between persons from different cultures, such as between Western-Europeans and Native Americans. Variations may also exist between groups with different views within the same broader culture, referred to as subcultures. For example, bird watchers and developers in the United States have drastically different perceptions of landscapes, birds and seasons.

When attempting to understand cultural relationships with Nature, it is also important to consider larger social contexts, historic events and cultural developments (Macnaghten and Urry 1998). Nature, with an N, is not static, but changes through time and space. Scientists and theologians, for instance, championed the separation of culture and Nature during the Scientific Revolution, which began in the sixteenth century (Worster 1994). During this shift, people in Western

cultures re-created Nature. In contrast to that of their pagan ancestors, the new Nature was no longer organic, but mechanical, and
set apart from civilization and people (Eisler 1987; Merchant 1980).
According to Barbara Noske (1992:226), modern biology emerged
from this context, viewing animals as specimens to be "controlled,
measured and quantified." With that shift, the animal-other and the
nature-other came into being. Thus, the conceptual split between
Nature and Society led to the subjugation of the former to the latter in Western traditions.

The meaning of Nature, then, is embedded within specific socio-
historical contexts and, consequently, Nature transforms as its context (i.e., culture) changes (Macnaghten and Urry 1998). William
Freudenberg, Scott Frickel and Robert Gramling (1995) illustrate this
phenomenon in their analysis of Iron Mountain, which is located in
the Upper Peninsula of Michigan. First, Native Americans constructed
Iron Mountain as a spiritual landscape rich in plants and animals.
As industrial economy and forestry came to dominate definitions of
the landscape, the timber industry imposed a new connotation on
Iron Mountain; from holy ground to the "logging capital of the
world," a boomtown and, eventually, a bust-town. With new forests
and new social values, most recently, local entrepreneurs and vaca-
tioners have reclaimed the trees and hills. Now Iron Mountain's construction is that of entertainment, a tourist attraction. Through time,
those having the power and position to define the environs of Iron
Mountain did so based on their own peculiar definition of Nature,
which was guided by culture in the form of knowledge, interests,
preferences, values and so on.

Of course, definitions of nature can vary between cultures and,
further, they can vary in the same place at the same time. Speaking
about differing definitions of landscapes, Thomas Greider and Lorraine
Garkovich (1994:2) explain that "meanings are not inherent." Rather,

> ... the symbols and meanings that comprise landscapes reflect what
> people in cultural groups define to be the proper and improper rela-
> tionships between themselves and between themselves and the physi-
> cal environment.

In a similar vein, James Proctor (1998:194) describes what he calls
"an ideological landscape" as the "... meaningful representation of
human values and interests, of social and human-environment relations,

embodied geographically in the land." Different groups of people relate to the natural world under the influence of their own culture or subculture. This multiplicity of constructions centering on the same nature (whether places or species) creates coexisting and, frequently, competing understandings about Nature and its components. As a result we can have opposing definitions of landscapes (Greider and Garkovich 1994), oceans (Steinberg 2001) and fish (Scarce 2000; Schreiber, Matthews and Elliott 2003) within a single society, all at the same time.

These coexisting constructions of Nature are often the source of social conflict over environmental and natural resource issues. Consider, for example, the ongoing battle over the use of Yucca Mountain, located in Nevada, as the answer for long-term storage of nuclear waste products in the United States. Valerie Kuletz (1998:139), in *The Tainted Desert*, explores the different meanings attached to Yucca Mountain:

> [I]f one sees Yucca Mountain as having *Puha* [spirit power], it becomes problematic to designate it as a burial tomb for toxic waste. If one sees Yucca Mountain as a mass of inanimate material, such as "welded tuft," with characteristics that discourage water permeability [. . .] then one might more easily consider its use as a toxic waste dump.

Even within the scientific community, the mountain takes on different meanings. Ecologists define the region as part of a desert ecosystem, while earth scientists peer through the prism of geology, hydrology and volcanology and see something different yet. This situation leads to the existence of varying definitions for the same mountain and, more importantly, spawns competing beliefs about what the appropriate human relationship to that mountain should be.

In situations where different groups of people disagree about appropriate human-environmental relationships, social scientists have used social problems analysis as one tool to understand resulting conflict. Social constructionists, building on ideas introduced by Peter Berger and Thomas Luckmann (1966), hold that environmental problems must be understood as subjective, social realties, in addition to physical conditions. John A. Hannigan (1995:56), who wrote the first comprehensive book on the application of constructionist theory to environmental problems from a sociological perspective, demonstrates that "environmentalism itself is a multi-faceted construction which welds together a clutch of philosophies, ideologies, scientific specialties and policy initiatives." His lesson is that when considering environmental conflicts, one must be aware of the multitude of definitions of Nature that come to bear as people debate and promote particular environmental issues as social problems.

The take-home point of viewing environmental issues as social problems is that "whether and how [environmental] changes come to be seen and treated as problematic is an inherently social process" (Burningham 1998:559–560). So, examination of these processes can answer questions like, why would a government create regulations to screen for Bovine Spongiform Encephalopathy (BSE) in cattle, but neglect policy to mitigate the possible long-term effects of climate change? A social scientist can find answers to such questions by investigating the social processes at work in 1) defining an environmental condition as problematic, and 2) making policy and other decisions about environmental, natural resource and public health issues. To examine environmental quandaries, social constructionists have investigated:

- the production of meanings about nature and environmental events;
- the rhetorical tools used and claims made by actors, often called claims-makers, who have an interest in particular issues, things, places or events;
- the arenas or social institutions wherein debate over issues takes place (e.g., the media, Internet, legislature, court system, etc.);
- the importance of an actor's social networks and political/social coalitions;
- the power relations between opposing groups (e.g., Greenpeace versus the D.R. Johnson logging company) and between groups as they stand before agencies and institutions of influence (e.g., Greenpeace versus the D.R. Johnson logging company as they both lobby the U.S. Congress).

Using a social problems framework, social constructionists have explored a variety of environmental and public health issues such as earthquakes (Stallings 1995), acid rain (Hannigan 1995), biodiversity loss (Hannigan 1995), bovine growth hormones (Hannigan 1995; MacMillan 2003), global warming (Demeritt 2000; Unger 1992), mushroom "overpick" (Fine 1997) and development of marshlands (Harrison and Burgess 1994). In each of these cases, claims-makers,

who can be media (see Schoenfeld, Meier and Griffin 1979), environmental movement organizations (see Čapek 1993), scientists (see
Hannigan 1995), government agencies and industry (see Litmanen
1995) and others, offer their own interpretation or *frame* of the issue.
Frames, or the particular rhetorical structures created by claims-makers to define a problem (Goffman 1974), are often presented using
persuasive verbal and visual imagery.

   Despite its potential for helping us better understand cultural relationships with the natural world, constructionist theory is criticized
by some as a destructive and dangerous pursuit within the environmental context (see Murphy 1994, 1997; Soulé 1995; Wilson 1998).
We would like, therefore, to briefly anticipate critiques of this volume by reclaiming the theory. The main point of criticism against
social constructionist work is that it distracts from real issues by shifting concern away from the objective reality of nature (e.g., the actual
ecological value of a wetland) or existing environmental problems
(e.g., arsenic in a river or lake). Ted Benton (1994:46) complained
that the sociologist "effectively excludes the environmental issues
themselves from investigation" by focusing on the competition between
cultural definitions of environmental problems. In short, these critics argue that constructionist approaches 1) deny the existence of the
physical environment in the absence of someone's construction of it,
and 2) are unconcerned with objective environmental conditions.

   The thrust of criticism against constructionist studies is waged
against strict constructionism – that espoused by Malcolm Spector,
John Kitsuse and Peter Ibarra[4] – which contends that objective conditions are unimportant and should not be part of social analysis.
Burningham and Cooper (1999:303) point out, however, that "the
majority" of environmental researchers doing constructionist work
rely on mild or contextual constructionism. Mild constructionism
focuses on processes involved in the formation of institutions and
meanings (artifacts of the social) while contextual constructionism
compares social realities against the actual environmental conditions
or natural facts (Best 1995; Burningham and Cooper 1999). Indeed,
the most persuasive critique of strict constructionism comes from
contextual constructionists who argue that constructionist researchers
cannot, merely out of theoretical purity, ignore "interesting" questions
that emerge from claims about objective conditions (see Best 1993).

   The studies we described above exemplify a constructionist approach that acknowledges the existence of "the environment" but

directs the researcher's attention to the social, that is, to our con-
textually-derived definitions of the environment and assertions of
"truth." While the approach advocated by strict constructionists pre-
cludes analysis of value statements about Nature and the environment, this introduction has highlighted numerous studies that
thoughtfully examine the context of claims-making about and around
environmental problems. Social constructions of environmental problems – about the problem's causes, consequences, nature, etc. – present a wealth of "interesting" and compelling questions. Their analysis
is important because the answers may provide valuable insight into
potential management and policy ramifications and actions in times
of social disagreement.

    There is an important link between studies examining the social
construction of Nature and those that examine environmental issues
as social problems: if different groups did not compete over varying
definitions of Nature, there would most likely be little conflict regarding environmental issues in general. For example, if we all believed
that Yucca Mountain was sacred then the question of whether or
not to store toxic, nuclear waste within it would be moot. That not
being the case, there is certainly a role for social scientists to play
in helping to untangle conflict over natural resources. Contributors
in the present volume hope to expand the efforts within environmental sociology to include issues of wildlife, a highly contested part
of nature in modern human society. To date we know of no volume that applies the theoretical perspective to *wildlife* issues. This
text attempts to step into that void.

Connections to Wild Things: Nature, Wildlife and Society

The body of scholarship exploring people's involvement with wildlife,
which is termed the human or social dimension of wildlife [man-
agement], has only gained prominence as an area of investigation
within the last three decades or so. Social scientists, by and large,
have overlooked wildlife as a subject of study, while natural scientists, particularly those schooled in natural resource management,
took the lead on these issues. The latter's interest, as resource practitioners, was and remains predominantly applied; it is focused on
the very pragmatic and pressing need to learn how to manipulate
wildlife and, while doing so, effectively manage the people who take

an interest in these issues. Considering the latter goal, scholars have urged managers and agencies to categorize people into publics, stake-holders, user groups, customers or constituents in order to manage them more effectively (Decker and Chase 1997; Wright, Backman and Wicks 1991). It is not surprising, therefore, that a body of research rooted predominantly in theories and practical considera-tions of marketing and public relations has emerged (see Responsive Management National Office 1998).

The dominant stream of literature on human relationships to wildlife, pioneered by Stephen R. Kellert (1980), has been driven by quantitative assessments of human attitudes toward and perceptions about various types of animals. Since the early 1980s researchers have considered public perceptions of wolves (Bright and Manfredo 1996; Kellert 1985a; Williams, Ericsson and Heberlein 2002), moun-tain sheep (Harris, Krausman and Shaw 1995), endangered species (Kellert 1985b) and bandicoots (Reading, Clark and Arnold 1994). Other researchers have emphasized attitudes toward conservation, restoration and reintroduction (Czech and Krausman 1997; Enck and Brown 2002; Pate et al. 1996; Reading and Kellert 1993), as well as particular management practices and philosophies (Reiter, Brunson and Schmidt 1999; Teel, Krannich and Schmidt 2002).

In addition to research specifically focusing on wildlife, quantita-tive researchers have also been interested in the wildlife-related activ-ities and recreation. They have explored, for example, opinions and preferences regarding hunting and fishing (Bissell and Duda 1993; Duda 1993; Heberlein and Willebrand 1998). Finally, some investi-gators have narrowed their emphasis to issues of valuation, asking how individuals and groups value, rate and rank particular animals or wildlife experiences (Driscoll 1995; Kellert 1984). All of these types of studies combined have allowed managers to understand how people might react to different management efforts, which has aided them to better tailor programs to particular groups and to promote their programs and policies more effectively to the public at large.

Quantitative assessments of human-wildlife issues have led to impor-tant insights about the attitudes of people toward wild animals and management. However, while identifying demographic predictors and creating typologies to gauge the public's orientation toward wildlife is serviceable, such efforts do little to explain *why* people have these value-orientations in the first place. Nor do such approaches pro-vide any inkling about which public sentiments are flexible or ephemeral and which are deeply enmeshed in the focal culture or subculture.

Consequently, the coarse data yielded from quantitative approaches cannot effectively shed light on the nuances of beliefs and ideologies that exist within and among people about wildlife. These types of studies cannot help us discover why and how a group's orientation to Nature might shape their social activism. As a result, quantitative studies are of dubious value when trying to reliably anticipate when social conflict will erupt over the range of wildlife and management policy issues. Moreover, they fail to provide critical information about how the multitude of views regarding issues might be understood and, perhaps, reconciled, thereby avoiding the manifestation of full-blown social conflict.

As the human population grows and space for wildlife shrinks correspondingly, American society will certainly experience more differences of perspective about how we ought to deal with wildlife-related issues (e.g., endangered species, hunting, animal damage control, etc.). In contemporary culture, where meanings of Nature grow more varied, groups of people will more frequently disagree with their neighbors over wildlife and management issues in their own backyard. As a result, we, as a society, will increasingly face the task of understanding and reconciling the demands of many groups of people with divergent views of Nature, from which emerge competing agendas about its relevance, use and management.

To meet this challenge, and because the stakes grow higher for both wildlife and people, it is necessary for us to more completely understand meanings, the basis of conflict, on multiple levels. We propose that, in addition to quantitative assessments, we must employ qualitative research to get at these nuances and to achieve finer levels of understanding. By allowing our investigations into human-wildlife issues to become more multidimensional, we will be better able to identify critical issues that create conflict and, hopefully, find additional, innovative ways to manage those disagreements. Recently, social scientists have begun work to expand thinking in this area by employing more detailed, qualitative studies on important social questions about wildlife.

Historians were among the first social scientists to look at wildlife issues in a qualitative way. Through their efforts we have seen the importance of culture in shaping human understandings and relationships to wildlife through time. Susan L. Flader (1974), for example,

chronicles the emergence and development of Aldo Leopold's ecological understanding of nature, a redefinition of Nature that eventually changed the face and form of professional wildlife management
in the United States. Similarly, Thomas R. Dunlap (1988) examines
the intertwining of popular knowledge and ecological ideology over
time, a phenomenon that ultimately affected America's approval of
unqualified federal predator control programs.[5] Dunlap (1991) also
critically considers the social context wherein the program to recover
Whooping Cranes originated and, later, evolved.

Other histories of wildlife, not necessarily written by historians,
enlighten us on the impacts that people have had on wildlife. For
example, David S. Wilcove (1999), an ecologist, documents the unfettered exploitation of wildlife and, in numerous cases, its consequent
destruction in the United States. Similarly, a number of historical
treatments by biologists and legal scholars document the activities of
government to protect and manage the wildlife remaining at the turn
of the last century (Alvarez 1993; Bean 1983; Clark and Westrum
1987; Tobin 1990; Yaffee 1995).

Recently, sociologists have entered the field, trying to contribute
new understandings about wildlife in human culture. As with trees
and mountains, people form cultural relationships to wildlife, which
are mediated by their own definition of Nature. Moreover, how people construct Nature necessarily governs how they understand and
regard 1) people who define or facilitate symbolic meanings about
wildlife (e.g., managers, biologists or hunters), and 2) practices that
are culturally-sanctioned, patterned human interactions with wildlife
and their habitat (e.g., legal protection, hunting or bulldozing).

Keith Tester (1991:46) suggests that ". . . animals are indeed a
blank paper which can be inscribed with any message, and symbolic
meaning, that the social wishes." Hence, meanings inscribe a set of
relationships between society and wildlife. Using a constructionist
theoretical grounding, therefore, sociologists have begun two broad
categories of study in an effort to divine these relationships. The first
is how people gain knowledge about wildlife, through scientific research
for instance, and how that knowledge base guides their definitions
or understandings. In these types of studies, social scientists have
examined the tools or processes through which meanings are made
for particular species, meanings that then serve as the bedrock for
deciding the appropriate human relationships to and interactions with
those animals.

Rik Scarce (2000), by taking up the question of what salmon are to the salmon biologists who study them, explains that there are a number of varying meanings imposed on this single type of fish. What salmon are and represent depends upon the particular sub-cultural standpoint, or view, created by different types of scientists within the scientific community. For instance, hatchery biologists produce a product for the economy while conservation biologists seek to preserve a vulnerable source of genetic heritage. Tim Clark and Ron Westrum (1987),[6] in a case study on scientific knowledge and the protection of the black-footed ferret, also discuss the practice of creating knowledge about wildlife. In this case, they explain that the practice of science is liable to "blind-spots" that can impede the construction of more accurate perceptions of Nature – that is, where and how many ferrets exist. Both studies, Scarce (2000) and Clark and Westrum (1987), drive home the point that power is a critical element in the creation and maintenance of dominant social definitions of wildlife and that the prevailing constructions will have a tremendous impact on the species in question.

A second group of wildlife studies utilizing a constructionist approach are focused on the symbolic meanings of species within human culture. These studies, collectively, try to unravel cultural connections to wildlife and remark on the social significance of these animals within social relationships between people. Gary Alan Fine and Lazaros Christoforides (1991), for example, discuss the connections between social disagreements over the management of exotic or "foreign" birds, specifically the English sparrow, and public debate over the influx of human immigrants from Southern and Eastern Europe. In this case, the birds bore the same negative attributes as people who were, by social definition, also undesirable additions to the national community and culture.

Looking at a more contemporary conflict, Matthew Wilson (1997) concludes that the dispute over wolves in Yellowstone National Park was indicative of a broader ideological debate over property control and natural resource management. Similarly, Sandy Rikoon and Robin Albee (1998) suggest that conflict over wild horse management in the Missouri Ozarks was a flashpoint for more diffuse arguments about the role of the federal government and intrusion of the same into local governance, identity and culture.

Other social scientists have looked closely at the construction of particular wild animals and have shown how those definitions are linked to how the public regards and treats these animals. For instance, Jody Emel (1998) demonstrates how, to justify the wolf's extirpation, people ascribed the animal with human qualities, but only the most base and ugly of them. Constance Russell (1995) considers the different categories or "stories" that ecotourists created to mediate their own relationship to orangutans as a child with human-like qualities and, conversely, the orangutan as emblematic of wild Nature. Finally, Andrea Gullo, Unna Lassiter and Jennifer Wolch (1998) describe the competing definitions of mountain lions in recent arguments about public safety. They find that the construction of mountain lions changed from symbol of wild Nature to cold-blooded killer. Consequently, the cultural value of the animals waned and people concluded that mountain lions were no longer worthy of protection and reverence.

These authors have embarked on a journey to understand the important place that wildlife holds in human society. Their investigations have been pioneering steps toward dissecting the intricate relationships woven by people as they interpret, relate, classify and control wild animals. Our primary interest in this volume is to contribute to and extend conversations about the cultural relationships between people and wildlife and to expand the application of constructionist theory to issues of wildlife and wildlife management. More specifically, this book continues recent efforts to discover how people give symbolic meaning to wildlife by examining the place people give to wild animals in Western cultures.

Looking at the Prism that is Wildlife

Often divergent meanings about Nature and the wild are most vivid and culturally divisive during times of social change, disagreement or conflict and that theme emerges in many of the chapters that follow. Our focus in this volume is on documenting the presence and types of Nature discourse emerging from particular human-wildlife issues. By so doing we can more clearly identify the social groups who create opposing symbolic meanings of Nature and the ways that those meanings influence wildlife, people generally, and management professionals.

Identifying the existence of competing symbolic meanings, however, is only helpful if we can bring some of the knowledge to bear on the more practical side of living in a world with wild creatures. Therefore, each author in this collection relates these issues back to two thematic questions that address applied, pragmatic issues. The first is: What insights are gained by using constructionist theory to examine the case study and how can those insights help us to better understand wildlife-related conflicts in general? And second, and perhaps most importantly, how might understanding more about Nature and meanings improve our relationships with each other and help us to better define our own place in the natural world?

To reach the goals stated above, our book is divided into three sections. Part I, "Constructing the Wildlife in Wildlife Management Issues," presents the reader with three case studies that examine the various meanings that are attached to nature and wildlife. Two of the case studies focus on particular species and demonstrate how competing definitions of wildlife and views of Nature are at the core of social conflicts over species management. Further, these chapters highlight how different claims-makers construct vastly different definitions of the same species and vie for power in an effort to persuade others, particularly managers, to accept their view of management in the context of Nature.

In "Devils, Angels or Animals: The Social Construction of Otters in Conflict Over Management," Theresa Goedeke examines the claims-making strategies and activities used to define the otter and, consequently, the otter problem. The claims-makers – pond owners and anglers, otter protectionists, and the Missouri Department of Conservation – offered different images of the river otter, with different management recommendations stemming from these constructions. Similarly, Ann Herda-Rapp and Karen Marotz ("Contested Meanings: The Social Construction of the Mourning Dove in Wisconsin") explore the contentious issue of a mourning dove hunt in Wisconsin and competing constructions of the dove. The authors argue that the issue cannot be simply reduced to hunters versus "anti-hunters," that it is, rather, the different meanings attributed to the dove that blur the lines between groups that have traditionally opposed each other. Together, these two chapters point out the importance of considering and incorporating an animal's multiple definitions – and those advancing them – into policy and conflict resolution processes.

Carol Miller ("Virtual Deer: Bagging the Mythical 'Big One' in Cyberspace") explores hunters' use of Internet bulletin boards to discuss deer hunting. By way of this online discussion format, Miller contends, hunters construct images of the deer they hunt, of the perfect hunt, and of themselves as their status as hunters is enhanced through the discussion. Miller shows that, while participants construct the deer as smart and cunning big game, they are also creating a deer hunter identity, with potential management implications stemming from this socially constructed reality.

Part II, "Constructing the People and Practices in Wildlife Management Issues," shifts the focus to managers, management practices and management systems, and to the social landscape surrounding wildlife issues to understand how constructions of each might lead to conflict eruptions or long-simmering antipathy. Véronique Campion-Vincent, in "The Restoration of Wolves in France: Story, Conflicts and Uses of Rumor," examines conflict surrounding wolves' return to France and the place of rumor in shaping the conflict. Likewise, in "More than Mere Wolves at the Door: Reconstructing Community amidst a Wildlife Controversy," Rik Scarce examines controversy surrounding the reintroduction of wolves, this time to Yellowstone National Park. Scarce analyzes the conflict not just for the constructions of wolves and Nature it reveals, but also for what it says about constructions of Community, closing with a discussion of the wildlife management implications associated with his analysis.

Robert Granfield and Paul Colomy take on wildlife law, wildlife's symbolic values and the poaching death of an emblematic elk, Samson, in "Paradise Lost: The Transformation of Wildlife Law in the Vanishing Wilderness." Theorizing from a social construction of law and deviance position, Granfield and Colomy show how the resulting Samson's Law was directed at the perceived poaching threat, in a class-tinged debate, while the more egregious threat to wildlife, habitat loss, escaped scrutiny. Richard Hummel and Theresa Goedeke ("The Hunters and the Hunted: Context and Evolution of Game Management in Germanic Countries Versus the United States") also examine the importance of law in mediating human interactions with wildlife. They highlight the importance of culture, history and polity in the formation of Germanic and American hunting systems by comparing the spatial and temporal contexts that helped to guide how people perceive wildlife, as well as understand Nature, game and hunting in these two cultures.

Part III, "Deconstructing and Reconstructing Wildlife Policy Approaches," brings the book full circle by highlighting the potential policy implications of deconstructing definitions of wildlife and nature when examining conflict over wildlife and natural resources. Stella Čapek addresses some of the ethical considerations that result from altering both time and space to suit human views of the landscape in "Of Time, Space, and Birds: Cattle Egrets and the Place of the Wild." Using a startling example of human interactions with cattle egrets, Čapek walks the reader through a powerful discussion about the potential value of looking at nature from a bird's point of view. Čapek offers novel recommendations for re-crafting policy at the local, national and international levels so that it might be more sensitive to the rhythms and spatial needs of nature.

Lawrence Felt ("You Can't Eat 'Paper Fish': Recent Attempts to Link Local Ecological Knowledge and Fisheries Science in Atlantic Canada") describes how local knowledge about Nature might be obtained from stakeholder groups and integrated into resource science and management. This, Felt asserts, can create more effective management while at the same time allay conflicts between resource users and managers. Felt explains how fishers' knowledge of Nature and their understandings of Newfoundland's cod fishery differ from and perhaps complement the "objective" and scientifically grounded understandings of fisheries researchers and managers that proved problematic in practice.

Brett Zollinger and Steven Daniels ("We All Can Just Get Along: The Social Constructions of Prairie Dog Stakeholders and the Use of a Transactional Management Approach in Devising a Species Conservation Plan") address conflict resolution at the state management level by examining Kansas's plan to bring together stakeholders over management of the Black Tailed Prairie Dog by recognizing the different meanings ascribed to the prairie dog. Zollinger and Daniels discuss the process of consensus-building by way of the transactional management approach, illustrating a practical application of constructionist theory.

Together, the chapters illustrate the significant, untapped utility of constructionist approaches for understanding conflict over wildlife issues and for managing natural resources in a way that acknowledges and incorporates different definitions of nature. This book, then, begins to undertake the "practical project of developing ways to manage environmental problems" (Burningham and Cooper 1999:312).

References

Alvarez, Ken. 1993. *Twilight of the Panther: Biology, Bureaucracy and Failure in an Endangered Species Program.* Sarasota, FL: Myakka River.

Bean, Michael J. 1983. *The Evolution of National Wildlife Law.* New York: Praeger.

Benton, Ted. 1994. "Biology and Social Theory in the Environmental Debate." Pp. 28–50 in *Social Theory and the Global Environment,* edited by M. Redclift and T. Benton. London: Routledge.

Berger, Peter and Thomas Luckmann. 1966. *The Social Construction of Reality: A Treatise in the Sociology of Knowledge.* Garden City, NY: Doubleday & Company.

Best, Joel. 1993. "But Seriously Folks: The Limitations of the Strict Constructionist Interpretation of Social Problems." Pp. 129–147 in *Reconsidering Social Constructionism: Debates in Social Problems Theory,* edited by J. Holstein and G. Miller. New York: Aldine De Gruyter.

———. 1995. "Constructionism in Context." Pp. 337–354 in *Images of Issues: Typifying Contemporary Social Problems,* edited by J. Best. New York: Aldine De Gruyter.

Bissell, Steven and Mark Damian Duda. 1993. *Factors Related to Hunting and Fishing Participation in the United States, Phase II: Hunting Focus Groups.* Harrisonburg, VA: Responsive Management, Western Association of Fish and Wildlife Agencies.

Bright, Alan D. and Michael J. Manfredo. 1996. "A Conceptual Model of Attitudes Toward Natural Resource Issues: A Case Study of Wolf Reintroduction." *Human Dimensions of Wildlife* 1(1):1–21.

Burningham, Kate. 1998. "A Noisy Road or Noisy Resident?: A Demonstration of the Utility of Social Constructionism for Analysing Environmental Problems." *The Sociological Review* 46(3):536–563.

Burningham, Kate and Geoff Cooper. 1999. "Being Constructive: Social Constructionism and the Environment." *Sociology* 33(2):297–316.

Čapek, Stella. 1993. "The 'Environmental Justice' Frame: A Conceptual Discussion and an Application." *Social Problems* 40(1):5–24.

Clark, Tim and Ron Westrum. 1987. "Paradigms and Ferrets." *Social Studies of Science* 17:3–33.

Czech, Brian and Paul R. Krausman. 1997. "Public Opinion on Species and Endangered Species Conservation." *Endangered Species UPDATE* 16(5/6):7.

Davis, Mike. 1998. *Ecology of Fear: Los Angeles and the Imagination of Disaster.* New York: Vintage Books.

Decker, Daniel and Lisa Chase. 1997. "Human Dimensions of Living with Wildlife – A Management Challenge for the 21st Century." *Wildlife Society Bulletin* 25(4):788–795.

Demeritt, David. 2000. "The Construction of Global Warming and the Politics of Science." *Annals of the Association of American Geographers* 91:307–337.

Driscoll, Janis Whiley. 1995. "Attitudes toward Animals: Species Ratings." *Society and Animals* 3(2):139–150.

Duda, Mark Damian. 1993. *Factors Related to Hunting and Fishing Participation in the United States, Phase I: Literature Review.* Harrisonburg, VA: Responsive Management, Western Association of Fish and Wildlife Agencies.

Dunlap, Thomas. 1988. *Saving America's Wildlife.* Princeton, NJ: Princeton University Press.

———. 1991. "Organization and Wildlife Preservation: The Case of the Whooping Crane in North America." *Social Studies of Science* 21:197–221.

Eisler, Raine. 1987. *The Chalice & the Blade: Our History, Our Future.* San Francisco: Harper Row.

Emel, Jody. 1998. "Are You Man Enough, Big and Bad Enough? Wolf Eradication in the US." Pp. 91–116 in *Animal Geographies: Place, Politics, and Identity in the Nature-Culture Borderlands,* edited by J. Wolch and J. Emel. London: Verso.

Enck, Jody and Tommy Brown. 2002. "New Yorkers' Attitudes toward Restoring Wolves to the Adirondack Park." *Wildlife Society Bulletin* 30(1):16–28.

Evernden, Neil. 1992. *The Social Creation of Nature.* Baltimore, MD: Johns Hopkins University Press.

Fine, Gary Alan. 1998. *Morel Tales: The Culture of Mushrooming.* Cambridge, MA: Harvard.

———. 1997. "Naturework and the Taming of the Wild: The Problem of 'Overpick' in the Culture of Mushroomers." *Social Problems* 44(1):68–88.

Fine, Gary Alan and Lazaros Christoforides. 1991. "Dirty Birds, Filthy Immigrants and the English Sparrow War: Metaphorical Linkage in Constructing Social Problems." *Symbolic Interaction* 14(4):375–394.

Flader, Susan. L. 1974. *Thinking Like a Mountain: Aldo Leopold and the Evolution of an Ecological Attitude toward Deer, Wolves, and Forests.* Madison: University of Wisconsin Press.

Freudenberg, William, Scott Frickel, and Robert Gramling. 1995. "Beyond the Nature/Society Divide: Learning to Think about a Mountain." *Sociological Forum* 10(3):361–392.

General Accounting Office, United States. 2001. *Wildlife Services Program: Information on Activities to Manage Wildlife Damage.* Washington, DC: Government Printing Office.

Goffman, Erving. 1974. *Frame Analysis: An Essay on the Organization of Experience.* New York: Harper.

Greider, Thomas and Lorraine Garkovich. 1994. "Landscapes: The Social Construction of Nature and the Environment." *Rural Sociology* 59(1):1–24.

Gulla, Andrea, Unna Lassiter, and Jennifer Wolch. 1998. "The Cougar's Tale." Pp. 139–161 in *Animal Geographies: Place, Politics, and Identity in the Nature-Culture Borderlands,* edited by J. Wolch and J. Emel. London: Verso.

Hannigan, John. 1995. *Environmental Sociology: A Social Constructionist Perspective.* London: Routledge.

Harris, Lisa, Paul Krausman, and William Shaw. 1995. "Human Attitudes and Mountain Sheep in a Wilderness Setting." *Wildlife Society Bulletin* 23(1):66–72.

Harrison, Carolyn and Jacquelin Burgess. 1994. "Social Constructions of Nature: A Case Study of Conflicts over the Development of Rainham Marshes." *Transactions of the Institute of British Geographers* 19(3):291–310.

Heberlein, Thomas and Tomas Willebrand. 1998. "Attitudes toward Hunting across Time and Continents." *Game and Wildlife* 15:1071–1080.

Holstein, James and Gale Miller, eds. 1993. *Reconsidering Social Constructionism: Debates in Social Problems Theory.* New York: Aldine de Gruyter.

Jeffers, Glenn. 2003. "Park District is Losing Turf War with Rabbits." *Chicago Tribune* (Metro), December 26, p. 1.

Kellert, Stephen R. 1980. "Americans' Attitudes and Knowledge of Animals." *Proceedings of the Forty-Fifth North American Wildlife Conference* 45:111–124.

———. 1984. "Assessing Wildlife and Environmental Values in Cost-Benefit Analysis." *Journal of Environmental Management* 18:355–363.

———. 1985a. "Public Perceptions of Predators, Particularly the Wolf and Coyote." *Biological Conservation* 31:167–189.

———. 1985b. "Social and Perceptual Factors in Endangered Species Management." *Journal of Wildlife Management* 49(2):528–536.

Kuletz, Valerie. 1998. *The Tainted Desert: Environmental and Social Ruin in the American West.* New York: Routledge.

Litmanen, Tapio. 1995. "Environmental Conflict as a Social Construction: Nuclear Waste Conflicts in Finland." *Society & Natural Resources* 9(5):523–535.

McIntyre, Rick. 1995. *War Against the Wolf: America's Campaign to Exterminate the Wolf.* Stillwater, MN: Voyageur.

MacMillan, Thomas. 2003. "Tales of Power in Biotechnology Regulation: The EU Ban on BST." *Geoforum* 34(2):187–201.

Macnaghten, Phil and John Urry. 1998. *Contested Natures.* London: Sage.

20   INTRODUCTION

Manning, Anita. 2003. "Wildlife Wanders into Urban, Suburban Landscapes." *USA TODAY*, September 22, pp. 8D.

Merchant, Carolyn. 1980. *The Death of Nature: Women, Ecology, and the Scientific Revolution*. San Francisco, CA: Harper & Row.

Murphy, Raymond. 1994. "The Sociological Construction of Science without Nature." *Sociology* 28(4):957–974.

———. 1997. *Sociology and Nature: Social Action in Context*. Boulder, CO: Westview.

Noske, Barbara. 1992. "Deconstructing the Animal Image: Toward an Anthropology of Animals." *Anthrozoös* 5(4):226–320.

Pate, Jennifer, Michael Manfredo, Alan Bright, and Geoff Tischbein. 1996. "Coloradans' Attitudes toward Reintroducing the Gray Wolf Into Colorado." *Wildlife Society Bulletin* 24(3):421–428.

Penprase, Mike. 2004. "Geese Thriving on Urban Life to Detriment of Selves, Cities." *Springfield News-Leader (MO)*, March 7, pp. 1A.

Proctor, James. 1998. "The Spotted Owl and the Contested Moral Landscape of the Pacific Northwest." Pp. 191–217 in *Animal Geographies: Place, Politics, and Identity in the Nature-Culture Borderlands*, edited by J. Wolch and J. Emel. London: Verso.

Reading, Richard, Tim Clark, and Andrew Arnold. 1994. "Attitudes toward the Eastern Barred Bandicoot." *Anthrozoös* 7(4):255–270.

Reading, Richard P. and Stephen R. Kellert. 1993. "Attitudes toward the Proposed Reintroduction of Black-Footed Ferrets." *Conservation Biology* 7(3):569–580.

Reiter, Douglas, Mark Brunson, and Robert Schmidt. 1999. "Public Attitudes toward Wildlife Damage Management and Policy." *Wildlife Society Bulletin* 27(3):746–758.

Responsive Management National Office. 1998. *Wildlife and the American Mind: Public Opinion on and Attitudes toward Fish and Wildlife Management*. Harrisonburg, VA: Responsive Management.

Rikoon, Sandy and Robin Albee. 1998. "'Wild and Free, Leave 'Em Be': Wild Horses and the Struggle over Nature in the Missouri Ozarks." *Journal of Folklore Research* 35(3):203–222.

Ruben, Barbara. 2003. "Racoons and Geese and Bears – Oh Deer! Wildlife Moves In, but Is Not Always Welcome." *Washington Post*, May 10, pp. F1.

Russell, Constance. 1995. "The Social Construction of Orangutans: An Ecotourist Experience." *Society and Animals* 3(2):151–171.

Scarce, Rik. 2000. *Fishy Business: Salmon, Biology, and the Social Construction of Nature*. Philadelphia: Temple University Press.

Schoenfeld, A. Clay, Robert Meier, and Robert Griffin. 1979. "Constructing a Social Problem: The Press and the Environment." *Social Problems* 27(1):38–61.

Schreiber, Dorothee, Ralph Matthews, and Brian Elliott. 2003. "The Framing of Farmed Fish: Product, Efficiency, and Technology." *Canadian Journal of Sociology* 28(2):153–169.

Singer, Lili. 2004. "The California Garden: When Deer Come Calling." *Los Angeles Times*, January 1, pp. F3.

Soulé, Michael. 1995. "The Social Siege of Nature." Pp. 137–170 in *Reinventing Nature? Responses to Postmodern Deconstruction*, edited by M. Soulé and G. Lease. Washington, D.C.: Island Press.

Spector, Malcolm and John Kitsuse. [1977] 1987. *Constructing Social Problems*. New Brunswick, NJ: Transaction Publishers.

Stallings, Robert A. 1995. *Promoting Risk: Constructing the Earthquake Threat*. New York: Aldine De Gruyter.

Stange, Mary Zeiss. 2004. "When Animals Stalk Humans, Hunters Should Shoot Back." *USA TODAY*, February 16, pp. 11A.

Steinberg, Philip E. 2001. *The Social Construction of the Ocean*. New York: Cambridge.

Teel, Tara, Richard Krannich, and Robert Schmidt. 2002. "Utah Stakeholders' Attitudes toward Selected Cougar and Black Bear Management Practices." *Wildlife Society Bulletin* 30(1):2–15.

Tester, Keith. 1991. *Animals and Society: The Humanity of Animal Rights*. London: Routledge.

Tobin, Richard. 1990. *The Expendable Future: U.S. Politics and the Protection of Biological Diversity*. Durham, NC: Duke University.

Unger, Sheldon. 1992. "The Rise and (Relative) Decline of Global Warming as a Social Problem." *Sociological Quarterly* 33:483–502.

Vanden Brook, Tom. 2000. "Deer Population Exploding across the USA." *USA TODAY* (News), December 22, pp. 17A.

Wilcove, David S. 1999. *The Condor's Shadow: The Loss and Recovery of Wildlife in America*. New York: Anchor Books.

Williams, Christopher, Goran Ericsson, and Thomas Heberlein. 2002. "A Quantitative Summary of Attitudes toward Wolves and Their Reintroduction (1972–2000)." *Wildlife Society Bulletin* 30(2):575–584.

Williams, Jerry. 1998. "Knowledge, Consequences and Experience: The Social Construction of Environmental Problems." *Sociological Inquiry* 68(4):476–497.

Wilson, Edward O. 1998. *Consilience: The Unity of Knowledge*. New York: Random House.

Wilson, Matthew. 1997. "The Wolf in Yellowstone: Science, Symbol, or Politics? Deconstructing the Conflict Between Environmentalism and Wise Use." *Society & Natural Resources* 10:453–468.

Worster, Donald. 1994. *Nature's Economy: A History of Ecological Ideas*. New York: Cambridge University Press.

Wright, Brett, Sheila Backman, and Bruce Wicks. 1991. "Operating at the 'Wildlife-Human Interface': A Marketing Approach to Wildlife Planning." Pp. 39–52 in *Public Policy Issues in Wildlife Management*, edited by W. Mangun. New York: Greenwood.

Yaffee, Steven. 1995. "Lessons about Leadership from the History of the Spotted Owl Controversy." *Natural Resources Journal* 35:381–412.

Notes

[1] Unless otherwise noted, the term "wildlife" in this volume is used broadly to include non-human animal species that are predominantly free-roaming, but that have not been domesticated (e.g., feral animals). In some cases the authors of particular chapters make further distinctions between the cultural classifications of wildlife, such as the division between game and non-game animals or protected versus unprotected species.

[2] Here we note a distinction between the person's assessment of an interaction versus how the animal(s) involved experiences or perhaps perceives the same encounter. We do not take up the latter question in this volume.

[3] For accounts of the population explosions of deer see Vanden Brook (2000), of Canada geese see Penprase (2004), and of rabbits see Jeffers (2003). For a full enumeration of the types of damage caused by wildlife see the 2001 report by the General Accounting Office cited herein.

[4] For a full elaboration of strict constructionism, see Holstein and Miller (1993) or Spector and Kitsuse (1987).

[5] See also *War Against the Wolf: America's Campaign to Exterminate the Wolf* (Stillwater, MN: Voyageur), edited by Rick McIntyre (1995) for an anthology of changing American attitudes toward the wolf explicitly.

[6] Tim Clark is a biologist; Ron Westrum is a sociologist.

PART ONE

CONSTRUCTING THE WILDLIFE
IN WILDLIFE MANAGEMENT ISSUES

DEVILS, ANGELS OR ANIMALS:
THE SOCIAL CONSTRUCTION OF OTTERS
IN CONFLICT OVER MANAGEMENT[1]

Theresa L. Goedeke

Introduction

The otter is an animal that has long captured the imagination of people and served as a cultural symbol of Nature at play. Images of otters sliding down mud banks and turning somersaults in the water are common in children's stories and in nature programming on television. On the other hand, the otter is a predatory animal and, in general, Americans have tended to dislike predators (Kellert 1985) resulting in a long and, often, sordid journey to achieve control over them (Dunlap 1988). Given such a background, it might be difficult to guess what would happen if the playful, yet predatory otter were restored to a vacant niche nearly fifty years after being trapped to near extinction. However, if the Missouri experience serves as an example, one could only conclude that intense social conflict would result.

In 1982, the state's wildlife management agency, the Missouri Department of Conservation (DOC), began efforts to restore the species to Missouri waters and, as the population of otters grew, so too did social conflict over their presence, behaviors and management. This chapter examines how each of the groups engaged in the controversy over river otters constructed and presented their own definition of the creatures. As each party engaged in discourse in both public and policy arenas, their rhetoric defined the otter's habits, motivations and behaviors. Each group cast the otter in ways that supported their own view about the problem and, ultimately, what should be done about it. Below is a discussion of how the otter was a predatory devil for some, an ecological angel for others or, simply, a useful species to be controlled and managed by people.

Otters, Claims-making and Social Problems

It may be somewhat perplexing to consider how river otters could have become a social problem. Therefore, some background on a social constructionist approach as it applies specifically to social problems is necessary. When considering social problems, it is important to recognize the difference between an objective condition and a social problem. According to Best (1989) an objective condition simply exists, but does not gain social problem status until someone or some group successfully works to have the condition defined as such. Having no otters or, conversely, having a million otters, for example, only becomes a *social problem* if someone comes to view the condition as problematic and, further, successfully promotes it as such. Therefore, it is not the actual state of the otter population that is important to the social problems researcher, but rather the perception of that condition and the value actors choose to place on it.

Successfully establishing a social problem, however, can be a rather up hill business. This is so because problem definition is a process. According to Best (1987), claims-makers define a problem by making statements that orient the condition in a particular way and, often, buttress such orientations with examples or evidentiary claims about the kind and extent of the problem. Such claims are made in certain public contexts or arenas, such as the media, in government forums and in the realm of public opinion, wherein it would be beneficial to have one's definition of the problem presented and accepted (Hilgartner and Bosk 1988).

To complicate matters further, these parties, or claims-makers, often find themselves competing with other groups who have a different take on the problem within these critical arenas. Given the diversity of attitudes toward wildlife and management practices (Conover 2002; Kellert 1993), it is not surprising that multiple groups with divergent perceptions of nature become involved in competitions to define social problems pertaining to wildlife and their management. Recent work in the social sciences has explored competing constructions of species or wildlife management solutions (Dizard 1994; Rikoon and Albee 1998; Scarce 1997, 2000; Wilson 1997).

Often the groups central to such conflicts are the management agencies themselves. Rikoon and Albee (1998), for example, studied conflict over management of wild horses in the Missouri Ozarks and described the competing constructions of the National Park Service and local residents. In Dizard (1994), the city management agency was at odds in their definition of a deer problem with those who condemned hunting deer where hunting was usually excluded. In the present research there were three distinct groups with competing constructions of the otter problem: anglers and pond owners, otter protection activists and the state's wildlife management agency.

When competing in arenas of influence claims-makers rely on various strategies to promote their definitions over those of competitors. Of those identified by Best (1987), two such strategies are applicable to this analysis. The first is "valuation." In Best's analysis this related to claims regarding the value of missing children. Groups attempting to discuss the problem of missing children defined children as the most valuable social resource, thus deserving of priority attention from government and society after they have gone missing. This same rhetorical tool was used in the controversy over river otters. However, as I will later discuss, the attributes of that value construction depended upon which group was engaged in the valuation.

The second rhetorical strategy, termed by Best as the "blameless victim," relates to the innocence or blame of a victim in bringing on some negative situation. In the context of research on wildlife conflict, however, the concept of victim must be refined to represent the blamelessness of the species in creation of a determined problem. The question becomes did the animal's own behavior or condition justify the situation, such as its own death, which was visited upon it? Or, conversely, was the animal undeserving of the situation because of its lack of culpability? In the case of social conflict over wildlife the perceived behaviors and activities of the animals themselves can complicate the matter. Thus, claims-making in such contexts will necessarily entail struggles amongst parties to define the species as either culprit or innocent victim. The otters, while portrayed as the victims by some in the controversy were, alternatively, constructed by other people as deserving such a fate because of their own behaviors.

Examining the rhetoric of groups competing in a social controversy helps to explain why conflict erupts over policy. Energy expended to successfully define a social problem in one or more arenas of influence is important because authority to define the problem translates into authority to define the appropriate solution (Best 1987). In the case of river otters, therefore, it was important for each group to define the behavior, value and character of the river otter. Only

by swaying opinions toward a particular view of the otter, its value
and impacts, could claims-makers in this controversy hope to win
the ultimate prize, which was to dictate acceptable solutions to the
problem.

Research Methods

To examine the claims-making activities of participants in the river
otter management conflict, I employed three methods of data collection. First, document analysis was used to gather information on
the claims-making activities within the public[2] and policy[3] arenas. I
analyzed newspaper articles and letters to the editor, publications
and literature from the various organizations involved in the conflict,
as well as agency memorandums and correspondence.

Newspaper articles were systematically gathered from two metro-
politan newspapers, the *St. Louis Post-Dispatch* and the *Columbia Daily
Tribune*, and one rural newspaper, *The Houston Herald*. Articles referring to Missouri otters were collected for the period of 1990 to 2000.
I collected non-newspaper documents by making requests for information; I also accessed the archives and clipping files of agencies,
organizations and individuals involved in otter issues. Approximately
two hundred documents were analyzed for this research.

In addition to document analysis, I conducted thirteen in-depth
interviews with key participants in the controversy representing each
of three positions: the state agency (hereafter referred to as DOC),
otter protection activists and pond owner/angler activists.[4] Finally,
three observations were conducted at public meetings, two during
meetings of the Otter Advisory Committee and one during a public otter presentation sponsored by DOC.

The Problem with Otters

The North American River Otter (*Lutra canadensis*) was not a problem in Missouri until the early 1990s. In fact, they were very rarely
seen and probably little thought of by the average person. This was
so because they had been rendered virtually extinct in Missouri by
the 1930s as a result of excessive trapping (Bennitt and Nagel 1937).
Although the "restocking" of otters had been suggested by Bennitt
and Nagel (1937), both biologists at the University of Missouri-

Columbia, this strand in Missouri's ecological web was all but lost for the next forty-five or so years as the landscape continued to change in their absence.

Eventually, the DOC did undertake a restoration program; they released a total of 845 river otters at forty-three sites throughout the state (Hamilton 1998). The first wave of Missouri's new otters hit the water in 1982 and the DOC freed the last group in 1992 (Simms 1992). Shortly after the restoration program came to a close citizens, mostly from rural areas in the state, began to suspect the otters of clandestine raids on fishing holes and farm ponds. By the middle 1990s, anglers and pond owners began to complain in earnest about the presence of otters and of what they perceived to be their impact. They accused the otters of depleting wild populations of sport fish, such as bass. In addition, they claimed that the otters were invading private fishing ponds paid for and stocked by individual landowners, cleaning out the fish completely. Angry anglers and pond owners directed their complaints and concerns to the DOC, as well as expressing their views in letters to the editor and newspaper articles.

At first DOC representatives doubted that otters could be culpable for declining fish stocks. They based their conclusions on scientific knowledge about otter eating habits. However, surprising findings from population growth indicators and models (the validity of which were rigorously debated by otter protection activists), combined with citizen complaints of otter damage led the department to begin preparations for the state's first trapping season since the early part of the twentieth century. The agency applied to the United States Fish and Wildlife Service for an export license in 1995, which would enable the export of otter pelts under the Convention on International Trade in Endangered Species, or CITES. Their request for export authorization was, ultimately, successful and otter trapping seasons have been held in Missouri since 1996.

Although pond owners and anglers might have been glad about the prospect of a trapping season, other Missouri citizens were not pleased about the agency's decision to legally sanction the killing of otters. The decision to open a trapping season engendered social conflict in other quarters. As preparations for the 1996–1997 trapping season were being made, citizens of Missouri who were against the trapping of otters wrote letters of protest to DOC officials and began to publish their own letters to the editor denouncing the decision to trap otters. Concerned citizens formed an activist group called

the Missouri River Otter Protection Coalition (ROPC) and began
to network and organize with other individuals and organizations
interested in delaying or halting the trapping season. National organizations also got involved in the effort to stop otter trapping, including the Animal Legal Defense Fund (ALDF) and the Humane Society
of the United States (HSUS).

In an effort to challenge the reasonableness of the trapping season, otter protection activists filed a state lawsuit against the DOC
in 1996. The court, however, ruled in favor of the agency (Westermann
v. Missouri Conservation Commission, Missouri Circuit Court for
the City of St. Louis 1996). A second lawsuit, seeking to stop the
export permits from being issued, was filed in U.S. District Court
in 1997. This suit was dismissed in 1998 (Animal Legal Defense
Fund v. Babbitt, U.S. District Court, D.C. 1998). Although litiga-
tion failed activists seeking to protect river otters, they continued
working for their cause through letter-writing and media campaigns
meant to sway public and bureaucratic opinion. Activists suggested
in news articles and letters to the editor that they might try placing
an anti-trapping measure on the state's election ballot in 2000.

In 1998 the DOC created the Otter Advisory Committee (OAC),
which was made up of a number of agency managers and scientists,
one university scientist, several people interested in sport fishing, a
couple of trappers and one otter protection activist. To diffuse social
tensions surrounding otters and their management, the OAC served
as an audience for fact-finding. In 2000 the OAC unanimously recommended otter trapping zones where bag limits would differ throughout
the state in relation to otter density projections. This recommendation was presented to the DOC Board of Conservation Commissioners,
a four-member body appointed by the governor and constitutionally
endowed with the authority to regulate wildlife in the State, who
approved the plan. The DOC implemented the new harvest regulations in 2001.

Constructing the Otter

Although rhetoric and claims-making with regard to otters likely
began in the early 1980s when the restoration project got under-
way, this research only focuses on the controversy that ensued after
the restoration was completed. The controversy over otter manage-

ment began in the early 1990s and, at least from a policy stand-point, culminated with the 2000 OAC recommendations about changes to the state's trapping regulations. Throughout this period, the claims-making activities of the different groups ebbed and flowed and, given the evolution of the conflict, it was not surprising that the nature of participant claims changed somewhat over time. Further, the arenas of discourse broadened from only a media or public arena to include a government arena as well, in the form of the OAC.

The agency along with pond owners and anglers participated in the conflict the longest and their claims-making shifted as the controversy progressed. Angler and pond owner activists were more vocal in public arenas until the DOC fell into step with their claims. The entrance of otter protection activists into the fray, which occurred with DOC preparations for a trapping season, led to somewhat of a unification of claims-making activities between the agency and pond owner/angler activists. Despite these changes, however, clear distinctions could be identified between the claims-making activities of each group as they constructed the otter throughout the course of the controversy.

The Hungry Little Devils

Anglers and pond owners, who were the first to define the otter as a problem, consistently described fish as more valuable than otters. One angler wrote, "I do not feel that the river otter is that valuable of an asset to the state of Missouri that we should allow the destruction of the state fisheries" (Citizen letter to DOC, April [no day] 2000). Instead of focusing on the value of the otter, angler and pond owner claims emphasized the social, familial and cultural importance of fishing. Letters to the editor and DOC correspondence contained references to how long anglers had been fishing and how important the activity was in their lives. Statements like, "My family has for years enjoyed getting together and fishing" and "My first love is flyfishing and have done it since I was 12 years old" often preceded complaints about otters and demands for agency action (Citizen letter to DOC, December [no day] 1999a; Citizen letter to DOC, December [no day] 1999b).

Claims-makers in this group described fish as an important part of Nature. In other words, sport fish enjoyed a prominent place in cultural traditions and were, therefore, included in local definitions about what Nature should include. Conversely, pond owners and anglers were apt to portray otters as out of place in the contemporary, natural system; otters were not a part of Nature, but were instead exotic interlopers. A DOC press release (October 2, 1998), reporting on the first OAC meeting, summed this view: "One citizen member of the committee agreed that otters and fish have coexisted in natural habitats in the past, but they have been reintroduced into unnatural habitats because of the changes in Ozark streams." Claims-makers within this group dwelt on the changes that had occurred in the landscape since the otter was extirpated and asserted that it could not now fit in.

Overall, for this group, the otters were neither missed when gone nor cared much for after they were restored. Comments such as the following from a local angler expressed the typical sentiment about the desirability of otters:

> Just the regular Ozarkers, the ones who live here, I haven't found any of them who are really too concerned if we have otters or not. It's the people away from here that we have to worry about. I haven't met any [local] people who say "well I'm glad they brought the otter back. I love to watch them." (interview)

Another angler expressed a similar sentiment, saying:

> But most of these people [those who are concerned about sport fish and pond fish] are what I call conservationists . . . they abide by the rules, they try to make things better. It's sad that they have to pay this price for somebody who wanted otters. Like I said we didn't miss them, we grew up without them and we were happy. (interview)

At best, otters were presented as a benign addition to the local environment and, at worst, their presence was described as problematic because their behaviors and needs were now incompatible with the modern landscape where human needs were the priority.

Most claims-making efforts, however, were focused on portraying the otter as a species with negative value, meaning destructive rather than good or benign. In claims-making, people described the otter's destructive character, along with its inevitable negative impact on the environment, meaning sport fisheries and ponds. People in this group focused on the otter's feeding behavior. For example, one person wrote:

I have often caught a glimpse of the not so elusive new fishing partner I have on this stream. Cute and very comical, it never occurred
to me that the rapid decline of my catch in the same water was a
result of this predator (Citizen letter to DOC, January 24, 2000).

In addition, members of this group emphasized what they viewed
as the otter's wasteful eating habits, that it could eat large amounts
of fish and, further, that it would eat as many fish as possible. In
letters to the editor, quotes in print media interviews, and in discourse during OAC meetings, angler and pond owners discussed the
large number of fish that were killed and the numerous fish left only
partially eaten by otters. A concerned angler's view of the issue was
reported in a print news article:

> "We must stop the fish kill that's going on in the Ozarks," said [the
> angler] of [a rural town]. [The angler] said streams that used to teem
> with large-mouth bass are nearly picked clean. As evidence of the
> otter's role, he showed commissioners photos of discarded, half-eaten
> catfish floating in the rivers (Gieich 1997:1).

Similarly, during an interview, a pond owner discussed the number
of dead fish found around her pond after an otter problem was
discovered:

> If you look at the highlight [referring to a portion of a photo circled
> in yellow], that's part of the fish. Here's another one. Then when we
> found the blood [and], of course, we circled to the back of the pond
> and this is what was floating out in the pond. It was still alive. Otters
> eat them from the back and it was trying to swim. We retrieved it
> because I can't stand to see something suffer. Here's another from at
> that time that was killed, but obviously we had scared [the offending
> otters] off. (interview)

The emphasis placed on the excessive amounts of fish that otters
ate, in addition to the wastefulness of their eating behaviors was
important because wastefulness was not a part of good conservation
as defined by anglers and pond owners.

In order to practice good conservation, according to this group,
resources such as fish should be used efficiently. Many interviewees
made reference to their own use-behaviors. They indicated that they
followed the rules of good conservation, including wildlife laws enforced
by the DOC, and some people explicitly complained that the otters
were not subject to those same rules. Claims about the otter's wan-
ton and destructive behavior were juxtaposed with what were viewed

as good, albeit human conservation practices. The otters were not following the proper standards set by humans for proper resource use and this was problematic.

The subtext of the waste discourse was that otters had a lower claim or no claim to the resource, which was fish, because of such behavior. Often, people in this group openly stated that otters had no right to the fish. One angler wrote:

> The idea of trappers taking care of them is out for now. A lot of trappers are not trapping because of the lousy fur prices [*sic*] therefore those otters that would have been taken by coon & muskrat trappers are out to reap their harvest of *our* fish (Citizen letter to DOC, January 3, 2000; emphasis original).

Because fish were portrayed as the rightful and exclusive property of people, the discourse regarding otter feeding habits cast the otter as a species that was intentionally stealing resources away from people. Claims made by this group explained or attributed meaning to the otter's motivations. This pond owner, for instance, explained otter behavior through a series of analogies:

> I think those little fellers are shaping the environment to suit themselves just like anybody else would. Also, I think they're a little bit like a cat. A cat will kill for the fun of it. Over back in [name of town] there was an old mother cat. She didn't just kill what she'd be able to eat it, she'd go in there and start killing all the mice she could. That was her job. And I think otters do the same thing. They're just like humans we like to catch a lot of fish, we catch a little more than we eat and put it in the deep freeze. I think that otter gets some enjoyment out of catching those fish and the bigger the better, I think. (interview)

Activists in this group imbued otters with the characteristics and motivations of other animals understood by people or compared them to people themselves. They portrayed the otter as a competitor.

Fish, particularly pond fish, were the property of people and so otters took fish that did not belong to them. In this way, the otters became criminals. This quote, taken from a pond owner's letter to DOC, described the otter as a thief in the night, "They [otters] are repeatedly robbing our fishing baskets. Last fall a family of 5 of these vermin robbed us of 65 fish in 3 successive nights" (Citizen letter to DOC, February 15, 2000). This is not surprising if we accept Mitchell's (1997:167, emphasis original) assertion that "what animals *do* may be the most important determinant for people's perceptions of their psychology." It appears logical that the otter's consumptive behaviors, which were perceived as excessive, were a passport to negative constructions about their motivations.

Thus, otters were no longer wildlife, but became "thieves" or "vermin" classed with other offensive and objectionable people and animals. Describing otters as intentionally and maliciously causing damage placed more culpability on them; they were in no way innocent. The otters knew what they were doing and, therefore, they deserved to be trapped or shot. Further, portraying the otter as a destructive foe with intent to destroy fish served to vilify the animal. This, in turn, justified activist desires to ameliorate or eliminate them.

Playful, Ecological Angels

While anglers and pond owner activists constructed an animal with little positive value, otter protection activists promoted a very different version of the otter. The otter, for this group, was an animal that was extremely important both to the landscape and to people, and it was more valuable alive than it was dead.

In claims offered by otter protection activists, restoring otters remedied an unnatural condition in Nature. A brochure for the ROPC (no date) stated that, "As with so many species, river otters played a critical role in the balance of nature in Missouri's rivers and streams." As a predator, it was an important component of the landscape and its newly established presence completed Missouri's aquatic systems. The otter's restoration brought the natural system one step closer to becoming true Nature.

Consequently, otter protection activists praised the otter's predatory status and the animal's value was defined by this critical, ecological role. The otter was not just a predator; it was the "capstone" or "pinnacle" predator for Missouri's aquatic systems. One editorial writer explained, "Otters have always been at the top of the food chain in Missouri and, except for trappers, are pinnacle predators" (Gruver 1996b:4). The otter's role was paramount because much of the health and balance of the system depended on its existence. One activist explained:

> I think that having a pinnacle predator type animal in the wild is important for other environmental reasons. . . . [N]umber one, [they] can act as a thinning or stabilization of their prey animals. Also, [they can] be an indication of the health of the environment of their prey

animals. That is the health of the water, the health of the woods,
[and] the land. All those things, I think, are a gauge that you need
to have. And that we as people benefit by having those pinnacle predator species coexists with us. (interview)

The river otter was not a thief. Instead, it was an animal that kept
prey populations in check, which was a desirable activity. Moreover,
the otter filled a broader purpose by serving as an environmental
indicator for the health of the habitat as a whole; if the otters were
doing fine, then the system was doing fine.

The ecological role of this predator was also used in claims-making about the animal's eating behaviors. Otter protection activists
argued that it was a native predator in this system, regardless of its
long absence. It had evolved with the landscape and its prey base
and, therefore, would not create declines in sport fish populations:

My whole contention [is] that you're not going to blame the total
decline of fish populations in a state on a predator; that's ludicrous.
They don't work like that. Predators don't work like that; they don't
wipe out prey populations. Look at other things. (interview)

In some cases, claims about the otter-fish relationship went beyond
the species having no impact on fish. Information provided in an
ROPC publication indicated that "generally otters are beneficial to
game fisheries because of their tendency to prey on less desirable
and competing fish species" (Missouri River Otter Protection Coalition
1998).[5] Thus, the otter as constructed by this group would not harm
wild fish populations and may, in fact, have been of great benefit
to sport fisheries.

In addition to being of ecological value, otters were portrayed as
having great recreational value. The species was important for the
viewing opportunities it offered to non-consumptive outdoor recreationists. One otter protection activist stated in a media interview
that "they are considered to be one of the most desirable species for
people who want to go out and view wildlife" (Keller 1999). Many
of the letters to the editor and media testimonials included comments
about the joy of seeing otters in the wild doing what otters do in
the wild, such as "playing on the riverbank" (Uhlenbrock 1999).

Otter protection activists, much like anglers and pond owners,
included claims about the otter's personality in their rhetoric. However,
they constructed a very different picture of the otter's character.
People wanting to protect otters used adjectives such as "playful"

and "beautiful" to describe the animal and focused on the pleasing qualities of the species, for example:

> The most compelling evidence on behalf of river otters is their personality. They're the most playful of the *Mustelidae*, or weasel, family . . . They have a frivolous manner throughout their adult lives and frequently immerse themselves in passionate games of hide-and-seek, wrestling or childishly skidding down mud and snowbanks into water (Gruver 1996a:17).

By describing the otter in this manner, trapping became a cruel and heartless activity. Thus, it is not surprising that language about the trapping of otters, for this group, went beyond rhetoric about "harvest" to defining trapping as "murder." One activist wrote:

> There exists virtually no market in the U.S. for this [otter pelts], and even if there was a market it does not condone for [*sic*] the heartless, selfish murdering of these beautiful, caring otters to take place (Citizen letter to DOC, March 27, 2000).

Such rhetorical strategies could be very important, particularly in the public arena, because casting the otter in this manner may have swayed public support toward no-trapping management solutions.

An Animal Like All Others

Finally, the DOC, which was responsible for both restoring and managing the otters, was caught between defending their decision to restore the species and, later, justifying their decision to open a trapping season on them. Their claims-making regarding the otter, perhaps as a result of this difficult position, largely presented a utilitarian value of the otter and cast the otter itself as a potentially destructive predator if left unchecked by human management.

Agency claims-makers made few claims about the value of the species during the period of the conflict, with the notable exception of their economic value. This finding is consistent with Scarce's (1997:124) conclusions on the social construction of Pacific salmon where the species had "increasingly come to be viewed in utilitarian terms, as entities for human use and little else." In DOC rhetoric over otters during the controversy, the otter was constructed as neither a varmint nor a fun-loving animal. It was simply a "natural resource," a "furbearer," that needed to be controlled and exploited if justifiable from a management perspective. A DOC press release (Conley 1997:B7) stated that:

[The agency] has always supported trapping as a legitimate means of regulating furbearer populations and as a way of allowing Missourians to make use of a valuable, renewable resource-fur.

Thus, for the DOC, the value of the otter was related to its use-value as a renewable crop to be harvested for pelts. In other words, Nature was essentially a commodity to be managed, produced and harvested by people.

In this context, the waste theme resurfaced in discourse over otters. As discussed earlier, angler and pond owner activists emphasized the rhetoric of waste to describe the negative aspects of otter character and behavior. The waste theme was characteristic of DOC rhetoric also, not only in relating to the species' wastefulness, but also relating to the utilitarian value of the animal. It was the non-use of otters, particularly those trapped incidentally or as nuisance animals, that was a problem. For example, in an editorial sympathetic to the otter protection position, the editorial's author questioned a DOC spokesman about the trapping issue. The passage read:

So this is really about money. "No," [the agency spokesman] said. "It's about waste. Now if a farmer traps the [nuisance] otter he just throws the carcass away," [he] said. "That is wasteful of a renewable resource" (Bertelson 1996:1B).

Thus, the economic value of harvesting otters was presented in the context of good conservation. An otter, having no value as a nuisance animal, meaning an animal that eats fish wanted by people, regains its value after having been killed and its pelt sold on the market. So, to not trap otters and sell pelts is poor conservation and wasteful of the value of the animal.

Unlike the otter activists, DOC claims-makers rarely invoked rhetoric about the otter's ecological role. In early publications agency representatives, as otter protection activists would later do, did characterize the otter as a species that had evolved with the system and one that would not likely cause damage to fisheries. In one newspaper article, a DOC representative was quoted as saying, "The way I look at it . . . is that before we got here, the otters were here, the bass were here, the crayfish were here, and everybody got along just fine" (*West Plains Daily Quill* 1997:C4). As the controversy progressed and otter protection activists became involved, however, such rhetoric did not dominate agency claims especially those made in public arenas.

As the DOC had a bureaucratic change of heart about the culpability of otters, associated with research findings and otter damage complaints, agency claims shifted to the species' predatory behaviors and its potential to be a destructive force in Nature. Much like that of angler and pond owner activists, agency rhetoric emphasized the negative aspects of the otter's predator status. DOC representatives and their supporters more frequently described otters as "efficient predators." While the otter's ability to catch fish was acknowledged, their tendency to catch all fish was emphasized, as in this example: "Otters are notoriously adept at catching fish and can clean out a small pond in a matter of a few nights, sometimes leaving dead fish on the bank to rot" (Hamilton 1999:22).

Perhaps in an attempt to neutralize the species' appeal as a cute, playful animal, DOC depictions of river otters emphasized its status as an "adept" or "expert" hunter. One OAC member, a retired agency biologist that still worked with the department doing public outreach and education on river otters, stated that:

> A lot of people don't understand the kind of problems that otters are causing now. They see the cute side of it. You know the charismatic otter image that the otters themselves project is one that would take your fancy. The image that they don't project is that "hey, we're a top of the line predator, we're hungry and we're going to eat." (interview)

In an effort to dilute the cute, cuddly image of the otter, much DOC rhetoric called to mind Alfred Tennyson's "nature, red in tooth and claw" (Worster 1994:47). For example, a news article written by an agency biologist declared that "Otters are efficient predators and will sometimes go into a frenzy, killing more fish than they can eat" (Hamilton 1999:22). This text, conjuring mental images of a chaotic 'feeding frenzy' (usually associated with sharks), captioned a photograph of bloody fish carcasses strewn across a snowy stream bank and was featured below a close-up photograph of an otter chewing the head off of a large fish.

Descriptions of the otter's predatory behavior were often accompanied by what I termed *potential pest arguments*. The potential for otters to run amok in the landscape and become a pest animal was stressed, as in the following passage: "Otters are loveable creatures and an important feature of Missouri's ecosystem. But if their population is not carefully managed, they stand poised to become viewed as damaging pests" (Hamilton 1999:24). In such a context, the agency began to characterize the otter's feeding habits as "damage." DOC compared the creatures to species commonly associated with over-population and property damage in Missouri, such as beaver and deer (observation field notes). One DOC representative wrote:

> "People love deer," says [the biologist], "but there is a limit to how many deer they want to live with. When automobile collisions with deer become too frequent or deer do excessive damage to crops or trees, people demand that conservation agencies reduce their numbers. The same thing could eventually happen with river otters in Missouri" (DOC Press Release, July 24, 1998).

Though there were acknowledgments of otter protection activists' view of otters as playful, fun-loving creatures in agency discourse, they were more likely to downplay this view of otters and, instead, focus on the predator otter with its damage potential. The DOC cast the otter as an efficient predator with potential to become a pest to people and a detriment to Nature if skilled resource managers did not properly control them.

How do you Solve a Problem like an Otter?

In claims-making, the way in which a social problem is defined often intimates or supports the solutions that are acceptable to the claims-makers. In the otter controversy, the differing manner in which each of the parties to the controversy constructed the value and image of the river otter related directly to the solutions that they promoted throughout the debate.

Get Rid of Them

The problem for anglers and pond owners was the impact otters were having on the ponds and local, wild fisheries. As discussed previously, this group placed little value on the otters themselves. Rather, the otter was cast as a destructive, exotic species that was wreaking havoc on the landscape and destroying those things meant for human use and recreation. The otters were poor conservationists wasting resources and ignoring the rules of resource consumption.

In rhetoric over what should be done about the otter problem, much emphasis was placed on the need to "control" the species. The animals were wasting fish and so their impact must be limited in some way or another. One activist explained:

I mean as far as animals we appreciate them more than someone who would be living in the city who never deals with them. I don't want to see any of them hurt or anything else, but I know that they have to be harvested. They have to be under control. (interview)

Not surprisingly, the consumptive wildlife activities of humans, as opposed to those of otters themselves, were presented as the necessary link in the ecological system. It was people who controlled the balance of Nature, a system that was now out of sync because of river otters. One editorial writer stated, "When the human element is taken out of the balance of nature, there is no balance. The human is at the top of the food chain and when that is tampered with, an imbalance is created" (Wood 1999:2). It was up to people to control the population of otters. With otters destroying the fisheries, human activities, meaning trapping or other harvest methods, were needed to again restore the natural balance.

For many angler activists, the ideal solution was to completely remove the otters once again from the landscape. Most called for a trapping season with generous take limits so that the otter population would be immediately reduced. One angler stated, "Well, boy, if enough people did trapping and they would liberalize seasons it might hurt it (the otter population) some" (interview). However, others expressed doubts that trapping alone would be helpful to remedy the problem quickly enough or on the scale necessary. One angler lamented that:

> I don't, personally, think trapping will ever help. There's not that many trappers. Trapping is a very, very hard occupation. It is extremely hard and there's not that many people that love it . . . a few years ago you could make at least an income by trapping, but not at the way wages are now. It's not worth it. (interview)

Because the goal was to eliminate as many otters as possible, more drastic reduction measures than currently allowed by the DOC were called for. One idea presented at the OAC meetings was the implementation of a state, otter bounty system, a system similar to those historically implemented for wolves, coyotes and mountain lions in the United States. Other ideas included longer and more liberal trapping seasons or the implementation of a rifle season, in addition to a trapping season (observation field notes).

Angler and pond owner solutions were synchronous with their construction of the river otter. The species was of little value and, thus, it could be reduced drastically or, better yet, completely removed with no ill effects on the environment. Indeed, such a scenario was certainly desirable for this group and, perhaps, necessary because the personal characteristics of the otter made it an impossible fit in the modern, human-dominated landscape.

Just Watch, Don't Meddle

Otter protection activists, on the other hand, presented a drastically different conception about what the appropriate solutions were to the management problem, a problem that in their view was the trapping of the otter, not the loss of wild fish. They directed much of their rhetoric to dispel the idea that otter behaviors were to blame for declines in wild fisheries:

> According to the things I have read, they (the DOC) were trying to say that the otters were eating up all of the game fish that people were out there trying to catch. Well that's not the reason, the game fish are just being over-fished and they don't look at the . . . who knows, maybe it's environmental because the streams are polluted and stuff. It's not because of a bunch of little otters. (interview)

Otters, for this group, did not pose a significant problem to wild fish and this construction augmented the view that if otters were trapped, it would not be for the security of sport fish, but solely for the recreation and economic benefit of trappers.

Unlike anglers and pond owners, or the DOC as I will later address, otter protection activists identified human interference in Nature as more problematic than non-interference. Claims were made about the otter's biological characteristics, which were presented as indications that otter populations were not likely to grow out of control. One editorial writer argued that trapping was unnecessary because, "By reproducing slowly they regulate their numbers naturally" (Gruver 1996b:4). A quote included in the Animal Legal Defense Fund promotional packet (no date) stated that "Predators, such as otters never need to be controlled." This was so, according to one otter activist, because 1) otters would not decimate their prey base wantonly, and 2) the natural system would balance out if predator-prey relationships were left to come to a state of equilibrium without human interference (interview). Thus, no management of otters was necessary at all.

If there were problems with the natural system it was not otters, their behaviors or abundance, but was instead the much broader

problem of people negatively impacting Nature. For example, one
interviewee stated:

> I don't know why they (the DOC) think [the otters] need to be man-
> aged. The whole problem is if we allowed the natural predators to
> exist, which we don't we kill them off, half of these issues wouldn't
> be issues. (interview)

Any solution to problems with Nature, then, should involve less interference by people, not more:

> It may be that if we had a moratorium on hunting, and I'm not advo-
> cating that, it may be that what is left behind are individuals that are
> genetically superior . . . and then they will then become the ones that
> the natural environment then controls their populations more. But the
> way we've got it set up now, we're telling everyone 'hey plant every-
> thing' so that we have these huge populations of animals and then we
> have to go out and kill them because it's for their own good. My feel-
> ing is that there's something wrong with that. (interview)

Otter protection activists argued that otters should be left alone to
find their own point of equilibrium in the natural system. Further,
they argued that the DOC should take a more comprehensive look
at a fishery problem to consider human usage and watershed pollution.

Lethal trapping was out of the question for this group, which naturally followed from their construction of the animal. The otter was
not culpable for the fishery problems for which it was accused, so
calls to kill the animals became unjustifiable. Moreover, trapping was
wrong because it was a waste of the animal's value. One otter sup-
porter wrote:

> If the [agency] were to encourage otter population growth and pro-
> mote tourist viewing of this engagingly beautiful and playful amphibi-
> ous mammal, I believe the state would receive untold financial benefits.
> Therefore, I strongly urge your department to reconsider its policy
> regarding the trapping of the river otter and adapt a management
> strategy that accurately reflects the interest of most Missourians (Citizen
> letter to DOC, June 11, 1999).

Their value, in addition to their ecological role, was attached to the
behaviors that made them a desirable species for non-consumptive
wildlife viewing. If the value of the species were related to watching its behaviors, then it would make little sense to kill the animal.

Moreover, to kill the otter, as constructed by otter protection activists, would be unconscionable. If the playful creature was guiltless

of harming wild fish stocks as accused, then trapping such an animal would go beyond wasting a valuable viewing opportunity to unnecessarily torturing and murdering an innocent, playful animal. The trapping of otters for pleasure and income was not a credible justification for their destruction.

Despite opposition to trapping, otter protection activists suggested policy options for animals that became a nuisance. In such cases, non-lethal methods were always recommended. One activist stated, "If the otters are truly becoming overpopulated, [then] investigate non-lethal means of fertility inhibitors" (interview). Other activists suggested that nuisance otters should be live-trapped and relocated. Many argued that in pond-raiding cases humans should change their own behavior by adapting ponds to thwart otters by building fences or managing their ponds differently (interviews; observation field notes).

Business As Usual

The DOC's position on the otter problem was similar to the anglers and pond owners, though tempered as to the extent of harvest necessary. For the agency, too, it was the role of people to keep Nature in balance. Because people had altered the natural system, the need for human intervention was even more important. In response to the otter protection activists' view that the otter population could achieve an acceptable environmental balance on its own, one DOC representative responded, "Yeah, but there won't be equilibrium. We used to have predators; we don't have predators now. Man is the predator. If man doesn't do it, we've eliminated the other predators" (interview). So, human intervention was not only necessary to manage the otters appropriately, it was the only responsible thing to do to in order to safeguard the balance of the system.

Given that humans were established as the most appropriate mechanism for manipulating otter populations, efforts to cast the otter as a potential pest species were in line with agency efforts to solve the otter problem. By constructing the otter as a potential pest species, this legitimated the use of trapping to control the animals because nuisance animals are commonly eliminated by landowners and by the State. A trapping season, then, was presented as the answer to otter damage and complaints:

[DOC] Wildlife Division Chief... said an annual otter harvest will help limit the increase in complaints from Missourians who experience problems with otters ... Missourians who are most likely to report otter problems include those who own fishing ponds or operate fish farms. For them, a substantial otter harvest is good news (DOC Press Release, February 21, 1997).

Another DOC representative stated in a press release that it was the agency's responsibility to protect the interest of people and the environment, in light of the otter's over-abundance. The representative wrote:

We are thrilled that river otters are being so successful in reclaiming their historic haunts in Missouri, but to be responsible, we have to be responsive to people's needs as well as those of the otters. If we find that increasing numbers of otters are causing problems for people or hurting other resources, we're going to respond with appropriate changes in management (DOC press release, July 24, 1999).

The DOC argued emphatically that "trapping is the only economically feasible way of controlling these species, which can become serious pests if their numbers go unchecked" (DOC Press Release, January 16, 1998).

Conclusions

Public controversy over wildlife policy and management is not new and, like claims-making regarding other social problems, parties interested in wildlife policy outcomes engage in claims-making activities that shape problem definitions and proposed solutions. Several constructions of the otter emerged as conflict over the otter problem and its solutions ensued. Wrangling over control of the public image of otters occurred as each group painted the otter, its habits and value in a manner that supported their definition of the problem and proposed solutions.

The value and need for otters became quite important within the debate. Not surprisingly, anglers and pond owners did not attribute value directly to the otter, while otter protection activists attributed a great deal of value to the mammal. The DOC stayed somewhat neutral on the ecological value of the otter, but did present claims about the species utilitarian value. In addition, within the context of the claims, the value of the otter became intertwined with construction of the species' personal character and motivations.

The ecological role of the river otter, whether for good or for bad, was also an important focus of claims-making. Most notably, the predatory nature of the otter was a focal point of discourse. Each group made different claims about the importance of the otter in the natural system, its ability to coexist with other species in that system and, finally, the effect the presence of the otter would ultimately have.

Although understanding how competing groups construct an animal differently is important, the goal of this research is to highlight the fact that differing constructions of wildlife, in this case the otter, inevitably lead to different views on what the appropriate management solutions should be. In the otter controversy, the contrasting constructions of the otter and its behavior related to the different solutions that each group proposed or supported, which were the elimination of as many otters as possible, the elimination of lethal trapping and the continuation of state-sanctioned trapping seasons.

Policy Implications

According to Kellert (1993:65), the diverse attitudes that exist in U.S. society regarding animals "may offer some insight as to why so much conflict and controversy surround the management and treatment of wildlife." In other words, there are many competing constructions of wildlife in modern society, which are based on a diversity of social and personal values, experiences and attitudes. Also, it is reasonable to suspect that the diversity of relationships and attitudes toward wildlife will grow more divergent in the future.

While discussing the social construction of endangered species in the context of policy actions, Czech and Krausman (2001:60–61) tell us that:

> Although nonhuman species cannot literally participate in the political arena, they do have unsolicited political power held in trust for them by interest groups, which are fundamental units of political power in pluralist theories of democracy.

This passage drives home a point that contemporary wildlife controversies have revealed. Different social groups are very willing to exert political power and bring vast amounts of resources to bear for or against the interests of particular species, however they are constructed. These two passages, together, suggest that developing an ability to meaningfully acknowledge and include diverse interests in wildlife conflict in the future would be very beneficial.

In the management context, it has long been recommended that management agencies should reach out to stakeholder groups and involve them in the policy process (Conover 2001; Gilbert and Dodds 1992; Tilt 1989). In order to meaningfully include stakeholder groups in conflict negotiation, the agency, and ideally all groups that are party to the conflict, should make an effort to objectively understand opponent constructions. This might be done with the assistance of an independent facilitator or an impartial assessment of the conflict. At any rate, moving beyond viewing controversy over wildlife as mere politicking or grandstanding by interested groups is a prerequisite to truly understanding alternative views of wildlife and nature.

Social constructionist approaches to understanding conflict, such as that employed in the present research, can enable those engaged in the policy-making process to more meaningfully understand and, consequently, incorporate alternative views of wildlife and nature into management policy. In the midst of controversy over wildlife issues it may be tempting for policy-makers and wildlife managers to dismiss the claims and constructions of other groups as self-interested, extreme, frivolous or wrong. However, this approach can lead to ineffective stakeholder inclusion and alienation from the negotiation process, which would do little to address core issues that will continue to crop up in future conflicts.

Instead, efforts to elucidate the differences between the constructions of different groups should be made and common ground for solutions must be sought. If this is accomplished, then understanding core differences in proposed solutions is made possible and this may be a more productive starting point for settling differences. Further, with genuine attempts to incorporate alternative views of wildlife, all stakeholders will be more invested in the negotiation process and have a more positive experience as a result. This could increase the likelihood of participants accepting and supporting compromise solutions. The establishment of the OAC by the DOC was one attempt to do just this, although their efforts began long after bad feelings and mistrust had permeated the conflict. Nevertheless, at the time of writing, their efforts seem to have paid off in Missouri's river otter conflict.

Another issue that this research highlights is that, although few agencies would view themselves as a stakeholder group, there may be some advantages to doing so. While texts on wildlife management often point out that there are multiple stakeholder groups or interested parties regarding any one wildlife issue (Anderson 1999; Gilbert and Dodds 1992), what is seldom discussed is that wildlife agencies themselves present their own constructions of animals and events. In addition, their policies and efforts very often support or benefit particular stakeholder groups over others for various reasons. Unfortunately, the implication of excluding agencies from being classified as a stakeholder group is that agency constructions then become privileged, which may unfairly privilege a particular group in turn.

Although this privileging might be deemed legitimate based on the scientific nature of debates or because of an agency's authority to define the species, problems and solutions, there may be disadvantages to forcing claims based on this status. As Tilt (1989:39) points out about public perception and endangered species policy, "if the general perception runs against an animal or plant's continued survival, all the biological data in the world will be useless against the perception." The same lesson must apply in the context of management of other species. Forcing definitions of a problem and subsequent solutions may be successful in the short-term, but the long-term prospects of conflict reoccurring may make the victory hard won. Until core differences in constructions are addressed, opposition will likely continue in different contexts and at different times.

If democratic problem-solving is the goal, it becomes important to get beyond arguments over the objective conditions that spur conflict and focus on what the social constructions of those conditions have become. This is so if we are to truly to make headway in addressing social problems, including conflict over wildlife management, and finding ways to more equitably manage and resolve conflicts that must spring from them.

References

Anderson, Stanley H. 1999. *Managing Our Wildlife Resources*, 3rd Ed. Upper Saddle River, NJ: Prentice Hall.
Animal Legal Defense Fund. (no date). Promotional packet on river otter trapping in Missouri.

Bennitt, Rudolf and Werner O. Nagel. 1937. *A Survey of the Resident Game and Furbearers of Missouri*. The University of Missouri Studies Series 12(2). University of Missouri: Columbia, MO.

Bertelson, Christine. 1996. Editorial, "Otter Trapping Policy Just Doesn't Make Good Sense." *St. Louis Post-Dispatch* (MO), August 6, pp. 1B.

Best, Joel. 1987. "Rhetoric in Claims-Making: Constructing the Missing Children Problem." *Social Problems* 34(2).

Best Joel, ed. 1989. *Images of Issues: Typifying Contemporary Social Problems*. New York: Aldine de Gruyter.

Citizen letter to DOC, June 11, 1999.

Citizen letter to DOC, December [no day] 1999a.

Citizen letter to DOC, December [no day] 1999b.

Citizen letter to DOC, January 3, 2000.

Citizen letter to DOC, January 24, 2000.

Citizen letter to DOC, February 15, 2000.

Citizen letter to DOC, March 27, 2000.

Citizen letter to DOC, April [no day], 2000.

Conover, Michael. 2001. *Resolving Human-Wildlife Conflict: The Science of Wildlife Damage Management*. Boca Raton, FL: Lewis Publishers.

Conley, Jerry. 1997. "Missouri's Conservation Principles." *St. Louis Post-Dispatch* (MO), December 8, pp. B7.

Czech, Brian and Paul R. Krausman. 2001. *The Endangered Species Act: History, Conservation Biology, and Public Policy*. Baltimore, MD: The Johns Hopkins University Press.

DOC [Missouri Department of Conservation] Press Release, February 21, 1997.

DOC [Missouri Department of Conservation] Press Release, January 16, 1998.

DOC [Missouri Department of Conservation] Press Release, October 2, 1998.

DOC [Missouri Department of Conservation] Press Release, July 24, 1998.

DOC [Missouri Department of Conservation] Press Release, July 24, 1999.

Dizard, Jan. 1994. *Going Wild: Hunting, Animal Rights and the Contested Meaning of Nature*. Amherst, MA: University of Massachusetts Press.

Dunlap, Thomas R. 1988. *Saving America's Wildlife: Ecology and the American Mind, 1850–1990*. Princeton, NJ: Princeton University Press.

Gieich, Terri. 1997. "Otters Hurting Ozarks Fishing." *Springfield News-Leader*, November 8, pp. 1.

Gilbert, Frederick F. and Donald G. Dodds. 1992. *The Philosophy and Practice of Wildlife Management*, 2nd Ed. Malabar, FL: Krieger Publishing Company.

Gruver, Mead. 1996a. *The Riverfront Times*, February 14–20, pp. 17.

———. 1996b. "Otter trapping unjustified." *Jefferson City News Tribune*, June 2, pp. 4.

Hamilton, Dave. 1998. *Missouri River Otter Population Assessment: Final Report – 1996–97 and 1997–98 Trapping Seasons and Petition for Multi-Year Export Authority*. Jefferson City, MO: Missouri Department of Conservation.

———. 1999. "Controversy in Times of Plenty." *Missouri Conservationist* 60(11):17–24.

Hilgartner, Stephen and Charles L. Bosk. 1988. "The Rise and Fall of Social Problems: A Public Arenas Model." *American Journal of Sociology* 94(1):53–78.

Keller, Rudi. 1999. "Feds Allow Export of River Otter Pelts by State's Trappers." *Columbia Daily Tribune*, January 10.

Kellert, Stephen R. 1985. "Public Perceptions of Predators, Particularly the Wolf and Coyote." *Biological Conservation* 31:167–189.

———. 1993. "Attitudes, Knowledge, and Behavior Toward Wildlife Among the Industrial Superpowers: United States, Japan, and Germany." *Journal of Social Issues* 49(1):53–69.

Missouri River Otter Protection Coalition. (No date.) Brochure, *Missouri's River Otters are in Big Trouble and You Can Help*.

———. 1998. (Handout).

Mitchell, Robert W. 1997. "Anthropomorphic Anecdotalism as Method." Pp. 151–169 in *Anthropomorphism, Anecdotes and Animals*, edited by R.W. Mitchell et al. Albany, NY: University of New York.

Rikoon, Sandy and Robin Albee. 1998. "'Wild and Free, Leave 'Em Be': Wild Horses and the Struggle Over Nature in the Missouri Ozarks." *Journal of Folklore Research* 35(3):203–222.

Scarce, Rik. 1997. "Socially Constructing Pacific Salmon." *Society and Animals* 5(2):117–135.

———. 2000. *Fishy Business: Salmon, Biology, and the Social Construction of Nature*. Philadelphia, PA: Temple University Press.

Simms, Lori. 1992. "Bringing the Otter Back." *Missouri Conservationist* 53(12):26–28.

Tilt, Whitney. 1989. "The Biopolitics of Endangered Species." *Endangered Species Update* 6(10):35–39.

Uhlenbrock, Tom. 1999. "Resurgent Otters Catch Ecological Cross Fire." *St. Louis Post-Dispatch*, January 1, p. F4.

West Plains Daily Quill. 1997. "DOC: Otters Unlikely Suspects in Stream Fishing Capers." May 7, p. C4.

Wilson, Matthew A. 1997. "The Wolf in Yellowstone: Science, Symbol, or Politics? Deconstructing the Conflict Between Environmentalism and Wise Use." *Society and Natural Resources* 10:453–468.

Wood, C. Russell. 1999. Opinion, "A Call for Rat and Cockroach Rights." *South Central Agri-Advertiser*, February 10, p. 2.

Worster, Donald. 1994. *Nature's Economy: The History of Ecological Ideas*, 2nd Ed. Cambridge, MA: Cambridge University Press.

Notes

[1] I would like to thank Ann Detwiler-Breidenbach who assisted with some of the early interviewing and document collection. I thank Diane Rodgers, Ann Herda-Rapp, Tina Evers, James Goedeke, Debo McKinney, Mary Jo Neitz and Gene Ertel for advice, feedback, ideas, editorial assistance or proofreading on various drafts of this paper or the research in general. A special thanks goes to all of my interviewees.

[2] Meaning claims-making that occurred in venues where discourse was readily available to the general public, which included newspapers, magazines, the internet and organization publication dispersed by members.

[3] Meaning claims-making that occurred in venues not readily accessible to the general public but where policy discourse occurred. Examples of documents from such venues include handouts at OAC meetings, correspondence to the agency from private citizens and internal organization publications not specifically authored for public distribution.

[4] Personal names of interviewees have been excluded from this document in order to ensure anonymity. To the extent possible, I have attempted to exclude the personal names of all people who were involved in the controversy. Only the names of individuals who published materials in the public domain (in newspapers or magazines) have been included.

[5] Cited in: Missouri River Otter Protection Coalition. 1998. (Handout). Within this publication, the quote is attributed to Melquist, Wayne. 1997. *Wild Furbearer Management and Conservation in North America*.

VIRTUAL DEER: BAGGING THE MYTHICAL "BIG ONE" IN CYBERSPACE

Carol D. Miller

Introduction

In the United States in 1996, 10.7 million hunters went out a total of 131 million days to hunt deer, and big game hunters spent $9.7 million on their trips and equipment (U.S. Fish and Wildlife Service 1997). Deer hunting is obviously an important activity for many people in the United States, so what are hunters' perceptions of the deer they pursue? Interestingly, sociologists Berger and Luckmann (1966:67) specifically discussed hunting as a social activity that allows individuals to define their identity:

> [Hunting] will produce a specific type of person, namely the hunter, whose identity and biography as a hunter have meaning only in a universe constituted by the aforementioned body of knowledge as a whole (say, in a hunter's society) or in part (say, in our own society, in which hunters come together in a subuniverse of their own).

In this chapter I explore how hunters attach special meanings to the deer they hunt by examining their discourse on Internet bulletin boards devoted to hunting. I argue that the deer they described were social constructions. That is, the descriptions were purposely created by the hunters' choices of words, to produce a specific reality.

I argue, however, that these socially constructed deer were distortions because of the electronic environment in which their discussions took place. Virtual deer, those described in cyberspace, had specific qualities because of the social nature of electronically mediated discussions. Cyberspace deer hunters described deer in a way that allowed them to enhance their own identities and their perceptions about hunting. This allowed them to escape into a fantasy woods, where, not unlike the children in Lake Wobegon, all the deer were above average. These distortions have implications for wildlife managers who need to remain aware of the hunters' perspectives as stakeholders in wildlife policy. If a hunter's perception of his or her self, their identity, is tied to the size of the deer they hunt and how challenging the hunt is, wildlife policy changes could possibly disrupt their self-perceptions and, in turn, be met with great resistance from the hunters. Wildlife policy-makers and enforcers need to keep in mind that hunting provides specific identities and meaning to the lives of hunters (Berger and Luckmann 1966). Hunters' discussions of deer on the Internet exhibited that identity construction.

Socially Constructing Animals

The reality of everyday life is a product of human interaction (Berger and Luckmann 1966). What we know about the existence of animals, human and nonhuman, is understood through the lens of culture that varies over place and time. Arluke (1994:143) claimed that although nonhuman animals are "real," humans construct meanings about animals that reflect their cultural concerns. "To say that animals are social constructions means that we have to look beyond what is regarded as innate in animals – beyond their physical appearance, observable behavior, and cognitive abilities – in order to understand how humans will think about and interact with them" (Arluke and Sanders 1996:9).

Analyses of social constructions of animals have focused on specific animals with which humans interact. Human perceptions of bears, for example, have changed over time and varied across cultures. Respect for bears was often shown in some Native American cultures by referring to them as "grandfather" or other honorable names, whereas, in Western civilization a separation between "man and beast" has been maintained (Lawrence 1986).

Within a specific group, supposedly sharing a culture, social constructions of animals can change over time. For example, Scarce (2000) described how some biologists changed the meanings and the cultural values they attached to salmon with each new piece of information published about the fish. Scarce found that there was a growing population of biologists that belonged to a "conservation biology" subdiscipline. Unlike most of the biologists that Scarce met in his research, these biologists saw the salmon as intrinsically valuable, as opposed to economically valuable only.

Hunters are one group that attach specific meanings to the animals they pursue. In her analysis of hunting in contemporary Dutch society, Dahles (1993) discussed how hunters classified the animals they hunted as "game." She claimed that this classification allowed wild, hunted animals to be associated with tame livestock that was consumed. The classification as game also allowed hunters to protect and care for animals that they simultaneously sought to kill.

The meanings that hunters and other groups attach to the animals depend on the situation or their own interests. Dizard (1994) analyzed the controversy that formed over a proposed deer hunt in the Quabbin Reservoir. In this case, many of the hunters who killed the deer on the Quabbin claimed the deer were smaller than normal and attributed that to their overpopulation, even though a comparison of the Quabbin deer with others found there was not a difference in average size (Dizard 1994:103). This suggested that their perceptions of the deer were affected by the specific beliefs and motivations they held. Those opposed to the hunt saw deer as representing the "grace, beauty and tranquility" of the reservoir (Dizard 1994:12). Other groups in favor of the hunt saw the deer as vermin chomping down on the ecosystem (Dizard 1994:2). From all of these examples, researchers showed that one's construction of animals was not only dependent upon culture or group membership, but it can vary from place and time.

It is important, especially for those involved in shaping wildlife management policy, to understand the hunters' *need* to think about deer the way they do. Hunters use the animals they pursue to construct their own identities. "In their cognitive schemas, hunters measure their power and abilities against strong, cunning and preferably male opponents" (Dahles 1993:182). Humans often use animals to express traits they desire in themselves. This is most evident in the use of animal mascots for sports teams. The Detroit Lions and the Chicago Bears are certainly perceived as fiercer and more competitive foes than would be the Detroit Kittens and the Chicago Hamsters. Sanders (1999) suggested that the breed of dog one chooses as a companion often exhibits characteristics of oneself one wishes to illustrate to others. "Powerful and aggressive dogs such as Rottweilers and German shepherds, for example, not only have a protective function but also reflect the owner's desire to present a social self that is correspondingly aggressive" (Sanders 1999:6).

Other examples can be found in entire cultures and specific sub-cultures. In the subculture of dog fighting, Forsyth and Evans (1998) explained how the dog owners described pit bull terriers as natural fighters. This social construction allowed the owners to neutralize the deviant status of the dogs and construct their own identities as non-criminal. In Vanuatu, pigs were used to enhance the identity of leaders (Miles 1997). Pig killing for a feast was a symbol of power and wealth. Humans use animals to construct specific cultural and subcultural identities. The social construction of animals depends on the culture, time, place and agenda of the group doing the con-structing. In cyberspace, ".... a subuniverse of their own" (Berger and Luckman 1966:67), hunters described deer in a specific way to enhance the culture and agenda of the group communicating and constructing reality on the bulletin board. More importantly, the deer described reflect the qualities the hunters desire in themselves.

Virtual Deer Constructed in Cyberspace

An entire industry of sporting goods stores like Cabelas or Gander Mountain exists for hunters, allowing them to wander around the selection of camouflage clothing, rifles and ammunition and other hunting supplies, while surrounded by taxidermy deer, bears and coyotes. In other words, they can experience aspects of hunting in an artificial reality. Another option for stepping into this reality is the hunting magazine. *Deer and Deer Hunting* magazine describes itself as the magazine "published for serious, analytical deer hunters who have a year-around passion for whitetail hunting." Hunters can get a dose of hunting even when their game is not in season. In such magazines, hunters can consume constructions of animals and hunt-ing experiences created by authors, magazine editors and advertisers.

Computers offer another option for animal/human interactions for hunters. The most popular selling computer game in the second quarter of 1998 was *Deer Hunter: An Interactive Hunting Experience* (Feldman 2004). It spawned five sequels and the software company claimed, "Every day should be a hunting day, and with Deer Hunter 3, it can be." Deer hunters can also get their deer fix on the Internet. They can discuss, share pictures and construct deer to fit their own desire on Internet bulletin board discussion forums.

Where hunters discuss deer is as important as the discourse. Internet bulletin boards are interactive and anonymous and this allows hunters to actively construct a reality about the deer and about themselves. Hunters who describe deer on Internet bulletin boards have a specific agenda and the electronic medium offers a type of liberation that allows them to construct deer in the very specific ways they desire. Hunters escape any physical inadequacies that they or their real deer might have by participating in an Internet bulletin board about deer hunting. Virtual deer can be as big and tough as the hunters wish to describe them, and they, themselves, can be as great in their sport as their deer reflect.

Methods

The research I present here includes analysis of participation on four different discussion forums or Internet bulletin boards in which "out-doors-people" of all types spent time interacting with others of their ilk. The research consisted of two parts: a survey and an examination of threads posted to two bulletin boards.

I started this study by posting a survey with open-ended questions on two Internet bulletin boards, *Deer Talk* and *The Coffee Shop Forum*, dedicated to discussing deer hunting. I posted the message and checked for responses daily until there were no new posts, for fifteen days after the initial post. I asked hunters to reflect on their experiences as hunters and to consider what they would miss if they could not hunt. Also, I asked if they were successful in their last hunt, in order to elicit a discussion about the kill and to see how they treated that discussion. Finally, I inquired if they hunted alone, with friends, family and/or their spouse or significant other. I asked this question to test other hypotheses about why they hunted as well as to explore how they felt about deer. Because the sample was purposive, it was limited to only those deer hunters who read and posted messages to these deer hunters' bulletin boards on the Internet. Responses from this part of the study are designated by "survey."

I received a total of thirty-four responses to my open-ended survey. The majority (thirty-one) of the responses were posted to the bulletin board, and three were emailed to me. Thirty-three men and one woman responded to my questions. Their ages ranged from sixteen to fifty-two years old. Most of the responses were lengthy (four or more paragraphs long) and detailed. I conducted a content analysis of each bulletin board post or e-mailed response in order to uncover the main themes in the hunters' answers. I did this by reading each post in its entirety, watching for specific characteristics of deer described. I created clusters of descriptions within the posts and then assigned themes to each cluster. Surprisingly, there were only three clusters or themes describing deer that emerged out of the data.

I conducted a follow-up investigation in which I analyzed independent posts to Internet bulletin boards. After my original results exposed very specific constructions of deer, I decided to test whether the results were a product of the method I used to obtain the data, so I returned to the bulletin boards. I found, though, that *Deer Talk* no longer existed, so I observed other discussion threads on *Coffee Shop, ModernSportsman.com* and *24HourCampfire.com* and analyzed posts for their constructs of deer. In other words, I lurked on the sites and read what people posted for readers on these forums. The discussions in these forums ranged in topics from which scope to use for whitetail hunting to what remedies work best for poison ivy. Some of the topics focused on political issues that affected hunters, such as Second Amendment rights and changes in the hunting regulations.

After reading through all of the discussion threads, I specifically chose to observe discussions that had descriptions of deer in them. For example, many of the threads focused on equipment and did not have any descriptions of deer. I analyzed threads having titles like, "Where do all the bucks go??" or "Anyone else scouting deer?" I selected these threads of discussion because specific deer were described to other members (or people like me who were lurking on the bulletin board).

This follow-up included an analysis of three more threads containing a total of forty-four posts. These threads came from *Coffee Shop*, one of the original forums and *24HourCampfire.com*, one of the newer forums. Although the newer forum did identify the gender of the discussant, other demographic information was not available unless it appeared in the post for some reason. Most of these posts were shorter (only one sentence to two paragraphs long) than those in the original stage of the study. Once again, I conducted a content analysis of the bulletin board messages. This time I specifically looked for the themes describing deer I previously uncovered in the first part of this study.

It is important to keep in mind the limitations of Internet research. Research conducted on-line is limited to the population connected to the Internet. There is a large fraction of the overall population not yet connected (Chambliss and Schutt 2003). Also, research on the Internet requires special ethical considerations (Hamilton 2004). The content analysis of the naturally occurring discussion threads in the follow-up stage was an unobtrusive method of analysis, similar to conducting content analysis on letters to editors in newspapers or magazines. The discussant is already aware that their posts are "published" on-line and available to anyone on the World Wide Web to read.

For the survey stage of this study, I was given approval from my university's Institutional Review Board to post the survey. I explained the purpose of the study to the discussion board participants. They were informed that by responding to the posted survey, they were agreeing to allow their posts or emails to be analyzed and included in presentations and published reports. I also assured them that I would maintain their anonymity and/or confidentiality. Anonymity is sometimes easier to maintain with Internet research because participants usually use aliases (Hamilton 2004).[1]

Results

In this section I discuss the results from both the survey I posted and the posts I analyzed in naturally occurring threads in the second stage of the study. Results from both stages revealed similar constructions of deer in cyberspace. The results of the Internet bulletin board survey revealed that the cyberspace hunters saw deer as beautiful, big, smart animals with very keen, well-developed senses of sight, hearing and smell. Nineteen of the thirty-four posts described characteristics of deer in general or a particular deer they had hunted and, perhaps, killed. Overall, the main themes that emerged from the analysis of their responses were that 1) deer are a challenge to hunt, 2) deer are "big game," and 3) deer are beautiful animals. In the follow-up observation of the naturally occurring discussion threads, thirty-two of the forty-four posts described deer. Two of the same themes of "deer are 'big game'" and "deer are a challenge to hunt" were evident in these posts, as well. The third, "deer are beautiful," did not appear in these posts.

On these bulletin boards, the hunters did not just exchange advice about hunting. Instead, they developed identities as knowledgeable, skilled hunters. Reporting that deer have enviable traits that the hunters "match" gave the hunters status. They used the imagery of the deer to enhance their own identities the same way humans have used their companion animals to express information about their own personalities (Sanders 1999). These posts revealed that hunting was not just a hobby or recreational activity; it is part of these hunters' identities and they are active agents in constructing that identity through their electronic discussions. They used deer and hunting to enhance their own identities and establish status within their group.

Deer are a Challenge

The most interesting and frequent responses discussed the challenge of hunting an animal that, to them, had very keen and well-developed senses and was skilled in its environment. When asked why they hunted, four of the survey respondents expressed this perception of deer and twelve of the thirty-two posts of the threads observed in the follow-up study constructed deer this way.

The first bulletin board member who posted to the thread I started wrote, "I enjoy being in the woods. The challenge of taking an animal that is the master of his domain." A different hunter offered:

> I hunt for many reasons. I do feel that I am a predator and the kill is the thrill and objective, but not near the full reason [for hunting]. *I want to match wits with the animals that smell, see, and hear better than me, and know the woods better than I. I love the challenge and the food I put on the table.* (survey, emphasis added)

A third respondent wrote, "It puts meat on the table, and challenges me to outsmart another living thing" (survey). Another said, "There is something almost spiritual for me now when I head out alone to match wits with a wild creature . . ." (survey). Finally, one hunter responded to the question, "Why do you hunt deer?" in the same way, explaining:

> Deer is the only "big game" in my area. *Deer are possibly the "smartest" of our big game animals,* though I wouldn't argue with anyone about that because I haven't hunted anything else, yet. All the guys who've been to Africa tell me that *a trophy whitetail is probably the hardest "trophy" to acquire, on average, at least as regards the matching of our wits with the quarry* [*sic*]. Other animals certainly offer harder terrain, though. "Winning" that contest is a bit more "meaningful" than shooting birds over a pointing dog or a field of feed. (survey, emphasis added)

These responses, as well as those reported below, exhibited how the emphasis on deer as wise and cunning was a reflection on the hunters themselves. They described, or constructed, deer in a manner that simultaneously boosted their own status as hunters within their community. Twelve of the thirty-two posts analyzed for deer descriptions in the follow-up study of bulletin board posts made a reference to deer being cunning or having better senses of sight and smell than the hunters. The thread in which most of these responses occurred was entitled, "camo or not?" The originator of the thread posed the following question:

> I would like to know your opinion on [camouflage clothing]. It is my understanding that deer, elk, pronghorn etc, can see very little color. What they can see very well is movement, which can be a bigger enemy to hunters. When watching shows on cable, you see these hunters all decked out in camo, then they wear the bright orange, packs, vests, & hats. I understand these are for safety. What do you think? (bulletin board post)

A bulletin board member responded in agreement by emphasizing the highly developed eyesight of deer and moose:

> I agree – movement, sound, and scent are the three biggies – a solid block of color/shade is the fourth, or maybe fifth in line, tho [*sic*]. Have to include ultraviolet light in there somewhere too – I would put it above solid color – after all, stumps, rocks and trees have pretty solid colors as well. As long as you are still . . . I have personally had game spook on me in late evening, when the only thing they could have been keying off was the UV "glow" of the clothes, including when I was wearing some brand new camo not UV killed. *The nocturnal/diurnal critters like deer and moose see farther down into the UV range than we do* – I don't know about pronghorns or other mostly daylight critters . . . (bulletin board post, emphasis added)

In a thread entitled "Where do the bucks go??" a bulletin board member posted that very question. He asked the other hunters if they knew where the bucks went during hunting season. He said that he noticed that when hunting season began, he usually saw some bucks, but as the season continued, the bucks seemed to disappear. Many of the responses attempted to explain the scarcity of bucks by discussing the bucks' skills in hiding and out-witting less skilled hunters. For example, one of the moderators on the discussion forum wrote:

Where do bucks go? Amazingly enough research has shown not far
at all. That's the easy part, the hard part is *the whitetail's ability to hide
almost before our eyes and stay put while ernest [sic] hunters crash the brush all
around them.* All of us at one time or another have suffered that ultimate of *deer insults* that of being "Flagged" by a whitetail buck. Indeed,
so widespread is this annoying of deer habits that all hunters can be
divided into two groups those who have been flagged and those who
will be. The sight of the big Whitetail bouncing away through the
brush from a spot that we had just passed within a few feet of answers
the question of where do bucks go better than I could. It's simply off
to teach another hunter just who is really in control of these Autumnal activities.
(bulletin board post, emphasis added)

Another response made a connection between the skills of the deer
and their size:

Once deer get the idea that the hunting season is in progress, their
patterns change pretty quickly. Here in Tennessee, the squirrel season
begins just about the same time as bow season for deer. It's not to
[sic] uncommon to see some pretty good bucks during early-morning
squirrel hunts, but in the same areas a month later at the beginning
of muzzleloader season, bucks will be noticeably less evident. By mid-
November when the center-fire season begins, only the immature bucks
with no previous hunting exposure will be following their summer
travel routes. The older, more experienced bucks have reacted to the
increased hunting pressure and gone into the deep cover and shifted
their feeding and travel times until well after dark. . . . *Big, older bucks
didn't get that way by being stupid.* The two biggest racks I've seen in 18
years of hunting my 100 acres were on a pair of bucks that stepped
up out of a deep ditch just before dark last muzzleloader season, and
a mistake with a set trigger caused me to miss one of them, a standing, broadside shot at 75 yards! *Big bucks do make dumb mistakes, just not
often!* Good luck this season! Jerry (bulletin board post, emphasis added)

Another post supported the above message:

One thing I learned over the years is that hunters make mistakes every
year, sometimes repeat them. Bucks don't seem to make the same mistake twice. Once a buck becomes mature and is past the rut, they
seem to get cagier and cagier each year. (bulletin board post)

The originator of the thread responded to some of the replies to his
post by suggesting that the deer were outsmarting the hunters by
hiding in places they would never look:

I used to live & hunt whitetails in Illinois. I mainly hunted public land
along with quite a few other hunters. One trick I discovered for finding

hard hunted deer was to look for a secluded, overlooked, walked past spot within a few hundred yards of the parking area. You wouldn't think it, but deer often seemed to stay near the parking lot and keep tabs on the hunters – none of which stayed close to their vehicles. I got a shot (missed :'( ) at one of the biggest bucks I ever saw in a for- gotten corner, not 25 yards from my vehicle a couple of years back! *He was old and wise enough to know how to duck an arrow.* (bulletin board post, emphasis added)

Finally, one member made a connection between the skills of the deer and his skills as a hunter. He associated his own willingness to endure strenuous hunting conditions with the ability to find these cunning, reclusive deer.

I hunt central Wisconsin and I can vouch for what you're saying. The big bucks DO disappear and right quick. From what I've seen they normally head to the thickest, nastiest, most God-awful chunk of brush you can imagine. I've been out still hunting, and ran across about a 3-acre chunk of nothing but Raspberry, Blackberry and Prickly Ash. Needless to say it was no picnic walking through this stuff. I did though, and was rewarded by jumping two VERY nice bucks. I had to prac- tically step on them before they would jump. *I think a lot of people would have just walked right by these bucks assuming they even had the balls to walk through that horrid mess.* (bulletin board post, emphasis added)

Smart, cunning deer are a social construction, a construction that may contrast with real experiences. Although deer do have keen senses of smell, sight and hearing, they can be gentle, affectionate and quite tame (Jackson 1961:419). The abundance of deer in many areas has made them less than challenging to even see or hit with an automobile. As a hunter in Dizard's study (1994:100–101) com- mented, "There are deer everywhere in there and they are tame as hell . . . any damn fool could get a deer there." In many cases the natural predators of deer, including puma, timber wolf and lynx, no longer pose a threat to deer, thus their populations have needed increased management (Jackson 1961:419). Research participants referred to abundant deer only three times in the total fifty-one posts analyzed in both stages of the study. Constructing deer as common, available, plentiful and tame would contradict the hunters' dominant construction of deer as elusive and challenging to hunt. Also, wily deer contribute to the hunters' perceptions of themselves as skillful sportsmen.

Deer are "Big Game"

Five survey respondents mentioned the large size of deer. Usually they just mentioned the deer's size as part of their description of their hunting experience or as an explanation for why they preferred to hunt deer over other game. As presented above, one hunter said that deer were "big game." Two other hunters expressed a desire to hunt deer for that reason. The first one wrote, "I hunt deer and wild hogs because I cannot seem to 'hunt up' enough spare money to head north and hunt moose and caribou very often. I hunt deer and hogs because the 'Cave Bear,' 'Mastodon,' 'Irish Elk,' 'Saber tooth Tiger' and 'Dire wolf' are long gone." The other respondent wrote that he hunts deer, "because that is the only 'big game' in these parts (Elk are being reintroduced though)" (survey).

The hunters continually focused on large deer, and many specifically made the link to large deer as desired "trophies" that further increased their status among other hunters or family members. Many associated pride with getting a large buck. Some did not list the size of deer as the reason for hunting them, but described a particular deer or desirable deer as being large. When asked how he would feel if he could no longer hunt, this is what one hunter wrote: "I would still go out in the woods to enjoy the moment. I would miss the feeling that comes from having a large Buck in my sights about ready to pull the trigger. I don't believe that feeling can be captured any other way" (survey). Four others mentioned the large size of their fantasy deer or the deer they have killed. The first wrote, "For 37 years now I have taken to the woods to hunt deer with the anticipation of bagging the mythical 'big one'. I never have . . . and in a very sincere sort of twist, hope that I never do" (survey). In one response, father-son pride was associated with shooting big deer:

> I personally have two "best" hunting experiences as far as deer are concerned. The first being my first deer and the fact that my dad was watching it through his scope when I shot. The deer was 80 yards out standing quartering away when I shot it with a pre 64.30–30 lever action with open sights. The second was a year or two later when I got to be in the same stand as my dad and watch him shoot *the biggest buck of his life.* (survey, emphasis added)

Another respondent specifically stated his own pride: ". . . with maybe 5 minutes of shooting light left, out popped 3 does, they circled around and the largest gave me a broadside shot. I took it and she ran. We took out after her and found her 150 yards away, nailed through both lungs with that little 6mm. Boy, was I proud" (survey). A third respondent wrote, "I first saw this buck in June, on the hillside behind my parents' home. I was shaken by the size of the rack and thought I was looking at an elk. It was larger than any buck I had ever seen in this area" (survey). This response was particularly interesting because he described how he spent the summer and fall tracking the deer with his camera and how people in the area were starting to talk about his buck. He finished the story by stating that because of this buck, he has held the record, since 1987, for the largest buck taken in the county. In other words, the size of this buck enhanced his status within the county, and then again on the discussion bulletin board to which he posted his response to the survey.

Large deer were mentioned in thirteen of the thirty-two bulletin board posts that discussed deer in the follow-up observation. Only one of the thirty-two posts mentioned a small deer. Most of the references to big deer were just brief, one-word descriptions embedded in the rest of the post. For example, one member described his experience hunting in the woods of New York. He included the comment that there were, "some large racks, viewed as they seek out a doe or two." Another discussant mentioned, "The sight of that big Whitetail bouncing away." Yet another noted that the "Big, older bucks didn't get that way by being stupid!" and another member found "the biggest bucks I ever saw." One member lamented, "The big bucks Do disappear."

One thread initiated by a member asked where he could hunt whitetails. He wanted "to go somewhere where the quality of animals is good and also where there is a decent buck to doe ratio" (bulletin board post). Many of the posts responding to his request questioned his criteria for a good hunting experience, and most assumed that he was after big bucks. One member wrote, "It sounds as if you want quite a bit! Most public land certainly doesn't sound like it will supply your needs, at least in the Midwest that is. Here in Illinois, there are some large racks and there are places where you have large tracts of public land to yourself, but you really have to work for it" (bulletin board post). A second member offered his state for hunting: "Nebraska has big (corn fed) whitetail and mule deer. . . . Eastern Nebraska and Western Iowa might be a good opportunity for that trophy buck" (bulletin board post). An Ohio

member wrote, "Big Midwest deer in Ohio. Cornfed bucks in western Ohio and reclusive bucks in southern and eastern Ohio. Gun
or bow" (bulletin board post). One member questioned what the
thread initiator really wanted:

> Now you said you would like to hunt whitetail deer. With what, bow,
> muzzleloader? or center-fire? Do you want a *huge rack*? or just a nice
> one? or just a doe to eat? How much are you willing to spend? All
> the land in Texas is private. *But we have the largest deer herd in the states
> and some huge racked bucks.* But the catch is, it is not cheap on ranches
> where *big bucks* are plentyful [*sic*] . . . (bulletin board post, emphasis
> added)

From these posts, it was obvious that the largeness of deer was
an important characteristic for these hunters. This last post suggested
that deer with huge racks were usually preferred over smaller bucks
and does. Along with the responses above, two hunters did not necessarily mention the size of the deer, but they referred to deer as
trophies. The use of the word trophy exhibited the idea that the
large deer were "a memento, as of one's personal achievements"
(The American Heritage Dictionary 1994).

Of course, characteristics of deer vary. Not all deer are large.
Deer species range in size. The European elk can average a height
of over seven feet. The South American pudu only gets to about
ten inches (*Microsoft Encarta Online Encyclopedia* 2000). A white-tailed
deer's weight can range from 70 to 400 pounds (Frazier 2001). The
average buck weighs around 240 pounds, while the largest buck
recorded in Wisconsin was 491 pounds. The average adult female
weighs around 160 pounds, but can range from 90 to 210 pounds.
The weight of deer, of course, varies with food availability and other
environmental conditions (Jackson 1961:415–416).

In fact, many hunters go out of their way to feed deer in order
to create that large size. This supports a claim that these big, trophy deer are social constructions. On one of the same bulletin boards
on which I posted my survey, discussions about baiting included
information on what foods increased a deer's size:

> A deer needs 1–1.5 oz./head/day of vitamin/mineral to make a
> difference. There is only one vitamin/mineral that has been researched
> for over 10 years and was designed just for deer, the Imperial Whitetail
> 30–06 vitamin/mineral. The 30–06 protein plus will make a big
> difference if it is put down now until July/August. Deer will start gain-
> ing 20–40 lbs. body weight in about a 3 year period. This is in addi-
> tion to a quality foodplot . . . (bulletin board post)

Not only are large-sized deer *social* constructions, they are a result of social actions taken by humans. The deer that are large are often the result of human interaction. They are not large, naturally, because of some superior trait they possess. They are large because hunters are feeding them foods to plump them up for deer season and large deer trophies increased the hunter's prestige.[2]

At the same time, the dominant belief that the deer that should be hunted each year during deer season should be large bucks with big racks has been challenged by policy changes in deer management. More and more agencies in charge of deer management have encouraged antlerless deer hunts to cull the large herds surviving through recent mild winters (Wisconsin Department of Natural Resources 1998; Wisconsin Department of Natural Resources 2000a). Antlerless permits have been handed out with regular permits or through other programs, like "Earn a Buck," which requires hunters to harvest an antlerless deer before being eligible to hunt a buck.[3] Sometimes three or more antlerless permits have been issued along with a buck permit. In these cases, in order to maintain sustainable population levels, the killing of younger, smaller and female deer is seen as as important as killing larger bucks.

However, the hunters posting messages on these bulletin boards rarely mentioned antlerless deer. Out of the fifty-one total posts containing descriptions of deer, only six mentioned antlerless deer. Those deer were not the deer that dominated the reality of hunting they constructed with their posts. Hunters did not mention smaller, antlerless deer as trophies that would reflect their own skills and achievements.

Deer are Beautiful

One other characteristic of deer that was only mentioned in the original thread was that deer were beautiful:

> I have been asked many times why I hunt. Each time it is a different answer because there are so many reasons why. I guess it is because where else can you get a chance to enjoy the outdoors on such a personal level. Sure you can go out in the woods without hunting, but there is some unexplainable thing about taking *one of god's most beautiful creatures*, and I thank him whenever I get to take one. (survey, emphasis added)

Another hunter wrote, "It must be primal, there is nothing that explains to me why I would walk around in the woods all day in any weather to try and kill *a beautiful animal*. It doesn't add up and

I certainly don't want to live without *this beautiful gift*" (survey, emphasis added).

No other specific descriptions of deer and their beauty were offered by these discussants, and only two of the original thirty-four survey responses describe deer this way. So, it may be argued that this unique portrayal of deer did not merit a separate theme. It was interesting that both of these posts described deer as beautiful while also discussing the dilemma they have about killing it. It was also interesting that this theme did not appear in the "naturally-occurring" threads observed in the follow-up study. This suggested that the "Deer are Beautiful" theme was the result of the questions asked in the open-ended survey.

Discussion

Virtual Deer Enhance the Hunters' Identities

Deer were social constructions created by the hunters discussing them in cyberspace. Deer are many things and have many qualities, but the hunters on these Internet bulletin boards chose to focus on only a few of them. These hunters perceived deer as big, smart animals that were challenging to hunt. The most remarkable finding was the lack of variation in the social constructions of deer, especially in comparison to how deer were described by wildlife biologists, like Jackson (1961).

These specific constructions of deer were a product of the cyberspace hunters' active creation of a specific reality. They allowed the hunters, themselves, to be seen as powerful beings who won at the contest with the big, beautiful animal who sees, smells, and hears better than humans. This was evidenced by the post included above, in which the author points out that, "Big, older bucks didn't get that way by being stupid." In another thread, the connection between the size and skill of the deer were associated with the hunter. The hunters were commenting on a picture in the *Detroit Free Press*. The picture was of a hunter and the buck he had killed. In the post discussing the picture, being a big deer was linked with being a smart deer. Further, for hunters, getting a big, smart deer was associated with hunting ability: "Apparently Mitch is a top flight deer hunter and the fact that he killed it with a bow makes it an even greater achievement. Bucks don't grow to be monsters like that by being dumb." Winning the contest with a big, smart animal constructed the individual as a good hunter.

One response to my questionnaire expressed this association. The hunter saw his father "matching" a deer's agility. In reply to the question, "Do you remember your first hunting experience? If you do, describe it," he wrote, "Watching my dad; he had incredible eyesight, reactions and shooting skills. I was in total amazement . . ."

One alternative explanation for the deer described in cyberspace might be that these deer were part of the hunters' fantasies of escape. Hunters usually spend up to one week in the woods during a normal gun season. The rest of the year is spent dreaming about their escape into the wilderness. Just like the actual experience of travel is often anti-climactic after planning a trip (Rojek 1993:9), the real deer do not live up to the fantasy deer. On the Internet, deer could be anything a hunter wanted them to be.

While at work or on their home computers, hunters can turn to an Internet bulletin board for daily hunting stimulation and make up for any lack of excitement in their workaday lives. They can escape into a story about the favorite hunt of someone else who has posted on the bulletin board or reconstruct the story of a hunt they had or wished they had themselves. If one accepts that the deer in cyberspace are the hunters' fantasy deer, then we are left with trying to explain why they were limited to specific characteristics. One explanation is that the environment in which the hunters exchange their descriptions of deer most likely played a role in shaping the way deer are constructed.

Cyberdeer are a Product of a Cyberculture

Because the place, time, culture or specific group membership affect how an animal is socially constructed, the deer described on these Internet bulletin boards took on specific characteristics based upon the social nature of electronic discussions. Discussants were not only exchanging helpful hints or interesting stories and comments. They were also members of an electronic community. Within that community they were involved in management of the *self*. They worked together to create and maintain a specific reality based upon the perceptions, beliefs and messages posted by members of the dominant culture within the electronic community.

Bulletin board discussions are a venue for identity construction.

Discussants write and edit messages to be posted on the bulletin board fully aware of how the text reflects on them. Internet bulletin boards are places where one's identity is dependent upon one's discourse. Who a person is depends on what she or he writes. Ostwald (1997:149) claims that participants in virtual communities like Internet bulletin boards are able to ". . . escape any social inequities and attitudes relating to various forms of embodiment." Through their digital messages, they can create the identity they desire, even if it is not what they have in their analog lives. "Individuals invent themselves and do so repeatedly and differentially in the course of conversing or messaging electronically" (Poster 1997:221).

Furthermore, the whole environment in which these discussions take place is a reality constructed by the participants. Virtual reality suggests that there are multiple realities. "Virtual reality is a computer-generated 'place' which is 'viewed' by the participant through 'goggles' but which responds to stimuli from the participant or participants" (Poster 1995:85). Although virtual reality usually refers to computer-generated images that an individual can "walk" through by maneuvering through computer software, it can also refer to the reality constructed by members of an electronic community, such as an Internet bulletin board. This reality is the one that they constructed through their interactions. Discussants on these Internet bulletin boards validated or denied each other's identities and opinions about their world through responses to each other's posts.

Ultimately, within Internet bulletin board communities dominant cultures persist so the identities within the dominant culture must coincide with it. This dominant culture, of specific values and beliefs, frames how reality is constructed through the discussions. Therefore, the deer discussed on the bulletin board had to fit into that dominant reality. Carstarphan and Lambiase (1998) liken what goes on in cyberspace to "land grabs" through discourse. Individuals who do not buy into the dominant reality are silenced. Hierarchies on Internet bulletin boards are established by those who control the topics and by how they are discussed.

Control is gained in a number of ways, but often by posting multiple, emotionally laden messages. This is referred to on these bulletin boards as "flaming." Those who challenge the dominant reality being constructed on the bulletin board are flamed off the board. "These tactics of a few powerful language users foil any chance for an egalitarian discussion of issues, because other members retreat in silence, withdraw from the group, or refrain from posting unpopular or trivialized topics" (Carstarphan and Lambiase 1998:126). So anyone not buying into the reality that dominates is marginalized and usually retreats from posting a counter-viewpoint. The identities and roles of the participants must fit into this dominant culture, so descriptions of or references to deer that did not fit into the dominant culture of the deer hunter bulletin board community were not posted. This explains a lack of variation in the type of deer described in cyberspace.

Therefore, hunters constructed deer in a specific way that enhanced their own identities and perpetuated the dominant culture of deer hunting. While reading and interpreting messages that described deer, by specifying mental images of deer, participants not only constructed a reality about deer, but also about the person who posted the message. Individuals shaped their identities while also socially constructing an ideal of deer. These bulletin boards were virtual communities in which people negotiated their statuses with the stories they told, how they described their lives, themselves, or through the jokes they made. For hunters, part of that is describing or exaggerating the "big one that got away" or even the one they shot last hunting season. At the same time, virtual deer were part of the virtual reality of Internet hunters. Hunters discussed deer they constructed in a reality about hunting that they designed with their own discourse. In cyberspace, deer were elusive trophies and the hunters were champions of the forest.

Conclusion

This study suggests that how hunters regard deer depends on the venue in which those deer are constructed. The deer they socially constructed were their fantasy deer, those about which they dreamed all year until hunting season finally arrived. The electronic forum in which these hunters communicated facilitated this specific social construction of deer. And how hunters perceived each other on the Internet bulletin board was important. In cyberspace, these hunters used the deer to negotiate their own identities with the other members of their community. They constructed virtual deer and a virtual reality about hunting that fed the fantasies of other hunters and established their status.

Virtual deer offer important evidence of how technology contributes to specific social constructions of animals and how hunters' perceptions of deer are shaped by their participation in a virtual community. Virtual deer could be anything cyberspace hunters wanted them to be. However, because the constructions of deer reflected on a specific reality in which hunters negotiated their own identities and perceptions about hunting as a sport, they regarded deer as large, handsome and magnificently gifted animals who were masters of their domain.

This study underscores one main implication for those who deal with wildlife management policies. As with all policies over which there might exist conflict, it is important to understand the perspective of each stakeholder. The narratives from the electronic bulletin board discussion illustrated how important hunting is in these people's lives. Deer and hunting were important to the construction of the self for these hunters and any policy change in wildlife management is a potential threat to these constructions.

All stakeholders – wildlife managers, environmentalists, hunters, landowners, and more – need to understand this specific perspective of hunters, that their activity is important to their identity. Without reading these narratives, a non-hunter might not understand the importance of specific characteristics of deer and hunting to a hunter's personal identity. Policy changes, like restrictions on buck permits or requiring antlerless hunts, mean that hunters have more at stake than just changing how they practice a hobby or sport. The hunter's personally constructed image of himself or herself is at risk each time a policy change is proposed.

References

The American Heritage Dictionary. 1994. 3rd Edition, Version 3.6a. Softkey International, Inc.

Arluke, Arnold. 1994 "'We Build a Better Beagle': Fantastic Creatures in Lab Animal Ads." *Qualitative Sociology* 17:2:143–158.

Arluke, Arnold and Clinton R. Sanders. 1996. *Regarding Animals*. Philadelphia: Temple University Press.

Berger, Peter L. and Thomas Luckmann. 1966. *The Social Construction of Reality: A Treatise in the Sociology of Knowledge*. New York: Anchor Books.

Carstarphan, Meta G. and Jacqueline Johnson Lambiase. 1998. "Domination and Democracy in Cyberspace: Reports from the Majority Media and Ethnic/Gender

Margins." Pp. 121–136 in *Cyberghetto or Cybertopia? Race, Class, and Gender on the Internet*, edited by B. Ebo. Westport, CT: Praeger.

Chambliss, William and Russell Schutt. 2003. *Making Sense of the World: Methods of Investigation*. Thousand Oaks, CA: Pine Forge Press.

Dahles, Heidi. 1993. "Game Killing and Killing Games: An Anthropologist Looking at Hunting in a Modern Society." *Society and Animals* 1(2):169–184.

Dizard, Jan E. 1994. *Going Wild: Hunting, Animal Rights, and the Contested Meaning of Nature*. Amherst: University of Massachusetts Press.

Feldman, Curt. 2004. "Deer Hunter Publisher Shuttered." *Gamespot NEWS*. Retrieved September 27, 2004 (http://www.gamespot.com/news/2004/03/29/news_6092469.html).

Forsyth, Craig J. and Rhonda D. Evans. 1998. "Dogmen: The Rationalization of Deviance." *Society and Animals* 6(3):203–218.

Frazier, Janice. 2001. "White-Tailed Deer." *The Pittsburgh Zoo*. Retrieved on February 8, 2001 (http://zoo.pgh.pa.us/wildlife).

Hamilton, James C. 2004. "The Ethics of Conducting Social Science Research on the Internet." Pp. 74–77 in *Readings in Social Research Methods*, 2nd Edition, edited by D. Kholos Wysocki. Belmont, CA: Wadsworth.

Jackson, Hartley H. 1961. *Mammals of Wisconsin*. Madison, WI: University of Wisconsin Press.

Lawrence, Elizabeth A. 1986. "Relationships with Animals: The Impact of Human Culture." *National Forum* 66(1):14–18.

Microsoft® Encarta® Online Encyclopedia 2000. "Deer." Retrieved February 8, 2001 (http://encarta.msn.com).

Miles, William F.S. 1997. "Pigs, Politics and Social Change in Vanuatu." *Society and Animals* 5(2):155–167.

Ostwald, Michael J. 1997. "Virtual Urban Futures." Pp. 125–144 in *Virtual Politics: Identity & Community in Cyberspace*, edited by D. Holmes. Thousand Oaks, CA: Sage Publications.

Poster, Mark. 1995. "Postmodern Virtualities." Pp. 79–95 in *Cyberspace, Cyberbodies, Cyberpunks: Cultures of Technological Embodiment*, edited by M. Featherstone and R. Burrows. Thousand Oaks, CA: Sage Publications.

——. 1997. "Cyberdemocracy: The Internet and the Public Sphere." Pp. 212–228 in *Virtual Politics: Identity & Community in Cyberspace*, edited by D. Holmes. Thousand Oaks, CA: Sage Publications.

Rojek, Chris. 1993. *Ways of Escape*. London: The MacMillan Press.

Sanders, Clinton. 1999. *Understanding Dogs: Living and Working with Canine Companions*. Philadelphia: Temple University Press.

Scarce, Rik. 2000. *Fishy Business: Salmon, Biology, and the Social Construction of Nature*. Philadelphia: Temple University Press.

U.S. Fish and Wildlife Service. 1997. *1996 National Survey Fishing, Hunting, and Recreation*. U.S. Department of Interior.

Wisconsin Department of Natural Resources. 1998. *Wisconsin's Deer Management Program: The Issues Involved in Decision-Making*, 2nd Edition. Madison, WI: Wisconsin Department of Natural Resources.

Wisconsin Department of Natural Resources. 2000a. "Remaining bonus antlerless permits to go on sale starting Sept. 11." Retrieved July 1, 2002 (www.dnr.state.wi.us).

Wisconsin Department of Natural Resources 2000b. "Deer 2000 Public Review of Recommendations Survey Results." Retrieved July 1, 2002 (www.dnr.state.wi.us).

Notes

[1] However, this anonymity also allows them to submit more than one response or to provide invalid information without the researcher's awareness, which could bias the findings (Hamilton 2004). I had no reason to believe that any responses to the survey or posts to the discussion threads analyzed in the follow-up study were fictitious, but I cannot rule out that possibility.

[2] Of course, the use of bait piles to consistently attract deer to a specific hunting site contradicts the construct of deer hunting as a challenging activity. However, the discussions I analyzed did not attempt to reconcile this contradiction.

[3] In a recent non-scientific survey conducted by the Wisconsin Conservation Congress, fifty percent (5,349) of the respondents "Oppose" or "Strongly Oppose" the "Earn a Buck" program as a deer management-unit specific policy (Wisconsin Department of Natural Resources 2000b).

CONTESTED MEANINGS: THE SOCIAL CONSTRUCTION OF THE MOURNING DOVE IN WISCONSIN

ANN HERDA-RAPP AND KAREN G. MAROTZ

Introduction

Since 1996 American voters in numerous states have voted on ballot measures addressing hunting. Measures to limit specific forms of hunting and trapping have drawn "disconnected urban voters" to the polls (Ritter 2001:6C).[1] By contrast, a handful of states – including Minnesota in 1998, North Dakota and Virginia in 2000, and Wisconsin in 2003[2] – have legally recognized hunting as part of their state heritage. These states have elevated hunting to the status of a right by guaranteeing it within each of their respective state Constitutions (Bowen 2001). In the past, hunting was an institution taken for granted in rural states, something so common as to go unnoticed. Once just a part of life in rural America, people in our increasingly urban/suburban/exurban nation are now redefining hunting. Hunting, as the aforementioned referenda suggest, is now on the political agenda, a reflection of population and lifestyle changes in the United States.

The proposal to hunt mourning doves in Wisconsin can best be understood as part of a context of socio-cultural-political change. While the dove was designated the state symbol of peace in 1971, presumably eliminating the possibility of establishing a hunting season in the state, a proposal surfaced in 1999 to initiate a dove hunt in Wisconsin. The proposal stalled for nearly two years as a court challenge was being considered. We can learn much from examining this case, an issue too simplistically described as a matter of "anti's versus hunters."

To understand this case, we draw on social constructionist theory and the meanings various groups attributed to the mourning dove. To some, the dove represented peace and innocence. To others it represented challenging game, another hunting opportunity. We show that these constructions do not simply follow from one's position on hunting in general – as in favor or against – but that the meanings of the dove, contested as they were, shaped one's position on the proposed hunt. We conclude by reflecting on the benefit of understanding these constructions, including benefits for sociologists, wildlife managers, politicians creating wildlife policy, and a general hunting public disturbed by the perceived erosion of their hunting rights.

Constructing Nature

To understand the mourning dove issue in Wisconsin, we must understand that the dove, like everything around us, is socially constructed. The meaning of that idea may not be self-evident. Berger and Luckmann (1966) argue that social facts – what we know to be true about the social world – are socially constructed. These facts are created and given meaning by the people in the culture, both during daily interactions and in interactions with social institutions, thereby creating a "reality." Politically and socially powerful claims-makers have the resources to offer more authoritative, and hence, dominant interpretations of reality. How we come to think about social problems, for instance, is shaped by claims-makers who vie for attention in public arenas recognized by policymakers (Hilgartner and Bosk 1988).

While it might at first seem odd, Nature is also a social construction. Obviously, there is a physical reality to nature. The physical characteristics each of us *sees* in the landscape will vary (you might see the deer browse line on the edge of a field, while someone else notices the soybeans growing *in* the field), but their existence can be confirmed. A black bear, white-tailed deer, red squirrel and mourning dove all exist, as do the white pine tree, trillium plant and blue stem grass. We can describe their physical properties, range, nutrient intake, reproduction cycles, etc. Yet, that same Nature is also socially constructed. That is, individuals attribute social meaning to Nature.

Social constructionist theory reminds us that, beyond their physical existence, wildlife too are symbols to whom we attach meaning (Munro 1997), meanings that are not always shared (Greider and Garkovich 1994). Rik Scarce (1998) shows that the wolf became a symbol of power and control for some and self-determination and freedom for others living around Yellowstone National Park during the 1990s when the wolf was reintroduced to the region. And Jan Dizard (1999) shows that, in the Quabbin Reservation in Massachusetts, residents, activists and wildlife managers constructed the resident white-tailed deer in very different ways. While some people saw the deer primarily for their qualities as a huntable species, others saw them as graceful, serene symbols of "the wild." Still others saw them as vermin, wild ungulates that were responsible for potentially cata-strophic overbrowsing of the landscape.

As objects of meaning, wildlife can become stand-ins for other social phenomena. Gary Alan Fine and Lazaros Christoforides (1991) show that, in the mid-1870s, the English sparrow, an exotic species that proliferated when introduced in the United States, became a nativist symbol of increased human immigration from Eastern and Southern Europe and Asia and the threats those immigrants posed. The sparrows were attributed with moral qualities as they were described as "un-American" and "foreign vulgarians," living in "avian ghettoes" (Fine and Christoforides 1991:381). Carol Miller (this vol-ume) shows that hunters' constructions of deer as challenging reflected the hunters' images of themselves as up to the challenge of stalking such formidable prey. Rik Scarce's (1998) research underscores the idea that the same object – in his case, wolves – can be inscribed with different meanings, meanings that are contested by others.

Moreover, the meanings ascribed to wildlife will change over time. Such changes correspond with the relationship to humans as Steven Yearley (1991:75) describes:

> Of course, the "popular" status of animals or other natural phenom-ena is subject to negotiation and change: tigers have been rehabili-tated from wild killers to majestic, endangered cats, and with this change many hunters have turned gamekeepers.

The wolf of fairy tales led many to fear the species as a predatory threat to humans. Today, the wolf has been transformed into a sym-bol of ecological balance as some seek to bring back such keystone species (Dunlap 1988; Scarce 1998).[3] The wolf's meanings and sym-bolisms have evolved as the social context evolved and as claims-makers reinterpreted the animal.

What we suggest is that social constructions are important not just as an academic exercise but because they are instructive of human relationships with Nature. Social constructions represent how we think about Nature and shape how others think about Nature. More importantly, they guide how we relate to and with Nature. Arnold Arluke and Clint Sanders (1996:9) summarize this perspective:

> To say that animals are social constructions means that we have to look beyond what is regarded as innate in animals – beyond their physical appearance, observable behavior, and cognitive abilities – in order to understand how humans will think about and interact with them.

As Thomas Greider and Lorraine Garkovich (1994:2) explain, constructions of the environment are revealing of relationships:

> Meanings are not inherent in the nature of things. Instead, the symbols and meanings that comprise landscapes reflect what people in cultural groups define to be proper and improper relationships among themselves and between themselves and the physical environment.

Conflict over wildlife is particularly instructive of the ways people construct wildlife. As Matthew Wilson (1997:465) put it in describing the controversy over wolf reintroduction in Yellowstone, "wolves are socially 'constructed' by environmentalists and wise users struggling to give meaning to their relationship with landscape in the [Greater Yellowstone Ecosystem]." These claims-makers make claims about the wildlife, wildlife managers, other stakeholders, and about the rest of the world. These claims about reality emerge, Rik Scarce (2000) notes, in particular socio-historical contexts. They are a reflection of that context, of the social, political and economic tensions and structures of a given historical moment.

In using social constructionist theory to study wildlife conflicts, language often becomes the focus, because it is through discourse that Nature is constructed. The discourse or the words with which we describe wildlife not only articulate the view of the wildlife in question, but also inscribe a set of relationships. These relationships are between the claims-maker and the wildlife, between the claims-maker and wildlife managers, and between the claims-maker and other publics.

In the case of the proposed mourning dove hunt in Wisconsin, one could break the argument down into those who are for the hunt and those who are against it and argue that each position is an outgrowth of larger positions on hunting. So, those against the hunt are just fanatical "anti's" and those for it are just "trigger-happy hunters." However, this is rather simplistic. The reality of the situation is much more complex and that complexity hinges on the fact that different groups have mobilized around different constructions of the mourning dove itself. Those constructions then shaped how the various activists believe they themselves and, more importantly, the rest of the public should interact with the dove.

The Mourning Dove in Wisconsin

The mourning dove – *Zenaida macroura* – is a medium-sized bird whose shape is similar to that of the common pigeon; both the pigeon and the mourning dove belong to the *Columbidae* family. The mourning dove is a light tan color and coos in the morning and evening. It is a migratory bird that is abundant throughout North America and inhabits both urban and rural areas. Its contested status is reflected in the *National Audubon Society Field Guide to North American Birds* that notes, "in some states it is hunted as a game bird, while in others it is protected as a 'songbird'" (Bull and Farrand 1994:536).

In 1971, the mourning dove was designated the state of Wisconsin's symbol of peace through an act of the state legislature. This was a gesture to recognize veterans returning from the Vietnam War. At that time, the state removed the mourning dove from the game list and it could not be hunted. Indeed, there has never been a mourning dove hunting season in Wisconsin. Efforts to establish a state hunting season on mourning doves failed in the early 1970s and again in 1989 (Sandin 2000). However, the effort gained momentum in April 1999 when a dove-hunt petition was advanced through the state's Conservation Congress, a citizen body that meets each spring in each county to advise Wisconsin's Department of Natural Resources (DNR) on wildlife and resource management issues in the state. As per its protocol, the Conservation Congress – a body traditionally dominated by hunters but technically comprised of any county residents who wish to attend an open meeting on conservation issues – then voted in each county across the state the following April (2000) to petition the DNR to open a hunt.

As a result, the DNR initiated a study of the issue and recommended opening a season. In May 2000, the Natural Resources Board, a body appointed by the governor, voted to proceed with a hunt. The DNR then prepared for a hunt to begin on September 1, 2001. In the interim, both houses of the state legislature held hearings on the issue. The state Assembly also considered administrative rule changes in the DNR to permit a hunt. However, no legislation to establish a hunt or, conversely, to override the Natural Resources Board's and the DNR's authority to go forward with a hunt made it out of committee.

Opposition to the hunt coalesced in 1999. That opposition brought together two camps with sometimes competing worldviews. One segment consisted of individuals opposed to all hunting and the other was a group of individuals who could otherwise be considered pro-hunting but who opposed the dove hunt. For ease, Table 4.1 delineates the divisions on the issue, the way we will refer to each throughout this chapter, and the organizations with which some of the respondents have been affiliated.

Table 4.1. Positions on the proposed dove hunt

Position	Name	Description	Related Group Affiliations
Opposed to dove hunt	Anti-hunting opponents	Those individuals opposed to all hunting, including the dove hunt.	The Alliance for Animals (based in Madison, WI), the Humane Society of the United States, Raising the Awareness of the Value of Endangered Nature (RAVEN).
	Pro-hunting opponents	Individuals who mostly supported hunting but did not support a dove hunt.	Wisconsin Citizens Concerned for Cranes and Doves (WCCCD).
Supportive of dove hunt	Pro-hunting proponents	Individuals supportive of hunting AND a dove hunt.	Wisconsin Dove Hunters Association, Sporting Heritage Coalition, National Rifle Association, Wisconsin Wildlife Federation, A Wisconsin Alliance for Resources and the Environment (AWARE).

Opponents to the dove hunt spoke at DNR and legislative hearings on the hunt and organized a petition drive. Ultimately, they brought a lawsuit to stop the hunt on the grounds that the DNR moved the dove back onto the game list without the necessary authorization of the state legislature. Just days before the hunt was set to open in September 2001, a judge ruled to temporarily stop the hunt. On March 27, 2003, the 4th District Court of Appeals, in a split decision, ruled that the DNR had the right to establish hunting seasons and this opened the door to a dove season (*Wisconsin Citizens Concerned for Cranes and Doves v. Wisconsin Department of Natural Resources*). In June 2003, the Wisconsin Supreme Court agreed to review the appellate court decision (Jones 2003). A dove hunt still proceeded on September 1, 2003, as the court's decision to hear the case did not stay the hunt. On April 6, 2004, the court upheld the DNR's authority to set a hunting season for mourning doves.

Methods and Data Sources

The results presented here are the product of two research methods: a survey of and in-depth interviews with claims-makers who spoke publicly on the issue of the dove hunt in Wisconsin.[4] We analyzed the constructions of doves and hunting issues, as revealed in interviews, that are fundamental to public claims. We selected study participants through a search of three Wisconsin newspapers: *The Capital Times* (Madison), *The Wisconsin State Journal* (Madison) and *The Milwaukee Journal-Sentinel*. The first author contacted any individuals who were quoted more than once in these newspapers during the period of June 1, 2000 through June 1, 2001 and asked them to participate in this research project.

This list of potential interviewees consisted of twenty-six individuals, eleven who spoke in favor of the hunt and fifteen who spoke against it. Of that list, nine could not be located or interviewed; this included three in favor of the hunt and six against the hunt. We also asked the individuals interviewed for the names of other activists who spoke on the issue and whom we might contact. If a person's name was given by more than one individual, he/she was contacted and interviewed. This resulted in three names being added to the pool of interviewees. In addition, we interviewed one official with the Wisconsin DNR. In total, twenty-one individuals were interviewed, which included ten for the hunt (nine men, one woman) and eleven against it (six men, five women).

We conducted in-depth interviews with the respondents. Three interviews were conducted over the phone; eighteen were conducted in-person. With the exception of the DNR official, respondents were

first asked to complete a short survey to obtain biographical information and to measure their overall views about hunting and the
proposed dove hunt. Interviews were then conducted and tape-
recorded. All interviews drew on a protocol of common questions
but we often asked follow-up and additional questions.

The surveys (N = 20) revealed that most of our respondents were
male (seventy-five percent), married (sixty-five percent), and had
hunted at least once in their lifetime (seventy percent). Most also
grew up in (sixty percent) and currently resided in (sixty percent) a
community of 75,000 or more residents. As one might expect, hunting experience seemed to be associated with feelings toward dove
hunting. All of the respondents who said they had never hunted (six
respondents) reported the least favorable possible view of the proposed dove hunt. However, as a reflection of the interesting complexities within this issue, those with previous hunting experience
showed some ambivalence about the hunt: thirty-five percent (five
respondents) reported the least favorable view of the proposed dove
hunt and thirty-five percent (five respondents) reported the most
favorable view. Thirty-percent (four respondents) of hunters reported
a view of the proposed hunt more toward the middle. This illustrates, as we will explain later, uncertainty and even disagreement
among hunters. While some hunters (referred to here as the "pro-
hunting proponents") *supported* the dove hunt, other hunters (referred
to here as the "pro-hunting opponents") *opposed* the dove hunt and
found themselves on the side of individuals who opposed all hunting (referred to as "anti-hunting opponents"). This illustrates why
constructions of this particular bird might be important and useful
for understanding wildlife issues and for creating wildlife policy.

Constructing the Mourning Dove

Stakeholders on the dove issue offered dramatically different constructions of the dove. This tan-colored bird took on symbolic importance as each side offered different interpretations of its behavior, its
personality and its role in the ecosystem and political landscape of
Wisconsin. Even the dove's classifications were contested.

Classifications: "Just Because You Call a Pig a Cow, Doesn't Mean It's a Cow"

At the heart of this issue is the question of the power to define wildlife like the mourning dove, over who has the power to make classifications. Kate Burningham and Geoff Cooper (1999) make the point that categories are social constructions. Keith Tester (1991:46) illustrates: "a fish is only a fish if it is socially classified as one." In saying this, Tester is not denying that animals have certain physical properties but that how animals are grouped, which properties become important for conceptually organizing them, is a social product. Classifications are socially created. This is true of the mourning dove as well. Both sides define the bird as a mourning dove. But beyond that, they part ways. That is, how they classify the bird – specifically, as a songbird or as a game bird – and the meanings attached to those categorizations, vary dramatically, dictating different interactions with and policies regarding the bird.

1. The "Friend at the Bird Feeder"
Those opposed to opening a dove hunt in Wisconsin offered a soft, gentle construction of the mourning dove. Dove hunt opponents described the dove as rare, as an old friend to which they were deeply attached. As one respondent put it, "it's a bird that most people are familiar with that comes into their yards. That they feed. That they see each day." Several respondents associated the bird with fond memories:

> [. . .] in the evening when I hear a mourning dove cooing it takes me back to my childhood when I could hear the same thing and person after person after person has told me that they relate the same way.

Many of the dove hunt opponents we interviewed emphasized that the dove is commonly designated as a songbird[5] in Wisconsin, although this designation does not preclude it from being hunted according to state statutes. One respondent, a retiree, noted that, "it's just a very enjoyable [bird], one of the songbird family. It is, in fact, my favorite songbird because of the sound it makes." Another respondent, when asked to describe the dove, underscored the contested nature of such classifications saying, "you could get into the definition of what a songbird is, but the mourning dove definitely has a song and it's definitely enjoyable." In a challenge to the hunting community and the Wisconsin DNR, one respondent said, "You want an easy definition of game? If it feeds in backyard feeders, it's not game."

The most common description dove hunt opponents invoked was of the dove as peaceful. This construction is structured around two contentions. The first is that it is the state symbol of peace and, second, that it is innocent of any wrongdoing. Nearly every dove hunt opponent that we interviewed noted that the dove is the state symbol of peace. (Interestingly, most dove hunt supporters we interviewed also noted the bird's status as the symbol of peace though, as we discuss later, they dismissed this as political maneuvering.) They described the dove as the symbolic expression of peace, particularly for Vietnam veterans: "I had enough killing and stuff in Vietnam. [. . .] [The mourning doves] welcomed us home in a time when not too many people welcomed us home."

Opponents also repeatedly constructed the dove as a non-destructive bird that does no harm, evoking both the image of the peace-inspiring white dove and a naïve, innocent victim. They described the bird as a "wobbly headed goofy bird who really doesn't have a clue about anything." Given this naivete, according to hunt opponents, it should therefore be protected, not hunted. More common was the assertion that the bird does no harm and, in fact, was beneficial because it ate weed seeds and insects. Again, therefore, it did not deserve to be hunted: "It's harmless. It does no harm to anyone and it's also a pretty good friend to farmers." Another explained that, "It's not an obnoxious bird, does no damage to the environment per se. In fact, it's probably helpful and picks up weed seeds and digests them." These respondents drew on the bird's role in the ecosystem, asserting that the bird was beneficial.

Other dove hunt opponents also noted the dove's benefits but went further by offering the image of a distinctly personified dove. When asked to describe the dove, one woman described it as:

> . . . probably the most non-abusive bird we have. It gives to everybody. Not only is it the symbol of peace in Wisconsin, it is just a peaceful bird to begin with. It doesn't argue with anybody. It always runs or flies away. [. . .] That's just who they are.

Another respondent described the gentle personality of the bird: "they're not detrimental to anything. You don't see them fighting. You don't see them hitting on each other, whacking each other. You don't see them swooping down at you." Others emphasized the monogamous nature of the doves, explaining that "they bond for life" and express affection. One respondent described this affection: "You go by and you see them sitting on a wire. Some of them just go alone by themselves and maybe two of them right close together, maybe rubbing on each other every once in a while."

All of these constructions depict a bird that is innocent, naïve and human-like in its attachments. Taken together, they anthropomorphize or extend human characteristics to the dove. In depicting doves as affectionate, monogamous, naïve, and peaceful, opponents of the hunt cast the dove as an innocent victim of hunting interests and hope to show how doves are similar to humans.

Fundamental to this construction is the primacy of *individual* doves. While opponents of the dove hunt expressed concern about the health of the dove population at large, most of their discourse focused on the individual dove. This focus on the individual *dove* was shared by both camps among the dove hunt opposition: those opposed to all hunting (the anti-hunting opponents) and those who supported hunting but opposed the dove hunt (the pro-hunting opponents). The two camps differ over whether their concern is for individual *doves* only or for *all individual animals*.

Anti-hunting opponents couched concern for the individual dove within a rhetoric of concern for *all* individual animals and their suffering. One respondent noted her disgust with hunting the dove, stating that what most bothered her was the scenario of hunting a dove "when it has its own family that it's trying to care for." Another anti-hunting opponent, when asked why she doesn't hunt, said, "[animals] feel pain and fear and it's not fair to hunt them. And most animals, so few of them are actually killed. Many more are wounded and maimed and left to suffer, to bleed to death." Similarly, when asked about the social, economic, personal, etc., costs of hunting in general a different respondent referred to emotional trauma experienced by hunted animals, explaining:

> To leave the animals that are left suffering and the animal's families that are left standing there and, especially in the case of deer, standing there and looking at this dead or wounded animal, that is the most tremendous cost that I see.

Each anti-hunting opponent in our study noted the family aspect of an animal's existence:

> What I see in the natural world is sentient, social, intelligent animals that participate in families. They participate in societies. They have complex nervous systems. They feel pain. They obviously have something that uses somewhat human emotions, different moods, fear, anxiety. They play. They run. They grow. They mate. Some species mate for life.

Most anti-hunting opponents also expressed concern for doves at the population level. That is, they expressed concern for the abundance and health of this particular species. It was their concern, however, for *all individual* animals that distinguished them from both pro-hunting opponents and pro-hunting proponents. One anti-hunting opponent spoke of her disgust with the DNR's and hunters' concern for species abundance only, in contrast with her and her compatriots' interest in the individual animal:

> Most of the people that I know that are active in this [animal protection] movement have had significant relationships with animals in their lives, that they've been caretaking or they've grown up with or they've had contact with and they are coming from that concern for the individual animal. Concern for the individual animal is the last thing that the DNR and hunters want. They want to preserve the species so that they can continue having part of the killing.

Another noted his concern for both the individual animal and the species at the population level, saying:

> If we valued nature differently, the value of the individual animals, not just a population that needs to be handled somehow through our wisdom, we would change our transportation policies, change our land-use policy.

These respondents suggest that healthy numbers of a given species are not enough; rather, the well-being of the individual animal must be the focus of land-use planning, development policy, and wildlife management.

In contrast to the anti-hunting opposition's focus on *all* individual animals, pro-hunting opponents of the dove hunt spoke instead of the need to protect individual *doves*. They invoked the image of the bird at their feeder, the pair on the telephone wire that mates for life, etc., while also speaking of the necessity of hunting *other* species. According to their discourse, it is necessary to hunt other animals out of concern over the health of those populations:

> Deer get overpopulated and they compete for food and cause disease and suffer through disease if they're not hunted. Squirrels and other

small game, the same thing can happen to them. If they get over-populated, it's not a benefit to them [to not be hunted]. It's a benefit to harvest them.

Another respondent noted, unlike doves whose numbers fluctuate from year to year, "Some [species] are capable of being hunted. Some can sustain it and some can't. Some of the numbers definitely need hunting. They need to be thinned or culled and some can't." In contrast to the anti-hunting opponents' empathy for all individual animals and their pain, pro-hunting opponents did not express across the board concern for all individual animals and their personal well-being.

2. "America's Most Popular Game Bird"

While those opposing the hunt constructed the dove as an innocent, non-destructive symbol of peace and a songbird, the advocates of a hunt presented a very different construction. Every respondent supportive of the hunt noted that the dove was the most popular game species in America because it was the most hunted. They cited that the bird was currently hunted in thirty-seven other states. Most pro-hunt respondents emphasized the dove's sporting quality: "I see the dove as a very challenging game bird, very quick, capable of changing directions in flight instantaneously. Good table fare." In line with the sportsman's ideal, hunting prey must be challenging and any game shot must be consumed (Dizard 1999). Hence, these claims-makers constructed the dove as a consumable, renewable resource: "It's a migratory bird with a very short life expectancy. I mean, if someone can utilize some of these, let them." The dove, then, was a resource available, in the words of dove hunt advocates, for "harvesting" and the dove hunter is "out there to harvest some birds [. . .] and to eat them."

While dove hunt opponents constructed the dove as the bird of peace, pro-hunt claims-makers emphasized the bird's more common roots, describing it as a pigeon. When asked to describe the mourning dove, one respondent said only "a small brown pigeon." Another claims-maker described the mourning dove as "a gray pigeon [. . .] They're cute. They waddle around. I have them at the bird feeder here. I don't think they're particularly bright." And yet another asserted that "a dove is a pigeon, no matter how you slice it. It's a pigeon. It's an edible food." And, the respondent added, "it's delicious."

Time and time again, pro-dove hunt respondents emphasized the bird's drab appearance, its lack of aesthetic appeal, as in this remark: "[It's] the most abundant bird in North America. An attractive bird? No. [. . .] it's not a good-looking bird." In contrast to the dove protectors' descriptions, they describe the bird as nothing special, aside from its hunting qualities, and only then for being an occasionally difficult target. The bird carried very little cultural significance, except as a symbol of hunting traditions and rights as we discuss below.

Notable in this construction of the dove is the relative emphasis on the species or population level, rather than the individual dove's well-being. Related to this, dove hunt advocates railed against emotional attachments to individual doves. Instead, they emphasized that the dove is an animal distinct from humans and a resource of utility to people. Time and time again, pro-hunt respondents referred to the dove's abundance, to the population's numbers, as in this response: "We wouldn't be harvesting enough to have any impact on the population whatsoever so it won't make any difference to the population whether it's hunted." Another respondent, after describing the dove as a pigeon, noted "[There are] huge blocks [of doves] in North America. There's no danger of it being endangered." One response is worth quoting at length to show the speaker's emphasis on the species' abundance:

> Currently, there's no biological reason not to have a dove season: the abundance of the birds, the absolutely no impact of hunting on the resource, the fact that the bird is so abundant and so prolific. [. . .] You take it to the anti-hunting extreme and if we can't have a dove hunting season which is the most prolific game bird in the country, where it's migratory, where it's being hunted in other areas regardless of what we do here, where it's not about the habitat, it's not about anything other than whether we can or cannot hunt in the state. [. . .] I am worried then that if we can't hunt the most abundant species, how then can we hunt anything else?

This individual went on to describe other species such as woodcock and various ducks that were not as abundant as the dove and, therefore, not hunted as intensively. To him, the dove hunt was about the size of the population rather than the well-being of the individual dove. This was important to hunt advocates because to describe the dove as being close to humans (in proximity or in their qualities) or to describe attachments to individual doves could promote the extension of rights to the dove. For example, when describing wildlife that are hunted, one pro-hunting proponent asserted that he has "great appreciation for that animal, what that animal can do [. . .] I guess it's a lot of respect and appreciation." However, for this respondent, it was an admiration from a distance because he emphasized how *different* wildlife is from humans:

> They're animals. So, not as beings with any rights in that sense but as living things, I think I have a responsibility to take them . . . to be a good enough shot. It's not an inherent right of the animal *not* to be taken.

This stood in stark contrast to one anti-hunting opponent's comment that "I don't make a sharp distinction between human animals and other animals."

It is instructive to also consider the Wisconsin DNR's constructions of the dove. A DNR official who was most involved in determining the biological appropriateness of a hunt, when asked what image comes to mind when he thinks of the mourning dove, described the dove in this way:

> As birds go, it's probably medium-sized to large, if you classify all of the species of birds. [. . .] From a game bird standpoint, it's on the small side of the scale. How do I picture the mourning dove? It's a drab, gray bird. You see them all over the place. Particularly this time of the year, they, it's just remarkable I guess, it seems to me, the numbers you see. Quick flyer. It's at home in both urban and non-urban or rural environments. [. . .] Very ubiquitous. Member of the *Columbidae* family. [. . .] Fairly long tail.

His description of the dove emphasized its physical aspects – its color, size, tail – in a scientific way, in keeping with his professional training in wildlife management. He also invoked the image of the *species* when emphasizing both its numbers and its classification in the *Columbidae* family. This construction, that of an official in the agency responsible for making recommendations on the question of a hunt, blended seamlessly with the pro-dove-hunt construction. Because of its institutional power, particularly when compared to the relative powerlessness of the anti-dove hunt activists (none of whom were DNR officials or felt DNR officials supported their position), the DNR construction and, consequently, the hunter's construction of the dove, could be considered the dominant construction.

Constructing the Dove: A Political Act

Both sides used their construction of the mourning dove to ground their argument for or against the proposed hunt. Not surprisingly, wrapped up in the issue of the dove hunt was the larger issue of hunting in general. Both sides suggested that the dove was a pawn in a greater political battle, the battle over hunting and the management of resources in Wisconsin. Both sides engaged in a discourse of dichotomy, casting the other side's position as grounded in emotion and fear and, by inference, their own as calm and rational.

As we suggested above, at issue with the dove hunt was who has the ability to define the dove. Whose constructions are legitimate and whose may be dismissed and on what grounds? Much of the discourse about legitimacy referred to the 1971 designation of the mourning dove as the state symbol of peace. The dove hunt opponents interpreted that legislative act as protecting the dove from any hunting season. Any attempt by the Wisconsin DNR to implement a hunt without the approval of the state legislature was, therefore, an illegitimate act. This was the nature of the lawsuit that temporarily staid the hunt. As one pro-hunting opponent indicated, the issue was about who had the ability to construct the meanings attributed to the dove: "This is more than just a bird, it's a symbol. [. . .] Legislation took [the dove] off the game bird species [list] and DNR is not a legislative body. They can't make laws or *resymbolize*."

The supporters of the dove hunt saw the mourning dove as a political pawn both for the way it was designated the state symbol of peace and for the larger anti-hunting effort it was allegedly part of. Pro-hunting proponents asserted that the peace symbol designation in 1971 was politically motivated, part of the anti-hunting effort to end all hunting one species at a time:

> Most [of the public had] no idea how it became the symbol of peace. They didn't know it was Defenders of Wildlife that made it a symbol of peace. They didn't understand the issue wasn't whether [. . .] you're going to hunt doves because it's biologically sound or not. We're not going to have one because some animal rights group made it the symbol of peace.

Dove hunt advocates claimed that the symbol designation was not important:

> Well [. . .] the state fish is the musky. The state wildlife animal is the deer, the whitetail deer, and those are two of the most sought after animals in the state. There's the dairy cow and we milk them and we eat them. [. . .] I don't see the connection. It can be someone's symbol of peace [. . .] it's someone else's pigeon.

Having status as a peace symbol and being hunted were, in this construction, not mutually exclusive. Another pro-hunting proponent, with sarcasm, noted the competing constructions: "terminology has nothing to do with it, the dove of peace. [. . .] If you are in India, cows are sacred. In Wisconsin, we raise them, we cherish them in our barn [. . .] they're food." In this respondent's view, different constructions of animals will prevail in different cultures. While there may be other definitions, the respondent claimed, in American culture, the dominant construction defined the dove as an edible game bird.

To dove hunt advocates, the dove issue was bigger than the dove. They charged that emotionalism, bias and attachment to individual animals leads to subjective wildlife policy, in contrast to policy that they considered to be the objective, population-based, and scientifically-supported. Here is how one respondent put it:

> I think the DNR is to be commended for providing an objective voice to this debate in stating that we have easily sustainable populations. [. . .] A scientific voice is welcome, a welcome one in this whole debate because so much of this debate has been done on an emotional level and not objectively and that's troubling to me if you set public policy.

Another pro-hunting proponent, referring to recent efforts to block a dove hunt, portrayed a slippery slope:

> With dove hunting, it should have nothing to do with whether you think they're cute. [It should be about] the biology: you can either hunt them or you can't. And that's how all of our hunting seasons are based. We don't have a cuteness factor put in when we do the bag limit or determine the season. The dove was the only animal we did that with. So I thought [this latest attempt] was kind of a dangerous precedent.

This was a predominant theme in the interviews. Pro-hunting proponents feared that constructing the dove and policy toward it by including subjective factors (i.e., "the cuteness factor") would open the door to other kinds of limitations on their hunting:

> That you could subjectively, on a whim, limit hunting a population that could sustain it, that would support it [. . .] There's the danger that once you do that, you've changed the whole dynamic and so it's not a matter of limiting hunting to protect a population so that you have it in the future. [. . .] If you can do it because you like to see the animals at your bird feeder, then you can do it because you like to see deer in your backyard too.

This same individual continued:

> If we start [. . .] to subjectively decide what we are going to hunt or
> not going to hunt because of the cuteness of the sound or whatever
> the factor is, then we are turning away from scientific management of
> the environment. We're turning away from responsibility. We're turn-
> ing away from being stewards of the environment and that's what
> hunters have always been. [. . .] So, that's dangerous not just for dove
> hunting in the future but it's dangerous for all.

The notion that this was about more than the dove dominated
our interviews with dove hunt proponents. Hunters, spurred by organizations like the Wisconsin Dove Hunters Association, took the organized resistance to the hunt by "animal rights groups" to mean that
all hunting was a potential target. That a season recommended by
the DNR and requested by hunters might not be approved, coupled
with the surprise election of an anti-hunting opponent as a Dane
County representative to the Conservation Congress, seemed to mobilize even rank-and-file hunters who then showed up in droves at the
following spring's Conservation Congress meeting.

That there had never been a dove season in Wisconsin seemed
to be a moot point. The dove hunt was constructed as a bellwether:
efforts to block the *extension* of hunting rights to include dove hunting were framed as an effort to *take away* hunting rights. For instance,
when asked why he supported the hunt, one individual said, "Several
reasons. One is, I feel this is a right that we do have to hunt and
I do not like to see people slowly chip away at what can be hunted."
His remark is at least in part a reflection of claims-making by one
of the organizations that lobbied for a hunt. The Wisconsin Dove
Hunters Association distributed thousands of copies of a poster in
which the heading "It's Not About DOVE HUNTING. It's about
ALL HUNTING" was prominently displayed on one-third of the
page. That theme and the construction of the dove as the first target of a concerted campaign resonated with hunters. That way of
framing the issue – and of the dove as a political pawn – struck a
chord. This was illustrated in one pro-hunting proponent's remarks:

> The argument was, if you are going to allow emotionalism and ani-
> mal rights activism to determine whether or not you have a dove sea-
> son, they may be determining other aspects of hunting too.

Yet, dove hunt opponents also constructed the dove as a pawn in
a political struggle. As they saw it, hunting groups were using the
dove – a bird that few hunters showed an interest in hunting – to

stir up hunters. Both camps on the anti-dove-hunt side were mystified by the argument that not allowing a *new* dove hunt could be equated with taking away hunting rights: "I can understand fighting not to lose something but you can't lose something if you never had it. They never had a dove hunt." Many dove hunt opponents noted that hunting groups – among them the Wisconsin Dove Hunters Association – introduced the idea that all hunting rights were now on the table and then worked to stir up that fear, as these remarks suggest:

- [Hunting and gun groups are] creating this issue to demonstrate to all their members that "all these anti-hunters are out here and you better keep up your dues," "you better give us more money," "you better join because all these anti-hunters are out there."
- [Hunting groups] are afraid to give any kind of a break [i.e., backing down on the dove hunt] [. . .] for fear that the dam will bust and a lot of things will happen that they don't like.
- They've been convinced [. . .] that they'd eventually lose their hunting privileges and maybe even have their guns threatened. [. . .] It's a fear factor. They really have done it by instilling fear. [. . .] I said, "thirty years ago, you lost the right to hunt doves. Your opportunities through Wisconsin's resources have only *increased* since then, so how is that a threat?"

The Wisconsin DNR is also seen as promoting that fear. One dove hunt opponent stated:

> [Hunting groups] feel that if they lose the ability to hunt doves, they're going to slowly lose their ability to hunt anything. [. . .] And then the DNR also said, "well, you might not want to hunt anymore but what about your kids?"

In an interesting turn, opponents of the hunt constructed the proponents of the hunt as emotional, even fanatical:

> Little by little, as I got into it, I felt that it was an emotional thing on the part of hunters, that they were losing their rights. [. . .] The hunting groups are out saying "we will show you [anti-hunters] that we can get any darn law passed that we want."

Hunters were viewed as being driven by an irrational fear. Hence, the proposal to hunt doves was also constructed as emotional, something that was not grounded in science or a sound management philosophy but, rather, fear, the fear of losing a hunting "right."

Conclusions and Implications

This case study of the proposed mourning dove hunt in Wisconsin offers several sociological lessons. For all parties, including sociologists observing the conflict, the dove issue is about more than biological facts. First, the dove issue illustrates that wildlife species can be thought of as vehicles, as repositories of culture. They are, as Matthew Wilson (1997:465) put it, "a symbolic medium – a social resource – through which differing social groups express deeply held beliefs about relationships to society and nature."

Interestingly, the pro-hunting proponents and the anti-hunting opponents share common ground. Both saw the dove as a symbol of something larger than the dove: it was the symbol of hunting in Wisconsin in the twenty-first century. That is, for supporters of the hunt, the dove – constructed as "game," a "harvestable resource," a "pigeon" – symbolized the struggle to retain the right to hunt. To lose the right to hunt the dove, a right never before granted in Wisconsin, signified an erosion of hunting rights. The anti-hunting opponents saw this as a battle over the power of hunters to dictate wildlife policy. For them, opposed as they were to all hunting, the dove – constructed as a "songbird," "innocent," the "symbol of peace" – signified a battle over the extension of hunting rights to one more species to keep hunters happy.

Yet, as we suggested at the start of this chapter, this issue cannot be reduced to "anti's versus hunters," with only the species varying from one battle to another. This is because the other part of the contingent against the hunt generally supported hunting but, because of their constructions of the mourning dove, could not support *this* hunt. Clearly, the various parties constructed the dove and hunting in remarkably different and complex ways, ways that would probably not be revealed in general surveys of attitudes toward wildlife.

Certain constructions, however, may become the dominant constructions, at least politically more powerful, in their effect on wildlife policy. Rik Scarce (1998) points to the importance of social and political institutions in constructing wildlife. Government agencies such as the Wisconsin DNR are uniquely situated as both experts and government, two facets of Joel Best's Iron Quadrangle of Institutionalization (1999). Agencies like the Wisconsin DNR – through legislative access and scientific authority – have the ability to define wildlife in certain ways, ways that become part of the discourse surrounding that wildlife.

In Wisconsin, DNR officials make recommendations to the Natural Resources Board and the state legislature, citing biological facts in support of their recommendation. Thomas Greider and Lorraine Garkovich (1994:18) note especially the importance of bureaucratic, routine access to the media for it has "direct consequences on whose symbolic definitions of nature and the environment get imposed, sometimes through the use of force, on others with less power." They go on to say that because policy extends from the way issues are framed, those who have the authority to define wildlife "influence social actions and the allocation of social resources" (1994:17).

This case underscores that game, as a classification, is a social construction. It is a social designation. We give meaning to species and to individual animals, meanings that will change, some of which will be shared while others are contested. In Wisconsin, what is considered game is wide open: state statutes define game as "all varieties of wild mammals or birds" (section 29.001). Some game is protected by federal or state legislation (i.e., endangered or protected species under the Endangered Species Act, those included in the Migratory Bird Treaty Act, the designation of a state bird, etc.). The state legislature, in conjunction with the Wisconsin DNR, may establish hunting seasons on certain species of game. Because it is sanctioned in state law, this is the dominant definition of game.

It is not, however, the common definition of game. In the United States, the average person's definition of game probably reflects that of *Webster's New World Dictionary* (1984): game is defined as "wild birds or animals *hunted for sport or for use as food*" (emphasis added). Even the definition of game, it seems, is contested terrain. It is instructive to note the power of the state in defining the concept. The definition starts broadly and is given specificity, as in what can be hunted, by its legislature and natural resource agencies. The state, it would seem, has the last word.

Yet the state has also defined the dove as the symbol of peace, a codified meaning grounded in a politically and socially important event, the Vietnam War. Hence, a competing cultural definition of the dove has been institutionalized. As we illustrated above, though, that designation has been challenged on political grounds as dove hunt proponents have charged the dove was, when designated the

state symbol of peace in 1971, even then a political pawn of "animal rights groups."

Perhaps this case is most instructive in underscoring that the state
does, in fact, not have the last word. The dove hunt went forward
on September 1, 2003 and Wisconsin's Supreme Court has weighed
in on the dove's classification as game and the DNR's authority to
set a hunt. But, more and more often citizen groups challenge the
way wildlife policy is set, suggesting that "non-consumptive" users –
itself a problematic notion – of Nature be given a greater voice in
how the state's resources are managed and used. As our nation
becomes more urban/suburban, division over hunting will continue
to grow. Hunting interests – stronger in rural areas of Wisconsin –
will find it difficult to add species to the list of new hunts.

Though the rhetoric of wildlife agencies and hunting organizations will emphasize "objective, scientific" criteria in supporting the
hunt, the subjective will become increasingly important as there is
less shared meaning about what wildlife are for and how we are to
interact with them. Part of the dissension, it seems, will be located
in the competing environmental ideologies and worldviews of modern preservationists and conservationists (including many hunters), as
noted in our case and by Thomas Dunlap (1988:96) in his historical overview of American wildlife policy:

> Americans continued to be interested in nature and more and more
> were committed to the "environmental-ecological idea and the anti-
> killing idea." These two ideas, however, were at odds. One valued the
> stability of the system. It thought in terms of species and populations,
> not individuals, and accepted animal death and hunting. The other
> was opposed, at least in principle, to all killing. It placed individuals
> and their suffering first.

Such ideologies and worldviews played out in the case of the mourning dove in Wisconsin.

The lesson herein is that once it surfaces, mending conflict that
becomes exaggerated when the non-hunting citizenry is not consulted
as to their definitions of game, is terribly difficult. Rather, our recommendation to management is to understand the different meanings associated with particular wildlife before supporting an initiative
to hunt it. Surveys, focus group interviews, public forums, working
groups, etc. can facilitate investigation of those meanings. The social
sciences are suited for the task; wildlife managers, especially if they

are too close to hunting interests or if they have a vested interest in reinforcing a particular construction of wildlife, may not be.

References

Arluke, Arnold and Clinton Sanders. 1996. *Regarding Animals*. Philadelphia: Temple University Press.
Berger, Peter and Thomas Luckmann. 1966. *The Social Construction of Reality: A Treatise in the Sociology of Knowledge*. Garden City, NY: Doubleday.
Best, Joel. 1999. *Random Violence: How We Talk about New Crimes and New Victims*. Berkeley: University of California Press.
Bowen, Scott. 2001. "State Hunting Amendments." *Outdoor Life*. March:17.
Bull, John and John Farrand, Jr., eds. 1994. *National Audubon Society Field Guide to North American Birds: Eastern Region*. New York: Alfred A. Knopf.
Burningham, Kate and Geoff Cooper. 1999. "Being Constructive: Social Constructionism and the Environment." *Sociology* 33(2):297–316.
Dizard, Jan. 1999. *Going Wild: Hunting, Animal Rights, and the Contested Meaning of Nature*, 2nd Edition. Amherst: University of Massachusetts Press.
Dunlap, Thomas. 1988. *Saving America's Wildlife*. Princeton, NJ: Princeton University Press.
Fine, Gary Alan and Lazaros Christoforides. 1991. "Dirty Birds, Filthy Immigrants, and the English Sparrow War: Metaphorical Linkage in Constructing Social Problems." *Symbolic Interaction* 14(4):375–393.
Greider, Thomas and Lorraine Garkovich. 1994. "Landscapes: The Social Construction of Nature and the Environment." *Rural Sociology* 59(1):1–24.
Hilgartner, Stephen and Charles Bosk. 1988. "The Rise and Fall of Social Problems." *American Journal of Sociology* 94(1):53–78.
Jones, Meg. 2003. "Court Will Review Dove Hunting." *Milwaukee Journal-Sentinel*, June 17, pp. 7B.
Meffe, Gary K. and C. Ronald Carroll, eds. 1997. *Principles of Conservation Biology*, 2nd Edition. Sunderland, MA: Sinauer Associates.
Miller, Carol. [this volume]. "Virtual Deer: Bagging the Mythical 'Big One' in Cyberspace." In *Mad About Wildlife: Looking at Social Conflict Over Wildlife*, edited by A. Herda-Rapp and T. Goedeke. Leiden, Netherlands: Brill Academic Publishers.
Munro, Lyle. 1997. "Framing Cruelty: The Construction of Duck Shooting as a Social Problem." *Society and Animals* 5(2):137–154.
Ritter, John. 2001. "Hunters Fear Political Clout is Waning." *Wausau Daily Herald*, January 7, pp. 6C.
Sandin, Jo. 2000. "Dove Hunting Clears Last Hurdle." *Milwaukee Journal-Sentinel*, July 12, pp. 15A.
Scarce, Rik. 1998. "What Do Wolves Mean? Conflicting Social Constructions of *Canis lupus* in 'Bordertown.'" *Human Dimensions of Wildlife* 3(3):26–45.
———. 2000. *Fishy Business: Salmon, Biology, and the Social Construction of Nature*. Philadelphia: Temple University Press.
Tester, Keith. 1991. *Animals and Society: The Humanity of Animal Rights*. London: Routledge.
Webster's New World Dictionary of the American Language. 1984. New York: Simon & Schuster.
Wilson, Matthew. 1997. "The Wolf in Yellowstone: Science, Symbol, or Politics? Deconstructing the Conflict Between Environmentalism and Wise Use." *Society & Natural Resources* 10:453–468.

Yearley, Steven. 1991. *The Green Case: A Sociology of Environmental Issues, Arguments and Politics*. London: HarperCollins *Academic*.

Notes

[1] Such voters were described by a spokesperson for the Wildlife Legislative Fund of America as having been educated about wildlife at "the Bambi school" (Ritter 2001:6C).

[2] The measure received the support of eighty-two percent of Wisconsin voters.

[3] Meffe and Carroll (1997) define a keystone species as a species that plays a disproportionately large role in the structure of the ecological community because of its interactions or behaviors.

[4] This research was generously supported by a UW-Madison – UW Colleges Summer Research grant, as well as grants from the University of Wisconsin – Marathon County Foundation and the UW Colleges Department of Anthropology and Sociology.

[5] The category of "songbird," according to the DNR official we interviewed, is not a biological classification. Rather, it is socially defined. It is subjective and fluid. One group might define a particular bird as a songbird, while another might not.

PART TWO

CONSTRUCTING THE PEOPLE AND PRACTICES
IN WILDLIFE MANAGEMENT ISSUES

THE RESTORATION OF WOLVES IN FRANCE: STORY, CONFLICTS AND USES OF RUMOR

Véronique Campion-Vincent

Introduction[1]

Since the beginning of the 1990s, the return of wolves in France has caused passionate controversies in which nature protectors oppose mountain sheep-farmers' position on wolves. If one wants to understand these debates, it is necessary to go beyond the stereotyped slogans and pay attention to the social discourse expressed through the detour of rumors. In this chapter, I show how the situation evolved from spring 1993, the first announcement of the "official" return of wolves in France, through the end of 2003. I then describe and assess the parties involved: mountain sheep-farmers; nature protectors' associations (NPAs) which include "ecologists," friends of the wolves and wild fauna defenders; and government administrations managing subsidies to mountain sheep-farmers or in charge of wildlife. Each party has tried to influence public opinion and has asserted to be the closest to "Nature," a blanket term that covers very different ideas. I will present the main arguments in the conflict and I will then present and analyze rumors about wild animals and the truths they express. Animal-release rumors that exist all over the planet correspond to the indirect expression of fears of the irruption of the wild amongst us. I will conclude with remarks on the probable future of wild wolves and predators in France.

While other predators did exist, for example bears, lynxes and wildcats, wolves have traditionally carried the strongest and most negative image in European societies, not only in folktales and legends but also in naturalists' descriptions since classical antiquity. In such stories, wolves regularly attacked livestock, especially sheep, occasionally humans, and especially children acting as shepherds. Numerous and recurrent episodes of rabies-infected wolves killing scores of humans from the seventeenth through the nineteenth centuries and the dramatic case of the Gévaudan Beast in 1764–1767[2] helped to turn wolves into a feared scourge of humans in France. Such stories supported heavy-handed anti-wolf measures: specialized wolf hunters, bounties, and systematic poisoning, all leading to the wolf's disappearance from France in the 1920s.

But the wolf held a major place in French popular culture and wolves, treated as quasi humans by popular culture, have come today to resemble pets, objects of emotional links and of individuation. Friends of the wolves, often passionate, have launched a major rehabilitation campaign of the animal, asserting that wolves have never killed any human – except wolves suffering from rabies, and maybe not even then. That campaign has involved a complete rewriting of the story of the Gévaudan Beast. Public opinion about wolves has changed completely, which is not minor, for this change overhauls our symbolic bestiary.

Research Methods

From autumn 1999 until the end of 2002, the assessment of conflicts sparked by the return of wild wolves in France – and especially of how seemingly unrelated "rumors" were relevant to understand these conflicts – was one of my main research subjects. However, during that period, I also co-authored a book on today's rumors (Campion-Vincent and Renard 2002) and published four research articles.

My research methods were indirect: interviews of key actors such as the author of the most recent report on the subject (interview with Pierre Bracque, Oct 10, 1999); the former director of the Environment Department's key agency in 1992–1993, when the wolves' return was noticed and announced who is also a member of the board of the main Nature Protectors' Associations (NPAs) lobbying for wolves (interview with Gilbert Simon, Dec 29, 1999); one of the main representatives of the sheep farmers, a sheep farmer himself (interview with Denis Grosjean, Nov 26, 1999).

In the bibliographical approach, my aim was to privilege the "internal" documents aimed at specialists and peers, more revealing for my purpose than the document addressing the general public, which are "tailored" for outsiders. I thus became an avid reader of administrative circulars and instructions, mostly of those available on the Internet, but also of the 1998 report authored by the Agricultural Chamber of the Alpes Maritimes county[3] asserting that the reintroduction of wolves had been deliberate and covered by secretive and lying authorities. I also studied systematically the NPAs' newsletters, media of internal information aimed at members of a small "community" which express their shared values: thirty-five issues for the main NPA (*Groupe Loup France* [France wolf group], which has become *FERUS* [latin term for predators]) and sixteen issues for the second (*Mission loup* de *France Nature Environnement* [Wolf mission of France nature environment]) were thoroughly analyzed to obtain an understanding of each group's worldview and culture. The fourteen issues of the Environment Department's official newsletter were studied too. This bibliographic endeavor extended to many of the numerous books published on the subject of wolves and nature magazines as well.

I lectured in the regional park of Luberon (Apt, Dec 2, 1999) and in several research conferences in 2000 and 2003. I also observed a meeting of the main pro-wolf association (Paris, Dec 18, 1999) and lately participated in an official conference convened by the Environment Department (Lyons, Dec 9–10, 2003). The feedback from these contacts was important as it enlivened the dusty words gathered.

When I reached the time of writing, the mobilization and rediscovery of the experience and ideas from my former fieldwork on the close subjects of animal-release stories – such as viper-release stories (Campion-Vincent 1990a), animal-release stories in general (Campion-Vincent 1990b) or mystery cats (Campion-Vincent 1992) – and of the problems raised by the return of lynxes (Campion-Vincent 1996b) were capital. Writing came in successive steps: the oral presentations of 1999 and 2000, a first research article, a second article inserted in a special issue on wolves which I co-edited (Campion-Vincent 2002) and now this contribution. The authorities' approach to the problems raised by the presence of wild wolves for the mountain sheep-farmers greatly evolved during the period of my research and a new set of interviews was conducted in 2002 and 2003 to cover this evolution.

The Return of Wolves in France

In the early 1990s wild populations of wolves reappeared on the French territory from which they had disappeared in the late 1920s. Since first reappearing on the French landscape wolves have spread throughout the country. In February of 2004, the *Office National de la Chasse et de la Faune Sauvage* [the national agency of hunting and wild fauna, ONCFS] estimated that "fifty five to seventy" wolves were present on the French territory in 2003 (Briet 2004). Their presence has been the subject of intense debate among parties with a stake in their return, a debate revealing different constructions of Nature.

The Events of the Wolf's Return

Wild wolves made their French debut with sightings in the national park of Mercantour on the border of Italy as early as 1990 (Bracque 1999:56) but with no official confirmation. Observations conducted during the winter of 1992–1993 confirmed the presence of a pack. With support from the Environment Department, their return was announced in a May 1993 special issue of the nature lovers' magazine *Terre Sauvage* [Wild Land] titled "Welcome to the wolf, now back in France." The special issue included fourteen pages in which pictures of wolves were dominant (mixing as is usual close-ups of frolicking wolves taken in captivity and traces of footprints in snow). The two authors were members of NPAs, and one of them, Geneviève Carbone, was then employed by the national park of Mercantour as an ethnozoologist. A lyrical editorial advised its readers to see in these "pioneers of animal reconquest [. . .] fragments of Celtic soul howling their freedom in the mountain" (Paccalet 1993:19).

The return of wolves was generally supported by the French public: the Environment Department sponsored a public opinion poll in May 1995 to assess support and found that seventy-nine percent judged that the return of wolves was good news (Dobremez 1996:84). Yet wolves were not well-received by mountain sheep-farmers due to concern over damage to flocks; their interests were supported by the Agriculture Department. In 1999, a committee of the National Assembly, pushed by political representatives of mountain sheep-farmers, published a report that concluded "wolves must be excluded from pastoralism[4] areas," while their presence "could be tolerated in 'wolves park' areas" (Chevallier 1999:31).

Slow to respond, the Environment[5] and Agriculture[6] Departments of the French government implemented measures in March 2000 to control wolves, designating areas where the wolves were totally protected (the national park of Mercantour and the natural regional park of Queyras, as well as "a traffic corridor linking the two parks") and areas in which "the population of wolves is controlled" (the rest of the Alps). And in July 2000 an additional protocol allowed decisions of capture or destruction of wolves to be made by the prefects on the local level. This "Wolf Plan" clearly took into account the clout of the political representatives of the mountain areas. A May 2003 report, commissioned by the French National Assembly, titled "Predators and mountain pastoralism. Priority to Man", suggested extending predator control to additional species, including bears and lynxes and called to dialogue of the Paris authorities with the local elites (Spagnou 2003a). A National Wolf Committee was set up in November 2003 and gave the major wolf management role to the Agriculture Department, "for all that concerns the help to pastoralism confronting the predation of wolves (prevention, better working conditions, etc.)" while the Environment Department's task was "to finance damage compensation, and to define a management plan of the species in France" (Programme Life 2003).

The Parties and Their Arguments

The discourse surrounding the wolf's reintroduction in France revolves around two issues: damage to flocks and the mode of the wolf's return. The reintroduction of wolves to the French landscape, however, may be best understood in the context of constructions of the landscape and humans' relationship to it.

Mountain sheep-farmers in the French Alps graze some 860,000 sheep over 8,660,000 square kilometers (Bracque 1999; Spagnou 2003a). Their incomes, subsidies included, are among the lowest of French farming even as their allowances and subsidies are twice the incomes mountain sheep-farmers derive from the sale of sheep. Mountain sheep-farmers, with support from the very large Agriculture Department, have shown strong antipathy toward wolves, basing their extreme dislike on figures showing loss of sheep to wolves. From 1993 to 2000, mountain sheep-farmers received 1 million euros in compensation for 5,760 sheep killed or maimed in the Alps. They received 301,595 euros as compensation for 1,828 animals lost in 2001 and 417,184 euros for 2,304 animals lost in 2002.[7] From 1993 to 2000, seventy-one percent of animal compensation (and sixty-four percent from 1993 to 2002) were from the Alpes Maritimes county, where the national park of Mercantour is located. Damage has spread in recent years: the more northern county of Isère, where only 182

animals were killed until 2000, had heavy predatory damage in 2001
(474) and 2002 (551) (Spagnou 2003a:153–154).

The wolf's return to France, by contrast, was lauded by the NPAs
and the Environment Department. NPAs consider themselves auxil-
iary scientists who help the Environment Department and the prestigious natural sciences institution, *Museum national d'histoire naturelle*,
to plan the management of natural areas and carry out the conservation of biodiversity. The NPAs have been keen to put in context
the damage to flocks, asserting that stray dog attacks are far more
numerous, aggressive, and damaging, even describing them as "mur-
derers" (Minga 1993:20). Soon after the wolves arrived in Mercantour,
this claim appeared in a magazine article:

> Nowadays dogs tarnish the animals' [wolves] image. More precisely
> stray dogs, more than 50,000 in France, who kill game, poultry and
> livestock while only wolves are accused. In six months there have been
> in Mercantour 60 attacks of dogs versus 33 of wolves (*Télé-loisirs* 1995:8,
> as quoted in Bobbé 1998:280–1).

NPAs put forward extravagant figures about the evils of stray dogs.
In the 1980s wolf advocate Gérard Ménatory (author of several books
on wolves since the mid 1970s and later director of the Wolf Park
of Gévaudan) routinely mentioned the figure of 50,000 sheep killed
each year by dogs, without any documentation of his assertions. A
booklet on how to manage guard dogs gives the highest figure, jux-
taposing the limited damage caused by "wild animals" against the
huge damage ascribed to "domestic dogs":

> Each year in France, domestic dogs cause the death of 500,000 sheep
> in a flock or some ten millions. The damage is important. Predation
> caused by wild animals (lynx, wolf and bear) is less than 1,000 sheep.
> Predation by domestic dogs concerns the whole territory. Predation by
> wild animals is limited to specific areas. It is therefore mostly to pro-
> tect themselves against the attacks of domestic dogs that French sheep-
> farmers have reintroduced guard dogs in their flocks (Wick 2002:8).

The general secretary of the National Ovine Federation, Denis
Grosjean (1998), responded to these assertions:

> Do not tell us that we accept from stray dogs what we reject from
> protected predators. Whether pest or cholera, we fight relentlessly all
> that slaughters our flocks. [. . .] Nothing is common between the sad
> toll of stray dogs, that intervene on the whole territory [. . .] and that
> of hyper protected beasts, slaughtering and stressing always the same
> flocks, with the encouragement of the public authorities.

Grosjean went on to cast sheep farmers as the true "managers of areas where they work" and articulated an anthropocentric view: "To protect nature, perfect! But not to the detriment of sheep-farmers, not to the detriment of their work, not against those that maintain the balance between pasture and forest" (Grosjean 1998). Indeed, there is no room for wolves in the livestock farming areas. The city dwellers who appreciate them so much, according to Grosjean, should take over their burden:

> If France wishes to experience beasts in the wild, let us start with the *Bois de Boulogne* and the *Bois de Vincennes*, with the forests of Fontainebleau and Rambouillet,[8] where it will not be our sheep's legs that will be at risk (Grosjean 1998).

Faced with the mounting protests of sheep-farmers, the NPAs endlessly repeat that the existence of wild wolves in the mountain areas is an enrichment of France's natural heritage. While they admit that conflicts between mountain sheep-farmers and wolves are inevitable, they assert that protection measures offered to the sheep-farmers (dogs, enclosures, assistants) are certainly enough to contain predators, and that national solidarity must be called upon to bolster compensations. NPAs firmly oppose any regulation (authorizing removal by capture or destruction) of the wolf population until the wild population reaches sustainable levels (as many as one hundred in about twenty wolf packs).[9]

The second point of contention for wolf opponents is over how wolves were reintroduced to France. A 1998 report, titled "A so-called natural return of wolves in France," of the Agricultural Chamber of the Alpes-Maritimes county, drew from an Italian inquiry its conclusion: that the reintroduction in France had been deliberate.[10] This conclusion, the report posited, legitimized the removal of wolves from the French territory. These accusations were not, however, included in the Spagnou Report (2003a), one of the two parliamentary reports, because, the authors concluded, the data was uncertain. Furthermore, except if the unrealistic thesis of a huge conspiracy was adopted, it was only isolated wolf enthusiasts that could have carried out these hypothetical reintroductions:

> The question of the natural return or of the reintroduction of the wolf in France has drawn the commission's attention. [. . .] Your reporter's conviction is that truth lies probably between the two: according to scientific knowledge now available, a natural return of the wolf from

Italy is quite possible [. . .] but cannot be proven. It is also probable
that clandestine releases of wolves have taken place but, once again,
without the possibility of proving this. Anyhow these releases have
probably not been the object of a conspiracy implicating the national
park of Mercantour and the Nature Protection Agency of the Environment Department. Irresponsible individuals passionate of nature have
probably enacted these releases. If there had been a conspiracy, it
would mean that more than half of the persons heard on the subject
would deliberately have lied to the commission while they deposited
under oath (Spagnou 2003a:25–26).

The Meaning of Nature

Mountain sheep-farmers and NPAs declare the same aim: to maintain and enrich natural territories and milieus. However, it is clear
that the words "nature" and "territories" do not correspond to the
same realities for each group. Nature as work tool or Nature as
ecosystem are two wildly different approaches to the concept.

In the early 1990s, conducting fieldwork in the Vosges, where
reintroduction of lynxes had been implemented by the Environment
Department, sociologist Anne Vourc'h (1991) analyzed the tensions
caused by the reintroduction in open spaces of a predator whose
disappearance had been deliberate. The naturalists promoting the
reintroductions and the locals who lived and worked in these open
spaces perceived the landscape differently. The naturalists saw themselves as protectors and managers of ecosystems and biological spaces,
spaces to be managed for public good by the restoration and maintenance of a biological diversity that included the predator, seen as
necessary for the maintenance of a natural balance. The locals, farmers, and hunters talked of the land as work tool and cast predators'
return as a threat to their traditional role as inhabitants and managers of their own living and working space.

Vourc'h concluded by asking a provocative question: Can the reintroductions of protected species be considered as the creation of a
new kind of zoo, "third type zoos"? After the early cages of classic
zoos and the enlarged spaces of animal parks, the first two types, it
is now rural areas that enclose the protected species, areas that are
controlled by scientific follow-up, while productive human activities
no longer master them.

At the end of the 1990s, in the debate raised by the return of
wolves, the same differences in space perception could be observed.
The mountain sheep-farmers present themselves as managers of areas

which, but for their arduous labor and the flocks' grazing, would only be impenetrable and monotonous bush. Denis Grosjean (1998) illustrated this in his Lyons speech:

> Sheep-farmers do not maim the landscapes. Armed with our flocks, we stop the thick bramble, crush dead wood, and aerate the under-wood. [. . .] Beneficial to nature, our activities, grazing, transhumance and mowing, maintain and develop a rich flora. As to fauna, scientists and hunters agree that the multiplicity of species and the abundance of animals are closely linked to sheep-farming. Sheep, this ill-appreciated livestock, is the ultimate detail before losing the fight to bush and firs.

The activist-ecologist invokes images of a land unpolluted by human presence, the lost paradise of an untouched and varied nature that can, however, be rebuilt. Thus a regular columnist of *Terre Sauvage* argued:

> We will never see again the virgin splendor of the forest before Vercingetorix.[11] At least we can try to safeguard some shreds of it; or to reinvent it. I would like fragments of France – let us say 1,000 square kilometers per Dept – where the powerful National Forest Agency lets trees grow as they please; where hunters allow deer, boars, martens and eagle owls to sort out their business; where we reintroduce lammergeyers and large grouse, beavers and European buffaloes, aurochs "reconstituted" through genetic engineering, brown bears and lynxes. Not to forget wolves (Paccalet 1993:19).

Integrating the Realities Expressed through Animal-Release Rumors

Amongst social reactions to the return of wild animals, some are judged uninteresting and not worth serious consideration by the authorities: these reactions are labeled *rumors*, i.e., untrue assertions. Yet, the study of these rumors, if conducted would have led to predictions and interpretations of unexpected social reactions. These rumors' central theme is animal-release, accidental or deliberate but covert, mostly of negatively perceived species (Campion-Vincent 1990a, 1990b, 1992, 1996b; Campion-Vincent and Renard 1992).

The social sciences take rumors seriously since the pioneering studies of Allport and Postman (1947) and Shibutani (1966). These first studies centered on rumors in the exceptional circumstances of riots or war; they tended to consider rumors as erroneous and pathological. The later studies of Rosnow and Fine (1976), Fine (1992) and

Fine and Turner (2001) adopted a more analytical approach and integrated the approaches of sociology and folklore (defined as a form of informal culture differing from popular culture because it is not marketed and from elite culture because it is not taught in schools). Rumors, often told in a short sentence, can be narrated and developed into stories; they then become contemporary (or urban) legends. Rumors and contemporary legends are truth claims that involve unsecured, unverified information; they are shared and transmitted because judged plausible. The common ideas about rumors, presenting them as always false and maliciously created, seem to validate their dismissal. But rumors can be accurate and "some rumors may be factually incorrect [. . .] yet reveal fundamental truths about the nature of the cultural order" (Fine and Turner 2001:56). Recurrent rumors of animal-release are meaningful and deserve interpretation. My hypothesis is that they indicate that the reintroductions of predators were not fully accepted.

Alligators in the Sewers

One of the most famous contemporary legends that appeared in the 1960s, the rumor of the alligators which are supposed to haunt the New York sewers (and sometimes bite the users of public toilets), is an animal-release story. Brought back from Florida by careless tourists to entertain the kids, the baby alligators have been flushed down the toilets into the sewers when they grow up into cumbersome large alligators. Many authentic facts correspond to this story, for example baby alligators were sold to tourists in Florida already in the 1930s. The rumor's widespread circulation – tales of alligators in the sewers are told in most big cities of the planet – is mostly linked, however, to the tale's symbolic value (Campion-Vincent 1996a). This tale is a metaphor of the impossibility of taming wild nature completely; it focuses "on the violation of a boundary between wild and civilized domains" (Oring 1996:330). It also comments upon the inhumanity of the great modern anonymous metropolis, the urban jungle encompassing all dangers.

Viper-Release Stories

Appearing in 1976, viper-release stories remained very active in France until 1985. They then stabilized into a belief, still alluded to in some social groups, to the "fact" that numerous vipers are or have been intentionally released. Their appearance is linked to measures protecting animal species adopted in 1979, which included reptiles.[12] In 1962, protective measures had already been adopted for negatively perceived birds of prey, such as buzzards and vultures. The expression "protected animal" shocks the public when applied to species such as buzzards and vipers.

These stories contain irrational elements, especially the popular assertions that vipers have been released through helicopters by groups hoping to covertly reintroduce them to the landscape. This fantasy element renders implausible the conspiracy interpretations asserting that these stories were constructed by hunters to denigrate friends of nature: one does not imagine propagandists using the fantasy element of helicopters in a concerted action of disinformation. The frequent usage of helicopters in rural and mountainous areas is not a more convincing explanation: "confusions" can only emerge if there are pre-existing "convictions." Yet the fantasy element of the helicopters is central to the story, as it unites opposed dimensions, one of the functions of symbolic thought.

Although its anonymous creators and disseminators are not conscious of it, the viper-release story echoes ancient legendary themes. For instance, the mysterious showers of lizards, snakes, salamanders, crabs, shrimps, prawns and snails, rains of frogs and fishes, of all types of slimy and negative creatures raining down from the sky, that are attested as dire omens in the ancient chronicles and still sporadically appear today (Mitchell and Rickard 1982:72–81, 89–96). These stories also echo the traditional tales about the death of the young nest robber, bit by a viper coiled in the nest he came to rob; in these tales the land-locked snake appears as close to the aerial birds.[13] It is equally possible to think of a link of contiguity between the rotating propeller blades of the helicopter and the undulating coils of the snake.[14]

This story is a collective symbolic production that permits the expression of half-formulated thoughts that circulate about practices of protection and reintroduction of tabooed species that are considered simultaneously positive and dangerous. It is also an accusatory tale, which declares that nature – including animal species dangerous for humans – is given priority over humans by ecologists. The viper-release story is the voice of those whose actions on nature are

judged illegitimate, of these "backwards" strata of society that authorities ignore when they make decisions (protecting buzzards and vipers)
inspired by the powerful orthodoxy of science.

Mystery Cats

In many animal-release accusations the sighting[15] of a "Beast" is
interpreted as indirect proof of the presence of a roaming feline, of
a big exotic cat: puma, panther or lion. These cases are sometimes
"closed" by the discovery of the authors of damage, stray dogs or
a circus escapee. The pattern is not new. A Swiss Jura case in 1895
ended with the discovery of stray dogs (*Almanach Vermot* 1895). In
Burgundy, a similar case in 1907 ended with the discovery of the
remains of a hyena escaped from a travelling circus (*L'Yonne Républicaine*
2003). However, almost all Mystery Cat cases remain unsolved,
"open" and mysterious. When official experts are called, they invari-
ably conclude that the anomaly can be explained by the presence
of a stray domestic animal (usually a dog) and by over-exaggerated
fears of the public. But the concerned public energetically rejects
these conclusions, maintains the thesis of a wild animal, or often
asserts that it is a captive animal, voluntarily released to harm.

These Mystery Cat cases are minor events, of opinion and interpretation rather than of material facts. However they have persisted
some forty years in France. The media strongly participate in the
elaboration of these "flaps" or cycles of agitation around anomalies,
often treating them as entertainment.

In France, twenty cases of Mystery Cats appearances reached the
press from 1978 until 1989 (Campion-Vincent 2002:44), twenty from
1991 until 2000 (Campion-Vincent 2002:45) (Brodu and Meurger
1984; Brodu 1999).

The Mystery Cats phenomenon exists all over the world and curi-
ously started in Great Britain (a country which possesses no big wild
animals roaming free) in the 1960s when the Surrey Puma became
a national celebrity (Goss 1992). The designation "Alien Big Cats"
(ABC), used by the British to designate these cases, underlines the
strangeness of the cat, as "alien," designating the foreigner but also
the extraterrestrial being. ABC maps have become a routine feature
of the British media as maps of the sightings are published each
year. The website of the British Big Cats Society claims that there
were 438 sightings of strange beasts, mostly black, in 2001 (www.british-

bigcats.org). Famous cases – including Surrey Puma (1962–1966), Black Beast of Exmoor (1994–1995), and Beast of Essex (1998) – have caused large-scale hunts and official enquiries that found either nothing or domestic animals. Folklorist John Widdowson (2003:20–21) has offered an interpretation:

> Could they [Big Cats] be regarded as manifestations of what is the same enduring English rural myth: that out there somewhere lies what-ever it is that we fear. [. . .] Often believed to be real, various kinds of big cats have silently taken over some of the habitats formerly haunted by Black Dogs [traditional phantom dogs] and their like.

The U.S. variants are briefly discussed in Brunvand (2001). The context is very different, as wild protected cougars *do* exist in sev-eral regions. However, the U.S. variants mention "panthers" and "lions." In "Big Cats Running Wild," Brunvand (2001:34–5) notices several successive panther sightings in Michigan (1984, 1985, 1989, 1992, 1995) and lion sightings near Philadelphia in 1995, all of which were investigated without results.

Mystery Cats cases correspond to a keen interest in the intrusions of the wild amongst us. They reuse and reinterpret traditional ele-ments (Meurger 1990, 1994) and often voice accusations of animal-release.

Metaphoric thought functions in several different contexts and assertions of animal-release (several other species than vipers or big cats are concerned, especially lynxes, bears and wolves) exist all over the world: in Italy as in the United States[16] wildlife managers are accused of releasing numerous species.

Wolf-Release Stories

In the case of wolves, whose former image was very poor in several circles, the protests about their return were often expressed openly. Rumors concerned mostly their introduction, said to have been covert and deliberate.

1. Italy and Sweden
The helicopter – or, in the following case, an airplane – regularly appears in accusations accompanying, in Italy, the expansion of wolves from the Abruzzes. In a cartoon playfully entitled *The throw of the wolves, or the favorite sport of the true conservationist*, planes with the inscription *Parco d'Abruzzo* on their sides throw parachute-equipped

"Siberian wolves." The wolves are shown dreaming of abundant sheep prey as they drift down to the Italian countryside.

A perplexed Italian zoologist (Marsan 1994:56) referred to "a sort of collective psychodrama" for such introduction tales. He emphasized that these tales do not respect biological knowledge of wolves:

> The tales of hunters, and generally those coming from rural areas describe a sort of collective psychodrama that sees hordes of wolves, parachuted from helicopters or at least fed through parachute drops, that are observed at any time of day or night and also are not shy of humans (Marsan 1994:56).

In a letter to the director of the national park of Mercantour, biologist Luigi Boitani pointed out that these recurring accusations ignore wolves' dynamic behavior:

> It is useful to recall how, even in Italy, each time that shepherds or sheep-farmers want to oppose wolves, they accuse the government, regional authorities, forest administrators, the WorldWide Fund for Nature and lots of other bodies to have reintroduced it, voluntarily ignoring the obvious dynamics of this species in Italy and its ability of dispersion (Dobremez 1996:162).

In Sweden, where wolves had almost disappeared from the south and center of the country in the 1870s, bounties for their shooting were maintained until the mid 1960s. In 1971, a protection project was started when only a few animals remained in the north. As in other countries, methods of development of the wolf stocks that were then discussed included the possibility to breed wolves in captivity and release them.[17] Swedish folklorist Per Peterson (1995:359) has discussed rumors circulating in Sweden in 1985. These asserted that wolves were:

> Let out in the forest by order of the Swedish Society of Nature Protection. [. . .] Similar motifs that have been attracted to rumours and legends [were noted that] deal with finds of empty wolf-cages in the forests or earmarks from zoological gardens on dead wolves or the presence of placed out meat in the forests. The latter should proceed from authorities, which provide wolves with flesh as they lack hunting training.

But Peterson does not conclude that the stories originated in the discovery of these provisions in international conventions. Discussing the problems wolves really raised in traditional agrarian Swedish society where resources were severely limited, he remarks that the fear of wolves had a real economic base then, as the loss of live-stock could be seriously damaging to a farm. It was mostly as killers of livestock that wolves were feared. Then wolves and their behav-ior were well known, which is not the case today. Today's folklore is not about wolves, but about their defenders who are presented as the real danger (Peterson 1995:362).

2. France

The return of the wolves in France in 1992 did not surprise the NPAs that waited for it eagerly and impatiently. A previous study I conducted (Campion-Vincent 1992) identified this expectation. In the 1980s activist media celebrities seized every occasion to proclaim the reintroduction of wolves, and books published by radicals or articles in the newspapers asserted that wolves were secretly released. Numerous inhabitants of the Lozère county believed that wolves were reintro-duced (already or soon) into the Margeride mountains. Local pro-jects of reintroduction did exist and were sustained by the Tourism Office – the Wolf Park of Gévaudan was already a major tourist attraction – while professional agricultural bodies of course rejected them. The ambiguity that existed then around wolves was marked by the repeated jocular April fool's announcements of escapes or official reintroduction of wolves. At the conference upon animal rein-troductions convened by the Environment Department's Protection of Nature Agency and the Cévennes National Park in December 1988, biologist François de Beaufort presented a proposal of wolf's reintroduction, suggesting the release of a wolf pack in the Chambord park estate (Beaufort 1990).

Social anthropologist Pierre Laurence has discussed the reasons the inhabitants of Cévennes National Park have to believe the national park authorities reintroduce predators, or are about to do it. The national park authorities' activities concerning wildlife protection, especially the help brought by the Cévennes National Park to the reintroduction operations of vultures and large grouse, are well known. The expressions "wolf park"[18] and "national park" are close, and even though no wolves have been seen in the Cévennes, rumors are recurrent; so much so that official denials have been published in the local press by the Cévennes authorities (*Lien des chercheurs cévenols* 1997; *La Lozère nouvelle* 1999).

From 1945 until 1989 in France, there were thirty-nine wolf sight-ings, of wild or captive origin: twenty-nine ending with the animal's capture or death, ten remaining mysterious but where the presence of a wolf was affirmed (Campion-Vincent 2002:30). Since 1989, there have been ten cases of sightings of wolves, eight ending with the capture or death of the animal, and two remaining mysterious (Campion-Vincent 2002:31).

The Spagnou Report, compiled from November 2002 to May 2003, published all its hearings (2003b: 863 pages, taken verbatim) which are a real information mine of attitudes towards wolves. The layman and the biologist thus successively describe the incident of a wolf sighting that occurred early in December of 2002.

The incident occurred in an isolated village of the regional park of Queyras, Ristolas (Altitude 1,600 meters, one hundred inhabitants) situated by the Italian frontier at the end of the Guil valley, in the Hautes Alpes county. Joel Giraud, the local political representative and member of the investigative committee, described it:

> A week ago, the inhabitants of Ristolas have seen six wolves cross the village in a single file [à la queue leu leu] by the day's fall. A legitimate worry has been generated (Spagnou 2003b, 1:90).

However two weeks later, the ONCFS biologist, Christophe Duchamp, who investigated the incident, stressed the wolves were not that close and expressed frustration that *he* never saw wolves:

> One must sort the data and the differences of interpretation of testimonies. [. . .] I have been there a week later, and the Mayor certified that they had been on the village square, that the wolves had entered the village, that they would end eating children and little girls . . . In fact it had snowed and we checked the wolves' passage. The tracks are really by the village, so people can have seen them from the village's last house, where they were no farther than a hundred meters away I admit, but the wolf has not crossed the village square! [. . .] Personally I've been studying the wolf for four years and I've only spotted it once, in the South-East of Poland. I've been out in the field for a whole year every day from 5 a.m. till 8 p.m. and I've only spotted it once (Spagnou 2003b, 1:154).

From this exchange, the reader can understand that the two approaches cannot be reconciled: the layman fears (and romanticizes) while the biologist stresses precision (and yet oddly seems disappointed that he has not seen the animal he tracks).

Cases of "erratic wolves" colonizing new Alpine valleys since 1993 often begin as mysterious "Beast" cases. Indeed, soon biological analyses (of feces and hair) confirm the predator's nature: it's a wolf, and it has the Italian wolves' genetic type. Yet not all accept the interpretation of these analyses suggested by the authorities and science: that is, that this wolf is a wild animal that has traveled "naturally" from its abode in the Abruzzes. They are inclined to think it's a released or escaped animal of captive origin.

Analysis

Through many cultural channels – the genres of conversation and of oral narrative, but also the productions of popular culture and of children's literature, by the means of "ostension"[19] or of performance and the elaborations of official culture: major literature and scientific knowledge – we build around wild animals, and especially around animals that stir negative emotions, collective symbolic creations that delimitate human society (Gillepsie and Mechling 1987). Although the dominant mode of thought rejects them, one can note the persistence of the negative use of animals in propaganda and publicity. Activists, who often do not reflect on the psychological and logical roots of these phobias, frequently and ritually denounce this persistence as "medieval superstitions." Wild in the sense of outlawed may have disappeared from the socially tolerated discourse, but in the jungle of modern cities, metaphors of wildness and uncontrolled animality (of which wolves remain the emblem) are always used to brand rebellious or delinquent youths.

Wild animals have been the pretext for a metaphoric and analogous discourse on human society. Scientists and ecologists reject this comparative mode of thought, and this rejection creates uneasiness in the general public that remains attached to ancient motifs, metaphors, associations, cultural symbols, and emblems. In this comparative approach the existence of negatively perceived and tabooed animal species is a logical necessity. If to talk about animals is to talk about humans, one must be able to express evil as well as good. To remark that negative animals are "good to think",[20] "that is they connect to a powerful cultural logic that makes sense to narrators and audiences" (Fine and Turner 2001:63), is not to defend cruel practices towards some animal categories.

For local human populations that have to cope with the disturbances caused by wolves' presence, the return of wolves corresponds to the intrusion of city dwellers in their narrowing universe. They feel these city dwellers dictate the rules of management of their environment

and that they almost live in "third type zoos" organized by naturalists (Vourc'h 1991).

Pierre Laurence (2002:193–194) has perceptively analyzed the fears
the local human populations of Cévennes feel and express about the
return of predators, for them the sign of the loss of human population and of the progressive "wilding" of the mountain:

> The Cévennes inhabitants long had to share their territory with the
> dangerous wolves and little by little our ancestors were able to get rid
> of this predator in an era when the whole territory was "humanized";
> then the losses of the First World War marked a first phase of loss of
> territory and of return of the wild with the arrival of boars; this was
> provisional as for a long time hunting contained the animal; today the
> boars pullulate, in a territory returned to the wild because of a lack
> of men and money to maintain it. In this perspective, the possibility
> of a return of the wolves with the protection of a national park that
> was set up to protect wild fauna – and their respective perceptions of
> "wild" are very different – would mean for many inhabitants the de-
> humanization and definitive "wilding" of their home country. The
> rumor of a possible wolves' reintroduction, following similar reintro-
> ductions, can be interpreted as "the end of Cévennes" those Cévennes
> that men had patiently managed and brought to "culture" in the word's
> two meanings.

The resistances, expressed through rumors and contradictory reactions, to the return of wild animals highlight the limits that actions
inspired by an ideology meet when they bring important changes
into local ways of life. It is well known that local resistances to change
have experienced an exponential growth over the past thirty years,
multiplying conflicts linked to management operations and making
very cumbersome the realization of any new equipment, electric utility, train or dam for example: it is the famous "NIMBY [Not In
My Back Yard] syndrome," a standard term in environmental literature regarding the treatment of hazardous waste.

The stakes of the manipulations of wild fauna, which possess their
legitimacy, would be clearer if there was less invocation of sacred
principles, less conjuring up of the loaded term of "Nature."
Manipulations of wild fauna are still often legitimized by a myth of
restoration, of reconstruction. This myth lessens or denies the artificial
management traits (radio-collars to ensure follow-up, feeding areas
for vultures) that inevitably accompany manipulations of wild fauna.
The very term of "reintroduction," whose use is general, sends back
"to this conception that Nature would have been complete in some

past era and that, therefore, one can only reconstruct it" (Micoud 1993:207). The search of "property rights" given to an animal on a territory by its past is, of course, more successful when the animal is very present in the symbolic bestiary; this is why the wolf's return in France was so meaningful to friends of nature.

Can we recognize that manipulations are necessary to modify Nature? Can we dream of the recovery of paradise lost but also understand that the environment must be managed with care? Nature, yes, but nature shaped and organized by humans, whether to culti-vate it or to re-establish animal species that had previously been removed.

Conclusion: What Will Happen?

The questions asked by ecologists are legitimate, and most reason-able people subscribe to the ideal of a diversified environment and accept that active conservation is necessary to maintain biodiversity. However, this ideal must be implemented through democratic means, not by the pressure groups of "deep ecology" as insists philosopher Luc Ferry (1992:237–238):

> Deep ecology raises antipathy amongst democrats. Nevertheless it chal-lenges the humanist ethic it claims to transcend [. . .] Deep ecology asks true questions, which a critical discourse denouncing its fascist or of ultra-leftist aspects cannot disqualify. Public opinion will never believe that ecology, however radical it may be, is more dangerous than the scores of Chernobyl threatening us. [. . .] It is because ecology is seri-ous business, that it should not be the monopoly of deep ecologists. [. . .] Questioning the liberal logic of production and consumption can-not leave us indifferent. [. . .] We do understand that mankind is not on earth to buy ever more sophisticated cars and TV sets.

It seems improbable that the controlled regulation measures adopted in 2000 or the management plan of 2004 might bring the disap-pearance of wild wolves in France. Such measures, adopted eleven years ago for lynxes, have not stopped the progression of that species. The quasi-disappearance of humans from the rural spaces will prob-ably free up areas for the predator.

However, adding to the prevalence of their contrasted image, the pack organization of wolves renders their presence difficult to toler-ate in sheep-farming areas. Conflicts will probably continue, but in 2004, the necessity of compromise is admitted by most of the actors.

The information policy of the Environment Department became more open after the adoption of the Wolf Plan. The bulletin *L'Infoloup* [Wolves Info] and the online site of the Programme Life (www.paca. environnement.gouv.fr), published a few articles emanating from sheep-farmers.

The attitudes of the local agents – of the County Agriculture and Forest Agencies of the Agriculture Department and also of some of the personnel hired by the Environment Department to manage the consequences of the reappearance of predators – have been important in the adoption of this spirit of compromise. In the meetings of the Summer 2003 aiming to organize the future, these county agents of the Agriculture Department pleaded for a choice of official terms closer to the sheep-farmer's sensitivities ("regulation" was suggested by them, but the NPAs strongly opposed it and the more neutral term of "management" was adopted). An equilibrium was re-established as these local agents listened to the dismayed mountain sheep-farmers more than to the noisy but sometimes irresponsible NPAs. This evolution was gradual, and it is still an ongoing process, but the mountain sheep-farmers have now a voice, which I think they won't lose.

References

Allport, Gordon W. and Leo J. Postman. 1947. *The Psychology of Rumor.* New York: H. Holt.
Almanach Vermot. 1895 "Les panthères du Jura [The Jura Panthers]." 6–8 septembre.
Beaufort, François de. 1990. "La réintroduction du loup en France [The reintroduction of the wolf in France]." Pp. 189–195 in *Réintroductions et renforcements de populations animales en France. Compte-rendu du Colloque de Saint Jean du Gard 6–8 décembre 1988,* edited by J. Lecomte, M. Bigan, and V. Barre. Paris: [Supplément 5 à la Revue d'écologie].
Bobbé, Sophie. 1998. *Du folklore à la science. Analyse anthropologique des représentations de l'ours et du loup dans l'imaginaire occidental* [From folklore to science. An anthropological analysis of the representations of the bear and of the wolf in western imaginary]. Paris: EHESS, Thèse de Doctorat.
Bracque, Pierre. 1999. *Rapport de mission interministérielle sur la cohabitation entre l'élevage et le loup* [Interdepartmental mission report on the cohabitation between animal farming and the wolf]. Paris: Ministère de l'Agriculture et de la Pêche, Inspection Générale de l'Agriculture, février.
Briet, Sylvie. 2004. "La France dans la gueule du loup [France in the wolf's throat]." *Libération,* 12 février.
Brodu, Jean-Louis. 1999. "Fauves et usage de fauves [Beast and uses of beasts]." *La Mandragore. Revue des littératures orales* 5:91–107.

Brodu, Jean-Louis, and Michel Meurger. 1984. *Les félins-mystère. Sur les traces d'un mythe moderne* [Mystery cats. On the tracks of a modern myth]. Paris: Pogonip.

Brunvand, Jan Harold. 2001. *Encyclopedia of Urban Legends*. Santa Barbara: ABC-CLIO Inc.

Campion-Vincent, Véronique. 1990a. "Viper-Release Stories: A Contemporary French Legend." Pp. 11–40 in *A Nest of Vipers. Perspectives on Contemporary Legend V*, edited by G. Bennett and P. Smith. Sheffield: Sheffield Academic Press.

———. 1990b. "Contemporary Legends about Animal-Releases in Rural France." *Fabula* 31:242–253.

———. 1992. "Appearances of Beasts and Mystery Cats in France." *Folklore* 103(2): 160–183.

———. 1996a. "Caimanes en las Alcantarillas de Nueva York [Alligators in the sewers of New York]." *Enigmas* VI(2):78–86.

———. 1996b. "Le retour du lynx [Return of the lynx]." *Anthropozoologica* 23:3–12.

———. 2002. "Les réactions au retour du loup en France. Une analyse tentant de prendre 'les rumeurs' au sérieux [Reactions to the return of the wolf in France. An analysis trying to take 'rumors' seriously]." *Le Monde Alpin et Rhodanien* 1–3 [Special Issue: *Le fait du loup* [Wolf fact] co-editors C. Abry, V. Campion-Vincent, J.-C. Duclos]:11–52.

Campion-Vincent, Véronique and Jean-Bruno Renard. 1992. *Légendes urbaines. Rumeurs d'aujourd'hui* [Urban legends. Rumors of today]. Paris: Payot.

———. 2002. *De source sûre. Nouvelles rumeurs d'aujourd'hui* [From a safe source. New rumors of today]. Paris: Payot.

Chevallier, Daniel. 1999. *De l'incompatibilité du loup et du maintien d'un pastoralisme durable* [On the incompatibility of the wolf and of the maintenance of a perennial pastoralism], Rapport n°1875, octobre. Paris: Assemblée nationale.

Delort, Robert. 1984. *Les animaux ont une histoire* [Animals have a history]. Paris: Seuil.

Dobremez, Jean-François. 1996. *Rapport à Madame le ministre de l'Environnement sur une mission d'inspection et de médiation sur le loup* [Report to the minister of the environment concerning an inquiry and mediation mission on wolves]. Paris, novembre.

Ferry, Luc. 1992. *Le nouvel ordre écologique. L'arbre, l'animal et l'homme* [The new ecological order. The tree, the animal and man]. Paris: Grasset.

Fine, Gary Alan. 1992. *Manufacturing Tales. Sex and Money in Contemporary Legends*. Knoxville: University of Tennessee Press.

Fine, Gary Alan and Patricia Turner. 2001. *Whispers on the Color Line. Rumor and Race in America*. Berkeley, Los Angeles, London: University of California Press.

Gillepsie, Angus and Jay Mechling. 1987. "Introduction." Pp. 1–14 in *American Wildlife in Symbol and Story*, edited by A.K. Gillespie and J. Mechling. Knoxville: The University of Tennessee Press.

Goss, Michael. 1992. "Alien Big Cat Sighting in Britain." *Folklore* 103:184–202.

Grosjean, Denis. 1998. "Address at Lyons protest rally." Lyons, October 15. [Manuscript sent by Denis Grosjean to author in February 2000].

L'Yonne Républicaine. 2003. "La bête de Noyers [The Noyers Beast]." 4–5 octobre.

La Lozère nouvelle. 1999. "Au Loup ! [Wolf !]." 17 décembre.

Laurence, Pierre. 2002. "'Ils finiront par nous bouffer'. Enquêtes contemporaines sur la mémoire du loup en Cévennes ['They'll end up eating us' Contemporary enquiries on the memory of the wolf in Cévennes]." *Le Monde Alpin et Rhodanien* 1–3 [Special issue of *Le fait du loup* [Wolf fact] co-editors C. Abry, V. Campion-Vincent, J.-C. Duclos]: 179–198.

Lévi-Strauss, Claude. [1962] 1963. *Totemism*. Boston: Beacon Press.

Lien des chercheurs cévenols. 1997. "Parc des Cévennes. Et si les loups revenaient naturellement [Cévennes park. And if wolves came back naturally]." Janvier-mars.

Marsan, A. 1994. "Indicatori di presenza del lupo sul territorio ed areale di diffusione della specie in Liguria [Indicators of presence of the wolf on the territory and area of diffusion of the species in Liguria]." Pp. 54–66 in *Appunti dal corso regionale di aggiornamento per veterinari su lo riconoscimento dei danni da predazione da canidi provocati al patrimonio zootecnico*. Regione Liguria: Servizio veterinario.

Meurger, Michel. 1990. "Les félins exotiques dans le légendaire français [Exotic felines in French legends]." *Communications* 52:175–196.

———. 1994. "The Leopards of the Great Turk." Pp. 198–209 in *Fortean Studies* (v.1), edited by S. Moore. London: John Brown Publishing.

Micoud, André. 1993. "Vers un nouvel animal sauvage : le sauvage 'naturalisé vivant'?" [Towards a new wild animal: the 'naturalized living' wild]. *Nature, Sciences, Sociétés* 1(3):202–210.

Minga, Marc. 1993. "Peur bleue. Et si les loups revenaient? [Great fear. And if wolves came back?]" *Grenoble mensuel* février: 20 [Declaration of Jean-François Noblet].

Mitchell, John and Bob Rickard. 1982. *Living Wonders. Mysteries and Curiosities of the Animal World*. London: Thames and Hudson.

Oring, Elliott. [1990] 1996. "Legend, Truth and News." Pp. 324–339 in *Contemporary Legend. A Reader*, edited by G. Bennett and P. Smith. New York and London: Garland Publishing.

Paccalet, Yves. 1993. "Au bonheur du gaulois [Happiness of the gaulois]." *Terre Sauvage* 73, May:19.

Pastoureau, Michel. 2001. *Les animaux célèbres* [Famous animals]. Paris: Bonneton.

Peterson, Per. 1995. "Attitudes and Folk Belief about Wolves in Swedish Tradition." Pp. 359–362 in *Folk Belief Today*, edited by M. Koiva and K. Vassiljeva. Tartu: Estonian Academy of Sciences.

Programme Life. 2003. *Rapport d'activité 2002* [Activity Report for 2002]. Retrieved November 8, 2003 (http://www.paca.environnement.gouv.fr/).

Renard, Jean-Bruno. 1999. *Rumeurs et légendes urbaines* [Rumors and urban legends]. Paris: PUF.

Rosnow, Ralph L. and Gary Alan Fine. 1976. *Rumor and Gossip. The Social Psychology of Hearsay*. New York: Elsevier.

Shibutani, Tamotsu. 1966. *Improvised News. A Sociological Study of Rumor*. Indianapolis: Bobbs-Merrill.

Spagnou, Daniel. 2003a. *Prédateurs et pastoralisme de montagne: priorité à l'Homme. Tome I: Rapport*. [Predators and mountain pastoralism: Priority to Man. Vol I: Report] Paris: Assemblée Nationale [Rapport n°825], mai.

———. 2003b. *Prédateurs et pastoralisme de montagne: priorité à l'Homme. Tomes II, Vols 1 and 2: Auditions*. [Predators and mountain pastoralism: Priority to Man. Vols II, 1 and 2 Hearings] Paris: Assemblée Nationale [Rapport n°825], mai.

Télé-loisirs. 1995. "Le danger des chiens errants." March, pp. 8.

Vourc'h, Anne. 1991. "Réintroduction du lynx dans les Vosges. Discours entre-croisés. [Reintroduction of the lynx in the Vosges. Interlaced discourses]." *Sociétés* 31:45–52.

Wick, Pascal. [1998] 2002. *Le chien de protection sur troupeau ovin* [The guard dog in an ovine flock]. Blois: ARTUS.

Widdowson, John. 2003. "From Black Dog to Big Cat: An Enduring English Rural Myth?" Paper presented at the 21st International Conference on Contemporary Legend Research, Corner Brook Newfoundland.

Notes

[1] Elements of this chapter have been presented orally in Apt and Aix (December 2, 1999), in Paris (March 1, 2000) and Rambouillet (October 2, 2000). A first publication occurred in France (Campion-Vincent 2002). I thank Adrienne Mayor for her revision and suggestions in 2002. All non-English quotations were translated by me.

[2] Murderous attacks on shepherds started in July 1764 and terrorised the region. Soldiers and later specialized wolf-hunters sent by the King met no success and France was laughed at in Europe. Casualties piled up until a gigantic wolf was killed on September 21, 1765 by the King's special envoy that received a huge bounty. But the deaths resumed in March 1767. The local nobility then took up the fight until another gigantic wolf was killed on June 19, 1767. The final toll was 250 attacks on humans in sixty-four parishes, 130 dead and seventy grievously wounded. Three victims out of four were under eighteen, two-thirds being women. As for wolves, 200 were killed in the region (Delort 1984:259–262; Pastoureau 2001:176–185). Today the story of the Gévaudan Beast is rewritten as fantasy so as to exonerate wolves. The latest well-known version is to be found in a popular film *The Brotherhood of the Wolf* (2001) that designated as culprit a Catholic priest motivated both by sadism and a desire to instill fear into his flock.

[3] Term used as equivalent to the French "Département.".

[4] This term, widely used in France, designates activities linked to open-air sheep-farming.

[5] Exact title *Ministère de l'Ecologie et du Développement Durable* [Department of Ecology and Sustainable Development] (MEDD).

[6] Exact title *Ministère de l'Agriculture, de l'Alimentation, de la Pêche et des Affaires Rurales* [Department of Agriculture, Food, Fishing and Rural Affairs] (MAAPAR). Of its 30,000 agents, only 2,000 are located in Paris.

[7] The euro/US dollar €/$ ratio oscillates between 0.80 and 1.20.

[8] Woodlands in Paris and the Paris region. These four areas are highly frequented by city dwellers for leisure activities.

[9] Gilbert Simon personal communication, December 29, 1999.

[10] The enquiry unequivocally revealed that no presence of wolves was signaled west of the city of Genoa. This fact is confirmed in a fax from Luigi Boitani, (a biologist and an authority on wolves, his subject since 1973, who inspired the protection measures adopted in Italy during the 1970s) to the director of the national park of Mercantour. However, this expert explains that these "jumps" in the species' progression are not surprising: "Re-colonization does not proceed as the spread of an oil stain, but rather through the irregular appearance of new population nuclei, [. . .] these appearances occur where there are optimal conditions of quietness, abundance of wild and mostly domestic preys. Feeble quantities of domestic flocks are available in the provinces of Imperia and Savone" (Dobremez 1996:161–4).

[11] Gaul leader whose surrender to Julius Cesar in 52 BC marked the end of Gaul's resistance to Roman colonization. All French children learn this name in their first history lessons.

[12] Buying, selling, exhibiting or transporting protected reptiles was banned by law, destruction remaining however authorized for the two most venomous species *Vipera Aspis* et *Vipera Berus*.

[13] Solange Pinton and Yvonne Verdier, anthropologists, personal communication, 1989. This tale has a naturalist basis, since some grass snakes, more common than vipers, also live in trees and rob the eggs (Gérard Naulleau, naturalist, personal communication, 1989).

[14] François Poplin, personal communication, March 1, 2000.

[15] And (rarely) damage to livestock. Episodes marked by important damage do exist: Cattle Mutilation Panics in the 1960s in the Western U.S.; Goat Suckers or *Chupacabras* that started in 1995 in Puerto Rico and expanded amongst U.S. Hispanics. However their discussion would take us beyond the focus of this chapter. These episodes are mostly promoted by "anomalists" and linked to extraterrestrial lore.

[16] Rumors asserting that the Kentucky Wildlife Service proceeded to release rattlesnakes, sometimes from helicopters, so as to control the population of wild turkeys were reported in the *Kentucky Herald* of January 9, 1997, leading to the disabused commentary of a spokesman: "these rumors surge periodically, we do not know how or why" (Jan Harold Brunvand, personal communication January 10, 1997).

[17] These methods: breeding wolves in captivity and later releasing them were proposed by IUCN The World Conservation Union.

[18] PL refers to the wolf park of Gévaudan, close to the Cévennes National Park and main tourist attraction of the Lozère county in which the national park is enclosed.

[19] "Behavior imitating the pattern of a rumor or of a legend, whether or not they are believed to be true" (Renard 1999:125).

[20] The expression originates in anthropologist Claude Lévi-Strauss's 1963 essay *Totemism*.

MORE THAN MERE WOLVES AT THE DOOR: RECONSTRUCTING COMMUNITY AMIDST A WILDLIFE CONTROVERSY

RIK SCARCE

Introduction

When I began my research on the social construction of nature in areas near Yellowstone National Park, my interests had nothing to do with community, only with what I called the "human-wolf interactions" that followed the 1995 reintroduction of wolves to the Park. I was only interested in how humans negotiated their newly-changed relationship with nature – or one part of nature, the wolves – and how, as a result of those negotiations, nature and the wolves were re-made by the residents.

However, in the course of interviews with ranchers who lived near the Park, I found that they were deeply concerned about other forces of change in their lives that predated the wolf reintroduction and were potentially more sweeping. New persons were moving to the Yellowstone area, buying up ranches, changing both the way the land was being used, and fundamentally altering the interactions between neighbors. These shifts in relationships with the land and with the community meant that the wolf reintroduction took place in an already tense climate, one of social upheaval that colored the reintroduction and added a level of complexity to it.

In this chapter I examine social constructions of the wolves and of one Yellowstone-area community by members of that community. I begin by discussing the difficulties that social theorists encounter as they attempt to grasp the meanings of both nature and community. I then present data from my interviews with ranchers living in wolf country. My analysis leads me to conclude that wildlife managers and policy-makers would do well to understand the constructions of *both* nature and community before embarking on new environmental initiatives in rural areas.

Getting "Nature" Right

One of the striking characteristics of many sociologists' thinking about the term nature is that, when they undertake the noble endeavor of remaking *nature* into Nature, they still end up with little-n nature. Little-n nature is the standard "received view" of nature, the one that "we all" have in mind whenever we use the word; that nature is facile and comfortable. On the other hand, *Nature* is an uncertain concept that reflects the fact that different social groups impose different meanings on nature. Michael Redclift and Grahame Woodgate (1994:55) penned one particularly hopeful beginning for this discussion when they wrote:

> Nature has become imbued with so many virtues that the term "natural" no longer confers unambiguous meaning. . . . We have refashioned nature, in our minds, as well as in test tubes and fields, transforming ecological processes into political axioms. . . . Differences surrounding "nature" and what is "natural" reflect differences between societies.

Redclift and Woodgate's explanation is helpful to that point. They develop a persuasive, if somewhat abstract, case that there is no one nature. Instead, they imply, there are multiple natures – Nature – each of which is created by certain social groups depending on how those groups are socially and historically situated. Moreover, they seem to be telling us, the dominant Nature handed down to us is one that serves certain political actors and does disservice to others.

Unfortunately, following that passage, Redclift and Woodgate quickly lapse into nature-ism: the unthinking, uncritical use of Nature. In other words, they completely forget the lesson they had just taught their readers, for they wrote, "Each society has developed *together with nature* under specific circumstances. At the same time, however, we also need to understand that all development is constrained by nature . . ." (Redclift and Woodgate 1994:55; emphasis original). Suddenly, the authors shift from seeing Nature as variable and culturally-dependent to something that all societies co-evolve with and that inevitably limits social behavior.

Similarly, Anthony Giddens, one of the leading sociological theorists of our time, has struggled with Nature. In one apt passage, he first plants the social constructivist's seed of doubt, writing, "Yet how should we understand the notion of 'environment' and more particularly that of 'nature'? For in any interpretation of ecological think-

ing an enormous amount hangs on these terms" (Giddens 1994:203).
Giddens proceeds to discuss Nature's variety, and he observes, "Most
such versions of green theory lack precision exactly because 'nature'
remains undefined or is understood in a catch-all way" (Giddens
1994:204). Nature, Giddens implies, is a squishy, uncertain concept,
but it needs an exacting definition. Here, he, too, slips into nature-
ism, as others have done (see, for example, Murphy 1994, 1997).

Giddens's longing for Natural exactitude leads him to attempt a
working definition of the concept. He writes:

> Several main domains or contexts in which "nature" (often also inter-
> woven with tradition) has disappeared, or is disappearing, can be dis-
> tinguished. Nature here means what is "natural" or pregiven in our
> lives; if this is not too paradoxical, a subcategory is understood as nature
> as the non-humanized physical environment (Giddens 1994:207).

Regrettably, when Giddens writes, "Nature here means what is 'natural' . . ." he all-but defines the term by invoking that very term. In
the process, he tells us nothing about Nature's constructedness. Instead,
he merely demonstrates how thoroughly meaning-laden the concept
is. Nature is as we make it.

What is there about Nature that makes it such a seductive notion
that even a thinker of Giddens' reputation may fall into its trap,
seeking to define a concept that resists definition as do few others
in the English language? C.S. Lewis (1967) said nature is one of the
most "dangerous" words we have. Because it is so vague, we risk
meaning nothing when we label something nature. Tentativeness and
situatedness characterize Nature. That is, what is natural seems to
be constantly shifting underfoot and it is dependent upon one's social
outlook. Nature *has never been* something that *all* societies emerge with,
nor do all societies feel constrained by it. Indeed, Nature simply does
not exist in some cultures (Scarce 2000; cf.: Simmons 1993).

I suspect there is another problem with the well-intentioned but
stumbling efforts of deductive theorists like Redclift, Woodgate, and
Giddens: they spend too little time away from their desks, out of
their offices, speaking with and observing people who are actively
creating Nature. They seem to have no understanding of the crucial role context plays in creating Nature. Inductivist Jan Dizard
(1999:160), who explored in-depth social constructions of Nature by
hunters and animal rights activists in Massachusetts, wrote:

> Nature might well be thought of as the original Rorschach. Like the
> suggestive, amorphous ink blots psychologists use to tap our innermost
> fears and longings, nature presents an open invitation to see what we
> want or need to see.

Dizard's hunters actively symbolized Nature based upon their personal experiences and those of others who lived in close proximity to them.

I advocate similar research that takes the would-be theorist of Nature into people's lives so that we can learn from them what Nature means, for it is in their lives that nature becomes Nature. Deductive theorists gather and systematically analyze little or no data. They read books, work out logical arguments and often produce insightful templates for how society operates. Not so with Nature, however. There is little context in a professor's office.

Given the growing body of scientific evidence indicating that industrial societies have brought the planet to the brink of multiple ecological catastrophes, deeper exploration of concepts like nature and closely related terms – environment and ecology – is of the utmost importance. What exactly are we seeing the end of when we proclaim that "the end of nature" is nigh (McKibben 1989; cf.: Evernden 1992)? The issue here is a fundamental one. If humans have the power to affect the global climate, pollute every fresh water source on the planet, and destroy dozens of species per day – or, in the case of the example I will use, to completely control the existence of wolves – is it not plain that *we make Nature what it is, not just in a conceptual sense, but physically?* In the process we give these things new meanings, meanings that both guide and reflect Nature's reality.

Those reality-embodying meanings are what my research explores, what Gary Alan Fine calls "naturework" (Fine 1998). I have examined salmon biologists' constructions of salmon (Scarce 1997, 1999, 2000) and the meanings that numerous stakeholders imbue to wolves (Scarce 1998). It is the latter research that I will use here to explore social constructions of nature and their link to constructions of community. First, however, the problematic "community" concept deserves some attention.

Accomplishing Community

Like Nature, community is a rebellious, dangerous term. A.L. Sinikka Dixon (1999:22) wrote, "Community is a difficult concept to deal with. It has become an 'omnibus' word, embracing 'a motley assortment of concepts and qualitatively different phenomena.'" As nature is Nature, so, too, community is Community. In their thoughtful examination of the Community concept and the challenge of theorizing about Community because it is so difficult to demarcate, "The Lumpen Society," a group of three authors, observed, "Community is everywhere" (Lumpen Society 1997:22). Community, like Nature, can mean anything, any group, any network, any place, whether it exists on the ground or on-line.

The Lumpen Society asserts that Community as actually practiced falls somewhere between the extremes of Tönnies's (1957) rose-colored pastoralism and more pessimistic, even nihilistic assertions that Community cannot exist. We do, after all, identify with others, communicate with them, live, work, and play with them, and these "others" often have beliefs, attitudes, skin colors, religions, genders, and lives that look very different from our own. "From this morass of difference," The Lumpen Society (1997:38) writes, "we seek to construct order, distinguishing entities called communities . . . in which we participate. We perceive the existence of community as a means of understanding and organizing experience." Community is something that is done. It is an accomplishment.

We create things that we call community out of what we are given in life, what we come across, and what we make for and of ourselves. In our daily lives we practice Community, cobbling together disparate things – space, people, outlooks, faiths, lifestyles, leisure activities – to make multiple communities. Our communities are at work, at play, where we worship, where our children attend school, and where we live. When we are participating in each of these communities, we share at least one important social characteristic with the others who are there, even if "there" is cyberspace, but none of our communities are perfect reflections of our social selves: our race, gender, economic class, religion, sexual preferences, recreational pursuits, tastes in food or film. If Community is the warp and woof of our lives, each of us is but one strand in a diverse weave.

This understanding of Community as something that people accomplish to provide their lives with order and stability is reflected in the

work of anthropologist Janet M. Fitchen. After spending years in
rural areas of upstate New York conducting ethnographic research,
Fitchen (1991:253) concluded:

> Social scientists have researched, written, and debated for decades
> about what the terms "community" and "rural community" mean, but
> the people who live in rural places have generally not had much trou-
> ble understanding that they do in fact live in and belong to a com-
> munity. If they cannot satisfactorily define what they mean by community,
> they nonetheless go about their business believing in its existence and
> certain of their own social existence within it. In a sense, without being
> told that they should, they do just what the social scientists say they
> do: "People construct community symbolically, making it a resource
> and repository of meaning, a referent of their identity."

Too much of the debate over Community, like much of the scholarly struggle over Nature, ignores what people believe, say, and do
in their day-to-day lives. Community *is* real to people. The particular
factors that shape it may vary from Community to Community, but
for ethnographers the challenge and the goal is to fairly reflect how
those people in those communities speak of themselves, their worlds,
and their relations with others – human and nonhuman alike –
whom they encounter in those lived worlds (Schutz and Luckmann
1973).

Some of the authors mentioned above noted the danger inherent
in overlaying researchers' pre-existing notions of Community onto
the communities that social scientists study. However, it is equally
dangerous to ignore a concept as important as Community when
fellow research participants ("subjects") invoke it themselves. When
participants do speak of Community, researchers need to do the
same thing they do when they explore Nature or some component
of it: treat that concept as an integral component of participants'
lives.

Studying Nature and Community

I was drawn to explore the Nature-Community connection because
of my methodology. Ethnographers get to know the people and places
that they research in a deep way. We tend to avoid "interviews"
preferring to turn our meetings with others into conversations, although
for ease of discussion this is the label we use to describe our primary

tool for data gathering,. We also recognize that even these conversations, because they take place between strangers and with a tape
recorder running, are not normal experiences for those conversing
with us. As such, researchers influence what is said by our mere
presence, not to mention the ways that we respond to statements
and a host of other factors. Thus, ethnographers and the persons
sharing their thoughts with us are all research "participants," working together to create knowledge.

The data below were drawn from approximately fifty-five interviews with persons from a wide range of stakeholder groups in the
Yellowstone National Park area. Some of the interviews were as brief
as fifteen minutes; others lasted more than two hours. Of particular
interest in this chapter are the results of a subset of those interviews
with fifteen current or former livestock operators near the Park. The
data were analyzed using the "grounded theory" approach, the most
popular system among sociologists for evaluating interview data.[1]

All of those with whom I spoke were "Oldtimers," persons who
had lived in the area for much of their adult lives, or who had been
involved in ranching elsewhere but had moved to the area. The
label Oldtimer is not meant to imply that all Oldtimers are aged;
few were older than sixty and many of them were younger than
fifty. They were all established in the "ranching community," and
nearly all of them were well known in the broader local Community
as well, although three of them had recently moved to the area to
manage cattle ranches.

It is important to note that I chose to emphasize the Oldtimers,
rather than those I term "Newcomers," recent arrivals to the area,
for theoretical and practical reasons. Theoretically, I wanted to explore
exactly what Oldtimers meant by Community change; it was, after
all, their concept of Community that was being affected by the
upheaval around them. In addition, although they clearly felt they
were losing power in their Community, for the most part they
remained the dominant group. They owned most of the land and
they remained the dominant decision-makers; politically powerful
groups are, of course, of special import to wildlife managers when
they work with communities.

On the practical side, the Oldtimers were more accessible than
were the Newcomers. Many Newcomers spent little time in the area,
and often they kept to themselves. For example, when I attempted

to interview one Newcomer family, I was encouraged instead to speak to their ranch/game preserve foreman. Were this broadly an examination of rural Community change, Newcomers' views might be as indispensable as the Oldtimers.' However, my concern is with the construction of the Yellowstone wolves and how it is affected by the reconstruction of the Oldtimer Community as the Oldtimers understand it. Powerful, long-term residents tend to show up at public hearings about resource issues, and they are the persons most likely to call upon natural resource managers for assistance. Thus, given the emphasis of this volume, residents like the Oldtimers deserve special attention.

New Neighbors

Longview Valley, a pseudonym, lies on the outskirts of Yellowstone National Park. It runs several tens of miles, and through it flows a large river with its headwaters in the Park. Bounded by two massive mountain ranges that stay snow covered for most of the year, "the Longview," as residents call it, seems to float near the clouds. The river provides a dependable source of irrigation water, and although winters can get bitterly cold and windy, the Longview is something of a "banana belt" compared to the rest of the region, its unusually warm conditions making it a good place to raise livestock.

Ranches ranging in size from several hundred to several thousands of acres fan out from both sides of the river, and the rounded Black Angus cattle graze silhouetted against snows in the winter and green pastures in the summer. Sheep are also raised in the Longview proper as well as high up in steeply-sloping secondary valleys and wide plateaus, some of which climb away from the river to 10,000 feet. The scene is as perfectly pastoral as any Romantic landscape artist could have desired. All is not well in the Longview, however. Some long-time residents insist the wolves are to blame, but all agree that humans are as well.

Living with Wolves

1. Disaster in the Making
Wolves once inhabited the Valley, but they were cleared out nearly a century ago, and the last wolf in Yellowstone Park was killed in

1926. Not long after, Aldo Leopold, already respected for his wildlife management theories, began arguing that wolves should be put back into the Park (Leopold 1995). That was not to happen for decades, however. Even twenty years after the passage of the Endangered Species Act (ESA), anti-wolf ranchers and their political allies had succeeded in keeping wolves out. Fearing that the vicious predators would leave the Park and ravage livestock up and down the Longview, as the 1990s arrived this group continued to fight what ultimately was a losing battle against the ESA, the wolves, and popular sentiment. In 1995, following the most extensive hearings ever held under the auspices of the ESA, the U.S. Fish and Wildlife Service captured wolves in Canada and brought them to the Park by helicopter, airplane, truck, and snowmobile. The wolves were penned for a month to break them of their homing instinct, and then released.

In its environmental impact statement developed before the wolves were reintroduced to the Park, the U.S. Fish and Wildlife Service (1994) speculated that wolves would leave Yellowstone and kill livestock. This was a virtual certainty because wolves disperse freely because of population pressures, the social structure of wolf packs, and other factors (Mech 1970), and because some wolves seem to have inherited a taste for livestock. This prediction, combined with the savage lore of wolves and the fact that generations earlier wolves were cleared out of the Longview country, led residents of the valley to reason that bringing wolves back likely would be disastrous. One of them told me:

> I had some old-timers that I was good friends with that seen 'em back in the turn-of-the-century, and all they could just say that, you know, there was a reason they got rid of them, 'cause they couldn't live with them. And, of course, times were tougher back then, maybe, but that timber wolf was just a terrible predator. He didn't care what he killed, when he killed it, so they just got rid of 'em.

It did not make sense to many Longview residents that the government and environmentalists wanted to bring back such a vicious animal. In these comments and others like them, wolves were constructed as a kind of disease not unlike smallpox or polio; once it was eliminated, some ranchers argued, what could possibly be the logic for bringing it back? Wolves spelled disaster to these ranchers who fought hard against the wolf during the reintroduction hearings, but lost.

It did not take long after the reintroduction for wolves to leave

the Park and to kill livestock in the Longview. It mattered little to
Oldtimers that the offending wolves killed far fewer head of sheep
and cattle than predicted, that the guilty ones were blasted by auto-
matic shotgun-wielding federal animal damage control agents, or that
an environmental group had established a fund to compensate ranchers for their losses. The pestilence was loose on the land and damage was being done to ranchers' psyches, pocketbooks, and their
sense of calm and security.

To those who opposed the reintroduction, wolves brought with
them a new level of uncertainty for ranchers. I asked one couple
about a conclusion that I had come to based on other ranchers'
comments that ranching families would ranch for nothing so long as
the essentials were taken care of (Scarce 1998). They responded –
him doing most of the talking, her interjecting a word or two here
or there:

> There's a lot of people who will carry unbearable debt and do without
> because (her) it's a way of life, (him) yeah, and they been in it all their
> lives. And what might break that camel's back is the timber wolf.

He spoke the last three words almost in a whisper. "You know, if
it really came in and they started finding dead livestock, it can be
devastating to some of those kind of people."

Here, wolves are constructed not merely as an amorphous disease
lurking in wait. They are, as well, a force promoting instability, an
immediate threat to hearth and home, home wreckers in the sense
that wolves possess the power to ruin everything that a ranching
family has struggled to create. Oldtimers in the Longview willingly
live a tenuous existence because they love the existence itself. They
possess an affinity for the place so profound that they *are* the Longview
and the Longview is them. Only the most powerful of forces, a disaster of some sort that exceeds in its enormity the run-of-the-mill
drought, flood, or blizzard, could, in combination with the rest, run
them off of the land. The wolves, some felt, had the potential for
being such a disaster.

2. Bringing Wolves Back – Or Inviting Them Back?

Not all Oldtime ranchers opposed the presence of wolves. Still, some
objected to the wolf reintroduction, preferring "restoration," where
the wolves would have been allowed to return on their own. The
distinction between, on one hand, reintroducing wolves by forcibly

bringing them down from Canada and, on the other, allowing wolves to restore themselves by making their own way down from Canada may seem like a fine point. For many ranchers it was not:

> I certainly am pro-wolf, as far as being pro- any wild animal that's trying to coexist. And I do understand that we have all kinds of talk and beliefs about wolves. When I was involved with the [state arts board], we'd have programming that dealt with the wolf and myth and folklore. Excellent stuff. From "Little Red Riding Hood" to Tolstoy – wolves were chasing the troikas with the bride and groom and they'd throw the bride out to the wolves and get back into the village. "Who's Afraid of the Big, Bad Wolf?" But even within that, this program has really been botched.

Her concern was that wolf mythology not be propagated through the reintroduction process. The belief among some pro-wolf Oldtimers, as well as some wolf biologists, was that if wolves were allowed to return to Yellowstone on their own – if they were essentially invited to return rather than being forcefully brought back – wolf politics would be considerably changed and the myths would whither in the face of a different reality. Instead of opposing the wolves, the Community might actually embrace them or at least tolerate them.

Another rancher explained this logic, commenting that:

> [T]he wolves that find their way down here by themselves, they're the ones that got this far because they stayed the hell out of the way. And I think that's a: Whether we could have waited ten years and whether there'd have been enough of them when they did get down here, whether there'd be enough of a population, how long it would take to create a population, you can ask all of those questions. But they sure are questions that need to be looked at.

The right wolves for Yellowstone, these Oldtimers insisted, were those that would have dispersed from the north and eventually found their way to the Park. Such recovered wolves, the argument went, would dispel wolf mythology and be accepted by locals because they would possess the skills to avoid conflicts with humans.

Implicit in the rancher's observation that recovered wolves would have "stayed the hell out of the way" is that any wolves that caused problems for humans would either be killed by humans – a federal offense under the ESA – or they would be moved to other locations by the U.S. Fish and Wildlife Service, a regular practice elsewhere in the region. Thus, for some Oldtimers even if they welcomed certain wolves, other wolves – those that were reintroduced – were

troublesome by their very presence. They became political poison to
the pro-wolf cause. The biologists and agency personnel with whom
I have spoken labeled wolves that came into conflict with humans
"bad wolves." For some ranchers who also are wolf advocates, a bad
wolf is one that was brought to Yellowstone by the government.

Other wolf proponents imposed different meanings on the reintroduced wolves. One rancher saw benefits in having wolves around,
but his comments led him to discuss the uncertainty of life in the
Longview, an uncertainty that wolves contribute to:

> When we were young, to see a few elk in the haystacks in the win-
> ter was a big thrill. Now we feel like we're being overrun by the elk.
> So you might say, I guess, wolves are good – they'll cut down on the
> elk numbers. But it's, it's a much bigger picture. Many more elk. The
> wolves now are a part of it. Grizzly bears: they're coming back, fol-
> lowing those elk when they're having their calves. There's been more
> grizzly bears seen on our place in the last couple of years than we
> saw for years. So you say, "Okay, we live in this very special place,
> and it's a wonderful combination to both live there, ranch, and be
> able to encounter a lot of wildlife." The balance is changing some-
> what, and it's having an impact on the ranch itself, the ability to run
> livestock. And I think we accept that as a fair tradeoff, because if we
> didn't like that we could move to somewhere else. You take that trade.
> The uncertainty about things like the security of one's Forest Service
> grazing lease, grazing on public land: All of those combine to make
> a rancher feel a lot less certain about what we may face a few years
> down the road in just this little livestock unit. I mean, will we really
> be thinking about bringing the cows into a corral every night? Probably
> not, but it would never have crossed our mind before. Now it's a fact.

Uncertainty is a consuming anxiety for ranching families, and this
pro-wolf rancher's comments imply a sympathy with wolf opponents
who are unwilling to go to great lengths to address the uncertainties that wolves and grizzly bears introduce to their lives. We all
want to live comfortably, yet ranchers have to be on guard against
factors as diverse as anti-public lands grazing activists, bitter cold
spells, drought, disease, low prices for the animals they produce, and
new predators.

Many livestock operators take precautions to address these uncertainties, including adopting new techniques to get along with wolves.
Regarding her and her husband's frequent midnight strolls to the
cow pasture during calving season to ward-off wolves, one rancher's
wife commented:

Yeah, you do preventative measures as much as you can. Not fancy technology and all that, but just hard labor. And it's tedious and it's exhausting and you lose a lot of weight, but it seemed to work. It seemed to really be a deterrent.

In comments like these, wolves emerge with almost human meanings. They and grizzly bears may be traded with and they behave like hunters, potentially curbing the Yellowstone-area elk irruption and aiding ranchers whose fields, intended for cattle grazing, sometimes are home to more elk than Angus.

Wolves also embody the potential to directly affect daily livestock operations, not unlike the cattle rustlers of old, although pro-wolf Oldtimers said they welcome the "balance" that wolves restore to the land and they are willing to take precautions to reduce conflicts between the wolves, their livestock, and themselves. Despite the hard work, exhaustion, disruption of decades-old management practices, and losses – this couple had had sheep and guard dogs killed by wolves – the wolf newcomers were welcomed. Far from being a pestilence, the wolves were seen as new neighbors that could contribute something of ecological and emotional importance to the Community. Although their presence came at cost, it was a cost these Oldtimers were willing to bear, in contrast to anti-wolf Oldtimers who saw only costs to pocketbooks, traditions, and routines.

The pro-wolf ranchers' constructions highlight the complexity of wolf-human interactions that emerged around 1990, when plans for the Yellowstone wolf reintroduction were first made public, and that persist to the present. First, there was the issue of whether to accept wolves in the Longview at all. For those who favored wolves in the valley, a second issue confronted them: to support the wolf reintroduction or to oppose it in favor of wolf recovery. Finally, today those who favored reintroduction – and, in practical terms, all ranchers, since the reintroduction is now a matter of historical fact – are confronted by the changes they must make in managing their herds and the corresponding lifestyle changes they undergo, such as purchasing guard dogs, corralling cows about to give birth, or waking up numerous times at night during calving season to check on one's herd at pasture. In a very real sense, the wolves were unwitting players in their own construction, compelling ranchers to alter their behaviors and their outlooks in light of the reality of dealing with the four-legged newcomers.

Human Newcomers

1. Gazing at the Big Gates

For at least as long as the wolf controversy has brewed, a human social controversy has been on Oldtimers' minds as well, so that when the wolves began to roam from their new Yellowstone home, they arrived in the middle of an already evolving human milieu. Newcomers had been coming to Longview Valley since the first white settler homesteaded there in the mid-1800s, and change in the Valley – whether it was a drought or an elk population out of control or a film star moving in – was a fact of life. More recently, however, from the Oldtimers' perspective the changes have been aimed at the fundamentals of Longview life.

The Valley's Community concept has always been one where diversity was tolerated, anticipating and reflecting the Lumpen Society scholars' observations regarding the strengths of Community. That tolerance had its limits, however. The first inkling I had of conflicts between indigenous human social groups – not between locals and outsiders, but between longtime locals and other, newer locals – came when a mention was made of "for-fee" hunting. Fee hunting, paying to hunt on land that someone manages largely, often entirely, to attract large game animals like elk, often takes place on *former* ranches. The result is considerable tension in the Community based in the fundamental change in land use necessary to accommodate elk or bear instead of cattle. One ranch manager said:

> Some people wouldn't care if we took every cow out of [the Longview]. You know, that might be their answer: "Just move the cows out." Well, you know, that's not really the answer, either ... It is already happening, but it's happening through: There's a transition [to] the investor, out-of-state owner that's buying up these lands for recreation and they're not restocking a lot of stock. So there is a trend going right now. And as, say, [our next door neighbors] get frustrated enough, then they're going to raise their hands and say, "I'll sell my place and move." And so you're forcing these people to go. The people who sold this ranch were very frustrated with all the elk eating all their vegetation. He didn't get to see the timber wolf, but that would have just been another nail in his coffin.

A dominant Oldtimer construction of the Newcomers is that of tourists or, perhaps more charitably, recreationists. The Newcomers want relaxation when they visit their homes in the Longview. They work elsewhere; when they come to the Northern Rockies, they want to play. Some, too, want the land to pay, but in new and foreign ways – thus the attraction of fee hunting.

Through the management of their land and the attitudes they share in encounters with Oldtimers, the Newcomers leave long-time residents with the unmistakable impression that they want to create a new Longview Valley. That revamped Valley may be ecologically friendlier and more complex, but that is of little concern to many of the Oldtimers. Implicit in the act of replacing livestock with wild animals is an attitude anathema to the Oldtimers, one that de-emphasizes intensive land management, production values, and an anthropocentric outlook. Ranching gets shoved aside, and with it goes a way of life that emphasizes extensive control of the land and the wildlife on that land.

Moreover, maximizing the land's potential for recreational purposes was not the only characteristic of the Newcomers that troubled long-term residents. Another rancher, part of a family that had lived on the land for generations and that favored wolf reintroduction, told me:

> The "Big Gate Syndrome," we call it. People come into the country and they need to make a big deal about it, make a statement. Naturally there's sort of this local provincial resentment against the manifestation of a lot of other things that people bring in with them, rather than people coming in who have a fairly humble approach to try and interact with other people. . . . When you personalize it, it's not too difficult to sort of neutralize that sense of style that people bring with them. But when it's not personalized, it's pretty easy to look at as just sort of this other culture statement that is hard to relate to.

Later in our conversation when I asked him about the differences between Oldtimers and Newcomers, he responded:

> For some reason commitment to this life – not necessarily ranching, but this life – comes to my mind immediately. The focus is a little different. This is, for a lot of people, recreation, and a lot of these people are literally here for two weeks a year. And a lot of the people who I'm talking about are the people who are building *that house*, the house two houses down.

A monstrous edifice, locally such houses were known as "trophy homes." "Great folks," the rancher continued, "but they're only here two weeks a year with a mega-million dollar home and a piece of land. That's hard to swallow sometimes." In these comments we see the subtleties of the Oldtimers' constructions of community. The well-settled residents welcome Newcomers to a point, but their tolerance ends when "commitment to this life" – not necessarily ranching, but commitment to the Community – ends.

And so another storm was welling even as the wolf controversy emerged. Newcomers give the Oldtimers, those whose roots in the Longview or in ranching go back generations, much to dislike. They use the land differently and they interact with their neighbors differently as well. The Newcomers build beautiful, lavish homes only to use them as hideaways from their normal lives rather than as doorways to a new life and a new Community. Because they visit the Longview so seldom, Oldtimers insist, the Newcomers fail to develop meaningful relationships with their neighbors. Many of the Newcomers close their "ranches" to cattle, and those who make some use of the land, as for fee hunting, often treat the land in radically different ways than Oldtimers do. They welcome elk, which eat forage once reserved for cattle. Since the elk have found refuge in the Valley, their numbers have increased, attracting the wolves and further compounding the problem in some Oldtimers' eyes. Regardless of how Oldtimer ranchers feel about the wolf issue, they are disturbed by the changes to the land that Newcomers bring with them.

2. Committing to Community

More importantly, though, the Oldtimers are troubled by the shifting notions of Community emerging around them. One does not have to ranch to be a respected and valued member of the Oldtimers' community, but to treat the land and the community as places to be briefly visited each year and then forgotten about is a slight to place and people. "Community" and "commitment" share more than just the same etymological root. With the former comes an expectation of the latter.

The Oldtimers, aware because it stares them in the face daily that they lead precipitous lives, are confronted by multiple social forces pushing them off of the land. Even if they are determined to stay, they told me that they increasingly find themselves strangers in their own Community, surrounded by either empty houses or people whom they do not know or recognize. Those people lack a commitment not only to others – how could they be dependable when they are not around fifty weeks of the year? – but to Community in the most general of senses. They do not understand what really matters, what makes one a part of a place. A woman who runs sheep on her land asked:

> What makes a person a part of a community? I think it is being involved in a community in educational aspects and environmental aspects and caring about your neighbors. So I would agree that people, when they're absentee, can oftentimes lose sight of the immediate: You know, if they don't give to the library often, but they'll give to Africa, you know, some relief in Africa, but they don't give to the local Chamber of Commerce, that sort of thing. . . . But things like a library: for people who come here two or three weeks a year, they're not giving to things that are community-based, but they are giving in Africa or giving around the world, but not necessarily to the little theater group. That's not a criticism. It's an observation. But oftentimes the people with money are the ones who are preserving the land, who are putting the conservation easements on it, versus other developers who are [locals] who may be sub-dividing it and so forth.

She was torn between condemning Newcomers for the social distance they keep from the Oldtimers and the Community and praising them for doing more to conserve the land than do many natives of the area. The Newcomers are so concerned about distant issues and doing what is correct in some universal sense of the term that they fail to see the needs of their new Community. Implicit in this construction is the observation that, when the Newcomers do act in the best interests of Community, as when they permanently protect land from development, they do so almost by accident.

Like the wolves, Newcomers are also constructed by the Oldtimers as powerful forces of change. Both the wolves and the Newcomers may bring ecological change; wolves keep elk herds under control and Newcomers apply conservation easements. And they both bring social change; wolves and Newcomers alike created new tensions in the Community. When I said to one couple, "The theme is not wolf reintroduction anymore for me. The theme has changed in people's lives." They interjected, she nodding her head and him saying, "I totally agree with that." I meant that the focus of my research had changed, but they thought I was putting words into their mouths, and they were telling me that I had gotten the words right. They heard me saying something like, "The theme is change in people's lives," I think, and by agreeing with my observation they indicated that the undercurrent in their Community had changed in only a few years. They found themselves living not in a stable community but in an uncertain Community, a place that they sometimes had difficulty recognizing.

Commitment to Community in the immediate sense, to one's neighbors, and to Community in the broader sense, to others living similar lives, is slackening in the Longview. This points toward a rending of the general social fabric. It is the little things that transform Community from an abstract and uncertain general concept to a real and vibrant *community* that is a lived and alive place: talking with neighbors and keeping up one's property, certainly, but also contributing to bake sales, donating time and money to the local library – in short, treating Community as a cause and sharing the community's commitment to common political purposes. That unity emerging out of diversity, according to Oldtimers, is increasingly a thing of the past in the Longview.

Conclusion

My underlying purpose in this chapter is simply to argue that wildlife management programs like the Yellowstone wolf reintroduction almost all take place in a rich milieu that needs to be appreciated by policy-makers and wildlife managers. That "richness" has two components. The first is residents' constructions of the species in question, and these in turn have a great deal to do with their reaction to any given management program: their resistance, acceptance, confusion, or ambivalence.

Second, wildlife managers need to understand that the meanings that residents give to plants, animals, and policies develop against a backdrop of *social complexity*. In the case of the Longview, that complexity took two forms. To begin with, not all residents share common constructions of the wolves. To some the wolves are a disaster or a pest that has brought another level of uncertainty into their already unpredictable lives, and, when combined with other forces, threatens to run them off of their land; to others, wolves are important players in a new, ecologically tolerant vision of the West – even if that vision is not *socially* tolerant. All of the Oldtimers with whom I spoke expressed anxiety about their changing Community, identifying the Newcomers as a primary force in shifting forms of land use and a lack of commitment to neighbors and the broader Community.

As managers well know, their work does not occur in a social vacuum. Previously, I wrote that for many wolf supporters and opponents near Yellowstone, wolves were surrogates for a federal government that seemed willing to ignore residents' concerns about wolves and about Park management in general (Scarce 1998). In that understanding, the major social force impinging upon local residents was a distant government that ignored locals' existence altogether. I reported that the opposition to the wolf reintroduction was widespread – even residents who liked the notion of having wolves around were troubled by how they were brought back, for they were almost jammed down their throats by what they saw as ruthless federal bureaucrats who cared more for another species and the law than about the humans who would have to change how they lived to accommodate the wolves.

However, I have come to understand that the struggle over wolf reintroduction was made even more difficult for residents in the Longview because wolves were not only a stand-in for government. They were also part of, and perhaps even were stand-ins for, Community change. Wolves are only one of the challenges confronting Longview Valley residents. The Oldtimers there live in a tumultuous world replete with an increasingly uncertain sense of Community that wracks their world – a world that was never idyllic, certainly not tranquil, but at least evolved somewhat manageably. Because of the fundamentals that connected them in the past – above all else an identification with the Longview and its land – individuals and the Community adapted well to changes. Now, however, according to the Oldtimers who remain, almost every ranching family that retires sells their land to someone who not only does not run cattle but will not allow their neighbors graze their land, either. Elk and even wolves seem to have more value to the Newcomers than do cattle and sheep, a fact that disturbs all of the Oldtimers, although some to lesser degrees than others.

What especially pains the Oldtimers, though, is the loss of a sense of connectedness to one another and of obligation and concern for the larger whole. The human Community is changing in fundamental ways, and it is against that backdrop that wolves returned to Longview Valley. According to the Oldtimers' construction, Newcomers seek bucolic havens for themselves far removed from big-city hustle and bustle. In the process, though, they undermine Community and alter ecology. Their close ties are with persons thousands of miles away, and the issues that compel them to action are similarly foreign to many in the Valley. At best they run a few head of livestock, but they do so almost for aesthetics; they let the land go to waste, many Oldtimers say, even if they are encouraging game like elk to graze on their land to take advantage of the lucrative market for fee hunting. That the Newcomers lack a fundamental connection to the Longview is evidenced by their rejection of traditional uses of the land, insist the Oldtimers.

Was the reception that the wolves received in the Longview *directly* affected by the Oldtimer/Newcomer struggle? My data do not directly support that conclusion, but it was implied. The ranching Oldtimers said they depend upon their neighbors for all kinds of support, including keeping an eye out for trouble, such as wolves in one another's pastures, and conveying the latest news and rumors. If one's next door neighbor is not out in the pasture working with their livestock because they have none to work with, and if they have no news to share about wolf whereabouts because they are not part of the networks that would convey that information to them, there is no basis for assuming that they will behave rancher-like when wolves are in the area. Those ranchers in the Longview who opposed the wolf reintroduction to Yellowstone Park likely would have opposed it regardless, but the changes that they are witnessing in their Community are also likely to have added to the urgency of their arguments and the extent of their anxiety – thus the sense that wolves may break the camel's back.

All of this leads me to my concluding observation, one that is tentative but tantalizing: Whenever members of a self-described Community socially construct Nature or a Natural entity like wolves, they also imbue meaning to Community. In saying this, I hark back to one of the earliest sociologists, Emile Durkheim. Durkheim ([1912] 1965) saw that in rituals like religious services, what was identified as sacred or profane was a reflection of society's ideals, its norms, expectations, and accepted values, beliefs, attitudes, and behaviors. So too, it appears, that Nature reflects Community. When Community members socially construct Nature, they remind themselves of the core of what matters to the social "us" – to us together, to us as community. In the Longview Valley residents gave wolves quite different meanings, but a common thread ran through those meanings: the land and its management matters deeply. This is so not simply because ranchland management is an obvious and integral part of living on ranches but because of the Oldtimers' profound connection to the land and the place. Whatever else separated the people of the Longview, that shared connection united them in their community.

Thus, in constructing wolves, whether as lifestyle destroyers or ecosystem saviors, the Oldtimers say a great deal more about what matters to them than the mere value of their livestock that might be lost to the fangs of *Canis lupus* (cf.: Greider and Garkovich 1994). Giddens observed:

> Most of the modes of life we have to deal with, however, are *ecosocial* systems: they concern the socially organized environment . . . In most environmental areas we couldn't begin to disentangle what is natural from what is social – more importantly it is usually irrelevant to policy-making endeavors to seek to do so (Giddens 1994:210; emphasis original).

The Longview Valley example supports Giddens's notion of ecosocial systems. The Oldtimers' meanings of wolves are social products, not natural entities, for there is nonesuch as nature.

There is, however, Nature, the stuff that we casually call nature, and Longview residents' constructs of wolves as a "natural" entity hinge not simply on wolves but on issues of lifestyle, values, and traditions. By the same token the wolf is only one player in communities being rended by sweeping human social changes, none of which the Oldtimers feel they can thwart. They have lost the battle over the wolf, as they knew they would. But their biggest foe walks on two legs, not four, and that foe does not wear the khaki and brown of a Park Service biologist.

Management Recommendations

Giddens is not correct, however, that distinguishing the social in nature is irrelevant to policy-making. In fact, identifying the Nature that we want to create is of extreme importance at the global level – as we stand on the brink of multiple ecological disasters – and locally as managers consider how to approach the practical problems that confront them, whether the project at-hand involves a species restoration or merely whether to change the dates for a deer hunting season. In the Longview the battle is really over the policies and politics of Community and ecological change. Who gets what, when, and how? Who gets to determine what life is like in the Longview and how the land will be used? When will the last rancher be run out by self-focused neighbors – and, some would add, marauding wolves? How will Community, in any meaningful sense, be maintained when connection to the land no longer unites those with diverse outlooks?

Perhaps it is a wildlife manager's dream to manage wolves in a place where there are no humans, although I doubt it. Management, after all, is about controlling nonhuman and human animals for the "benefit and enjoyment" (to borrow words chiseled on the north gate of Yellowstone Park) of both, and no meaningful decisions about the fate of a wildlife population take place in a social vacuum. The challenge, it seems to me as an outsider to wildlife management, is to develop strategies that are as effective for communicating with the public as they are for directing the behavior of wildlife. Notice that I do not recommend "directing the behavior of the public;" to do so is arrogant, undemocratic, and futile. And in order to communicate with the public, one has to understand it. Fundamentally, managers want to encourage the development of new constructions of nature. How can they do these things?

My sense is that on-the-ground research that gives managers an understanding of the public, the meanings that the public creates, and the underlying dynamics of communities is of great potential value. Ideally, no manager would knowingly place a species in an inappropriate ecosystem. If humans are intimately part of the ecosystems around them, to the point that they are the most powerful members of those ecosystems, their Communities must be seen as integral to ecosystems. Thus, managers must gather information about the factors that shape the human social Community's ability and willingness to listen and to cooperate.

Methodologically, ethnographic research such as I undertook in the Yellowstone area may yield substantial and useful understandings of communities' social constructions of wildlife and of the communities themselves. So, too, may focus groups. Ethnographers pride themselves on their ability to "get into" people's lives and reveal their worlds through in-depth interviews and observations. A strength of focus groups is that they bring small numbers of persons together who can respond to one another as the subject matter is discussed, offering supporting and contradictory observations and explanations. The ever-popular social science survey, while appropriate for inquiring about attitudes, values, and to a lesser extent behaviors, lacks the sort of depth of insight that these other methods can provide.

Unlike surveys, ethnographies and focus groups do not readily yield the sorts of quantitative data that many researchers and managers find attractive and persuasive. However, my sense is that qualitative research is the only effective means for plumbing the depths of persons' lived worlds, and the resulting findings have the potential for contributing significantly to management decisions and managers' interactions with communities.

References

Charmaz, Kathy. 2000. "Grounded Theory: Objectivist and Constructivist Methods." Pp. 509–535 in *Handbook of Qualitative Research*, 2nd ed., edited by N.K. Denzin and Y.S. Lincoln. Thousand Oaks, CA: Sage.

Dixon, A.L. Sinikka. 1999. "The Hidden Community: Spatial Dimensions of Urban Life." Pp. 287–308 in *Research in Community Sociology*, edited by D. Chekki. Stamford, CT: JAI.

Dizard, Jan E. 1999. *Going Wild: Hunting, Animal Rights, and the Contested Meanings of Nature*. Amherst: University of Massachusetts Press.

Durkheim, Emile. [1912] 1965. *Elementary Forms of the Religious Life*. New York: Free Press.

Evernden, Neil. 1992. *The Social Creation of Nature*. Baltimore: The Johns Hopkins University Press.

Fine, Gary Alan. 1998. *Morel Tales: The Culture of Mushrooming*. Cambridge, MA: Harvard University Press.

Fitchen, Janet M. 1991. *Endangered Spaces, Enduring Spaces: Change, Identity, and Survival in Rural America*. Boulder, CO: Westview.

Giddens, Anthony. 1994. *Beyond Left and Right: The Future of Radical Politics*. Stanford, CA: Stanford University Press.

Glaser, Barney G. and Anselm L Strauss. 1967. *The Discovery of Grounded Theory: Strategies for Qualitative Research*. New York: Aldine de Gruyter.

Greider, Thomas and Lorraine Garkovich. 1994. "Landscapes: The Social Construction of Nature and the Environment." *Rural Sociology* 59(1):1–24.

Leopold, Aldo. 1995. Unpublished foreword to *A Sand County Almanac: Sketches Here and There*. Pp. 321–325 in *War against the Wolf: America's Campaign to Exterminate the Wolf*, edited by R. McIntyre. Stillwater, MN: Voyager.

Lewis, C.S. 1967. *Studies in Words*. New York: Cambridge University Press.

Lumpen Society. 1997. "The End of Community? Forms, Process and Pattern." Pp. 21–59 in *Research in Community Sociology*, edited by D. Chekki. Stamford, CT: JAI.

McKibben, Bill. 1989. *The End of Nature*. New York: Anchor Books.

Mech, L. David. 1970. *The Wolf*. Minneapolis: University of Minnesota Press.

Murphy, Raymond. 1994. *Rationality and Nature: A Sociological Inquiry into a Changing Relationship*. Boulder, CO: Westview.

———. 1997. *Sociology and Nature: Social Action in Context*. Boulder, CO: Westview.

Redclift, Michael and Graham Woodgate. 1994. "Sociology and the Environment: Discordant Discourse?" Pp. 51–66 in *Social Theory and the Global Environment*, edited by M. Redclift and T. Benton. London: Routledge.

Scarce, Rik. 1997. "Socially Constructing Pacific Salmon." *Society and Animals* 5(2):117–135.

———. 1998. "What Do Wolves Mean? Social Constructions of *Canis lupus* by 'Bordertown' Residents." *Human Dimensions of Wildlife* 3(3):26–45.

———. 1999. "Who – or What – Is in Control Here? The Social Context of Salmon Biology." *Society and Natural Resources* 12(8):763–776.

———. 2000. *Fishy Business: Salmon, Biology, and the Social Construction of Nature.* Philadelphia: Temple University Press.

Schutz, Alfred and Thomas Luckmann. 1973. *The Structures of the Life World.* Evanston, IL: Northwestern University Press.

Simmons, I.G. 1993. *Interpreting Nature: Cultural Constructions of the Environment.* New York: Routledge.

Tönnies, Ferdinand. 1957. *Community and Society (Gemeinschaft und Gesellschaft)*, trans. and edited by C.P. Loomis. East Lansing: Michigan State University Press.

U.S. Fish and Wildlife Service. 1994. *The Reintroduction of Gray Wolves to Yellowstone National Park and Central Idaho: Final Environmental Impact Statement.* Helena, MT: U.S. Fish and Wildlife Service.

Note

[1] Grounded theory is a meticulous process of inductive theory construction (Charmaz 2000; Glaser and Strauss 1967). Beginning with a small set of interviews, the researcher identifies key concepts that seem to be the most prominent. In succeeding rounds of interviews, those concepts are explored in more depth with new participants until the researcher identifies a small number of key theoretical notions that appear to explain much of what the researcher has observed. The results are "grounded" in the data because the theory is directly traceable to the words spoken in interviews or to field observations, and in publications the researcher's theoretical conclusions are supported by presenting exemplary data: excerpts from interviews and field notes.

PARADISE LOST: THE TRANSFORMATION OF WILDLIFE LAW IN THE VANISHING WILDERNESS[1]

ROBERT GRANFIELD AND PAUL COLOMY

Introduction

Sociologists have given scant attention to the subject of wildlife crime and law. Although there has been empirical examination of environmental issues in the sociology of law, interest had not extended to the subject of wildlife law and criminalization. This lack of detailed socio-legal analysis may be due to the secondary status that has been accorded to rural issues and animal issues. For instance, crimes perpetrated against wildlife, such as poaching or the illegal killing of game animals, have been typically seen as folk crimes. These crimes have little moral stigma associated with them and, though violations are not generally approved, such crimes are relatively numerous and often treated as unimportant by law enforcement authorities. However, the enforcement of wildlife law may be in the process of flux for a variety of reasons.

First, the animal rights movement has gained considerable strength and popularity over the past several years. There has been growing opposition to the use of animals in experiments and efforts to protect animals from human exploitation and persecution have moved into the legal arena. In Boulder, Colorado, for example, a new law restricts killing and displacing prairie dogs, a species considered by many to be a growing urban nuisance, thereby according them rights to land use; citizens and businesses are encouraged to live in peaceful coexistence with their rodent brethren.[2] Similarly, in Denver a law passed in 2002, dubbed "Westy's Law" in honor of a cat that was tortured by two teenage boys, makes cruelty to animals a felony punishable by up to three years in prison and up to $100,000 in fines (Martinez 2002). In California, Proposition 197, which would have reopened a hunting season on mountain lions, was narrowly defeated in 1996. Most remarkably, in Germany animals have recently been accorded legal rights under that country's constitution. On an international level, increased public attention has been given to the unethical treatment of animals for food production as well as to the commercialization of big game hunting (Scully 2002).

A second reason for the growth of interest in wildlife and other animal issues may be due to the rise of animal "edu-tainment" programs, that is, television programs such as Discovery, Animal Planet, The Crocodile Hunter and others that deal with non-human animal issues. There is even a television program called "Busted" that is like the "Cops" of the non-human animal world in which daring game wardens, wildlife law enforcement agents and animal rescue officials do battle with unsavory poachers and assorted animal abusers. Perhaps a more global reason for the increasing attention to the legal issues involving animals has to do with increasing urbanization and growth within the rural landscape. Sampson and Groves (1989) have indicated that increased population growth is associated with an increase in deviance, either real or constructed. During periods of growth, old accepted practices may give way to new legal regulations. What was once considered a form of normal deviance such as the case of poaching becomes redefined as a significant malfeasance.

In this chapter, we present a preliminary analysis of the transformation of wildlife law and consider how law emerges out of, or is constituted within, local, concrete, and historically specific situations (Ewick and Silby 1998). Specifically, the subject of this chapter is the recent enhancement of legal sanctions associated with hunting and game laws in Colorado. Although poaching of game animals, for the most part, is on the fringe of public consciousness, it continues to persist in advanced industrial society (Muth 1998). Some observers have argued that poaching has become increasingly attractive, particularly in light of the expanding market for trophies.

In the sociological literature the subject of poaching has received some limited attention. However, much of this research tends to focus on the neutralization techniques employed by poachers to account for their crime (Eliason and Dodder 1999). By contrast we explore how one incident of poaching led to the collective mobilization of a community and passage of more punitive legislation. We begin this chapter with a brief discussion of the relationship between hunting law and social change in England and America. Transformations in social life brought on by modernization and industrialization have had profound effects on hunting regulations and law and on the criminalization of poaching. Next, we present a case study of the emergence and development of "Samson's Law," a recent law that significantly increases the penalties for the poaching of trophy class big game in Colorado. We conclude with a discussion of the symbolic significance of this law and the challenges faced by wildlife officials who enforce the law.

Social Change and Wildlife Law in England and America

One of the first systematic treatments of the importance of the social context of game laws was Thompson's (1976) detailed analysis of the Black Act. This English law, passed in 1793, made it a capital offense to engage in a wide variety of activities involving wildlife and the wilderness. Killing deer, damaging fish ponds and cutting trees, acts that had traditionally been practiced in the commons, were criminalized and the efforts of landlords to prosecute individuals under these new laws received the support of the state. These traditional acts of commoners, formerly considered natural rights, were transformed into illegal acts of poaching. Thompson maintains that enclosing once common land and restricting its use by local communities was a response to changing social conditions of the time.

The rise of capitalism created new conceptions of property that were inconsistent with the natural rights view of land use. How to transform common land to private property, an ideology that was consistent with emerging capitalist views of land use, posed a dilemma for the State. By creating laws prohibiting and punishing the illegal taking of game animals and other wilderness resources, members of local communities could be increasingly subject to criminal law as the law extended beyond crimes against persons to include crimes against property. In pure capitalist logic, deer and trees were defined as the property of wealthy landlords who wished to exact increased control on commoners, as well as utilize the wilderness territories surrounding towns, for their own recreational and commercial purposes.

For Thompson, law is more than simply class power. It is a site of conflict and contradiction that is mediated by various interests. What was at issue in the Black Act was alternative and conflicting definitions of property rights; for the landowner, enclosure; for the cottager, common rights; for the forest officials and game wardens, preserved grounds for the deer; for those living in the forests, the right to take animals. As Chambliss (1993:46) notes:

> Law is a living institution, created by people occupying roles and positions within the social structure. It does not arise automatically in response to social needs. It reflects the fundamental contradictions of the time.

Thompson's analysis of game laws in England points to these underlying contradictions as well as to the fact that law is embedded within a broader social context.

Although organized low-level wars between poachers and estate game wardens along with allegations of class bias and elitism occurred in England, no such situation existed in the New World. Nevertheless, game laws in the United States reflect similar conflicts and contradictions. In twentieth century America, the reification of wild animals as public goods immunized the state against charges of bias and elitism in game laws (Warren 1997). Contrary to English game law, wildlife was democratized under the banner of conservation in the United States. This is not meant to imply that the state, acting independently, simply enacted laws to protect wildlife. The history of hunting in America is a complex one. Colonial and Puritan settlers generally saw large game animals like deer and wolves as nuisances to be eliminated in order to pave the way for agricultural development (Warren 1997). However, while early settlers considered these animals to be a threat to their livelihoods on local farms, they nevertheless did not generally approve of hunting. Eliminating animals to promote agriculture was one thing; hunting animals for the purpose of subsistence or pleasure was quite another. Hunters at the time were often reviled by Puritans who not only saw subsistence hunting as savage, but also objected to the elitist tradition of sport hunting in England.

This generalized reserve towards hunting underwent a dramatic transformation in the late 1800s after the Revolutionary War. The hunter-soldier became a lionized figure on the American landscape and frontiersmen took on mythic proportion. An idealized image of hunting as an expression of rugged individualism and independence gained considerable strength among the emerging middle and upper classes (Warren 1997). With the wilderness in decline as a result of encroaching urbanization, the myth of the frontiersman became an attractive icon to be emulated among middle and upper class males. Ideas about the nobility of an unspoiled wilderness became increasingly popular. The writings of James Fenimore Cooper, James Audubon, John Muir, and Henry David Thoreau spawned romantic descriptions of the wilderness while the paintings of Thomas Cole and Albert Bierstadt depicted idealized images of the wilderness landscape.

Between 1865 and 1900, thirty-nine separate periodicals devoted to stories of sport hunting came into circulation (Herman 2001). The Jacksonian and antebellum periods of American history represent the ascendance of sport hunting, made increasingly popular by a growing industrial society that produced mass alienation. As Herman (2001:149) points out:

> [M]achines threatened to destroy individualism itself by reducing humans to operatives, caretakers for the mechanical behemoths they had created. . . . To enter to wilds with one's gun was to become a perfect atom, a free man, fearless, bold, and in harmony with nature. Gun and wilderness were bound together.

These romantic and increasingly elite views of hunting led to the establishment of a sharp fault-line between the legitimate hunter who was seen as respecting nature and the animals they killed, and those individuals who killed indiscriminately and who possessed none of the ideals associated with the sportsman. In various locations throughout the country, some of the first poaching laws were enacted against subsistence and market hunters. Laws increasingly defined local subsistence hunters, often consisting of farmers and ethnic groups, particularly Native Americans, as outlaws who were subject to fines and imprisonment.

This was particularly the case in the Rocky Mountain region where sport hunters of the middle and upper classes pressured the government to pass laws to limit the amount of hunting by indigenous people. There are numerous legal cases in Colorado, Wyoming, and Utah involving Native Americans accused of poaching game animals, although the game was taken only for the purpose of subsistence. Confrontations between Native Americans and game wardens often escalated into violence (Warren 1997). In recent years, Native Americans have offered cultural defense pleas in these kinds of poaching cases.

In addition to conflicts with local subsistence hunters, conflicts between market or commercial hunters and sportsmen grew to a head in the late nineteenth century. The expansion of capitalism in the west and with it the railroads, brought large numbers of people to the Rocky Mountain region, including commercial hunters. Market

152 ROBERT GRANFIELD & PAUL COLOMY

hunters did not per se live off the animals they killed, but rather harvested the meat, hides and antlers to be sold on the market.

The combination of unregulated local and market hunting led to a massive decimation of the animal populations in the west. Elk, buffalo, wolves, mountain lions and coyotes were all brought to the verge of extinction, and in some cases, completely eliminated. Elk were once plentiful in Colorado, which led Milton Estes, the first white pioneer to settle what became known as Estes Park, to comment in 1860 that "great bands of elk ... were everywhere" in the area (Lee 1997:1). However, by 1910 there were only about 1,000 elk remaining in the state with only a handful found in the Estes Valley.

This reduction was aided by the ascendance of agriculture and ranching in the west in which game animals were considered a nuisance since these animals competed with farmers and ranchers for similar resources. In fact, Native Americans were often encouraged to hunt game on private farms and ranches to help these emerging businesses reduce the animal population. As the game population declined in the late nineteenth century, more subsistence and market hunters turned to the remaining animals to meet their demands. As this happened, "local subsistence and market hunters in America faced off against elite, urban sportsmen who demanded state and federal regulation of hunting in accordance with their own ideology of the hunt" (Warren 1997:13).

These struggles were about nothing less than the place of human society in the natural world. In the end, middle class and upper class sportsmen lobbied lawmakers to pass game laws that effectively wrote their ideology of hunting onto the wilderness landscape. Hunting, consequently, became increasingly regulated through licensing and limits. Local market and subsistence hunters were increasingly prosecuted for their failure to abide by the ideology of the sportsman. As Davis (1999:226–227) commented:

> The campaign against market hunting (in California) seamlessly coalesced with a nativist crusade against Chinese shrimpmen, black and Italian birdtrappers, and native Californian subsistence hunters who did not honor the animal loving ethos of the Anglo-Saxon.

Eventually, elite recreational hunters began to set the standards of behavior for other hunters, cleansing the fields of all who did not abide by the sportsmen's ethic (Warren 1997). It is in this way that these hunters were converted into conservationists. Indeed, the ethic of sportsmen became institutionalized and has served as the backbone for much of America's burgeoning conservation movement.

Thus, in both the English and American cases, the emergence of game laws and the criminalization of poaching were closely connected to broader social transformations occurring at the time. In England, the expansion of capitalism and its impact on concepts of property, land use and ownership created definitions of the forests and wilderness areas that were incompatible with local use by those who subsisted off the land. In the U.S., the rising middle and upper classes in the east and their mobility into the west, combined with increasing industrialization, served as the impetus for increasing federal and state regulation of hunting. How social transformations may be affecting current developments in wildlife law is explored in the remainder of this chapter.

Method

In the fall of 2002, the authors initiated an investigation into the 1995 poaching of a large bull elk in Estes Park, Colorado known as "Samson." Data necessary to examine the transformation of wildlife law in Colorado were collected from multiple sources. In-depth interviews were conducted with several Estes Park residents familiar with the poaching incident, as well as law enforcement officials who investigated the case. We relied on snowball sampling techniques; at the end of each interview interviewees were asked to identify other individuals who might offer insight into the celebrated case. Using this technique we were able to speak with a wide range of key individuals. We interviewed a total of twenty-eight people including:

• the director of the YMCA where Samson the elk was killed,
• the father of the young woman who witnessed the incident,
• local officials from the Division of Wildlife who investigated the crime and eventually arrested the perpetrator,
• the prosecutor at the trial of the man charged with the poaching incident,
• and the town mayor at the time of the incident.

We also interviewed several other town residents who were familiar with the poaching incident. Interviews varied in length from two to four hours. During this period, we examined issues pertaining to the community reaction to the incident.

In addition to these sources, we conducted an extensive analysis of the various newspaper accounts and follow-up stories on the case. Most of these articles were gathered from a local library that maintains a large file devoted to Samson the elk. Over 200 newspaper stories about Samson were analyzed. These articles were used mainly as a way of providing information pertaining to the broader context surrounding the case.

In addition, we employed observational strategies as part of this study. Each of the authors visited Estes Park where they paid particular attention to the actual and symbolic presence of elk in the community. We toured the grounds of the YMCA where Samson was killed, visited shops that displayed Samson artifacts, and walked the town with residents and tourists observing the elk herd as they wandered through the busy streets. We also attended the annual "Elk Fest" which provided information on hunting and featured simulated elk hunting video games, talks from local wildlife experts and law enforcement officials and a guided tour in open-bed trucks to view the elk that had taken up residence at a local golf course. The Elk Fest also offered a memorial to Samson whose head is displayed each year at the festival to "educate" visitors on the evils of poaching.

Finally, the authors collected legislative information on Samson's Law that was contained in archives located at the State House in Denver. We not only reviewed drafts of the law but we also "dubbed" audio-tapes from the assorted legislative committee hearings. Testimonies from various constituencies including government as well as private citizen groups were later transcribed.

Killing an Icon

Milton Estes first visited the Estes valley on a hunting trip in October of 1859 and described it as a paradise. Soon others came from the east to trap, hunt and view the scenery. Ranching and tourism provided a livelihood for most of the 200 citizens recorded in the 1900 census. The two principal sources of commerce in the area, ranching and tourist hunting, eventually took a toll on the elk population in Estes Park reducing it to a tiny fraction of its original size by 1910. To sustain the tourist economy, a group of concerned citizens brought in elk from Yellowstone National Park to replenish the local herd, twenty-five in 1913 and another twenty-five in 1915. The Rocky Mountain National Park was established in 1915 and the town of Estes Park, nestled at its base, was incorporated just two years later. Because of conservation efforts to protect the herd, the population of elk grew rapidly. The herd also grew because there were no longer natural predators such as wolves to control them. By 1945 a reduction and management system was enacted to limit damage to the landscape from elk.

The town of Estes Park has continued to grow both in terms of people and in elk over the years. The human population has more than tripled since 1970 reaching the current population of nearly 10,000 people. Over the past decade, the town has extended its geographical borders further and further into wilderness areas as housing developments, golf courses, restaurants, coffee shops, motels, and strip malls have appeared, transforming the landscape into an increasingly upscale mountain retreat for the financially well-heeled. The elk population has grown as well to an estimated 4,000 animals, each of which is considered to be a rightful citizen of Estes Park. This number is much higher than what game experts refer to as the carrying capacity of the local environment.

Every year thousands of hunters descend upon the Estes Park area hoping for the opportunity to bring down a large elk. Although female elk were considered attractive by hunters in years past because of the higher quality of their meat, hunters have increasingly sought out large male "bull" elk as their quarry, primarily for the antlers or "rack" that drape their head. Because of the increasing value of trophy-sized animals to both sportsmen and commercial hunters, poaching or the illegal taking of an animal has been a relatively common occurrence in the area.[3] Although the people of Estes Park oppose poaching, little has been done over the years to prevent it from occurring. In interviews, several people commented that Estes Park was known as a relatively safe haven for poachers and that when poachers were apprehended, fines were nominal and the county court judge refused to impose stiff fines.

All this changed on November 11, 1995 when late in the afternoon in Estes Park a single arrow shot from a crossbow ended the life of a large male elk. The elk that was killed, however, was no ordinary elk. Local residents knew this elk as "Samson." Samson was thought to be the largest bull elk in the Estes Valley and was well-known through the region and beyond as a national celebrity who had been photographed by thousands of Estes Park guests (Asbury 1995).

Weighing approximately 1,000 pounds and estimated to be about twelve years old, Samson was an 8 × 9 point elk who, over the years, had become like a mascot to the community, particularly people at the local YMCA camp where Samson spent most of his winter months. It was on the YMCA grounds that a commercial poacher from nearby Lakewood, Colorado, who reportedly had a $10,000 offer for Samson's head, approached to within ten yards of the icon to deliver the fatal shot.

As news of Samson's death spread, phone calls came in from around the country. The story of his killing was covered by the local and national media including *Headline News* and *U.S.A. Today*. Producers at *Court TV* had even made plans to televise the trial had it not been settled. More recently, *Animal Planet* aired the story of Samson, complete with a re-enactment of the crime, on its popular "Busted" program.

In interviews with residents of the area, as well as in the many newspaper articles and accounts of his death that were printed over the next several weeks, Samson was "ecopomorphized." We use this term as a way of describing the meaning this animal had for citizens in relation to the surrounding environment. While anthropomorphization implies that individuals attribute human qualities to animals, ecopomorphization suggests that individuals attribute ecological qualities to animals. Samson was frequently described as "awe-inspiring," or "majestic" and "noble." These images were very romantic and reminiscent of the wilderness imagery discussed earlier. Local people also anthropomorphized Samson by attributing agency to him. As one local resident commented, "He (Samson) enjoyed having his picture taken. He was a wild animal who had this affinity for people and this place. He felt safe here [at the YMCA]." Another commented that Samson "was always a willing model for photographers and if he got tired of posing he never complained. He was aware of his fame and importance." One resident who often illegally fed Samson described him as a "neat friend," and another described his death as a deep "personal loss."

News of Samson's death spread rapidly throughout the town of

Estes Park. A local radio announcer stayed on the air the entire day to report breaking news to residents as well as to take calls from angry and distraught citizens. Within days of the elk's death, residents began holding town meetings calling for stiffer sentencing for poachers and increased law enforcement in the area. One individual inquired into whether a class action suit against the poacher could be filed because wildlife is the property of the state and because there were several victims who could claim damages (Hutchins 1995). Some people even went so far as to suggest that the poacher should be put to death.

Death threats were taken seriously by local law enforcement agents who refused to release the name of the poacher to the press for fear of reprisals. As a result of this decision citizens perceived local law enforcement as not acting quickly enough to prosecute the poacher. There was much consternation. Letters and petitions demanding the prosecution and punishment of the offender to the full extent of the law poured into the offices of district attorney and county judge.

Most residents and law enforcement personnel in the area agreed that the killing of Samson was the biggest single event to have taken place in Estes Park in the past decade. The district attorney responsible for prosecuting the case claimed that, in all of his years of prosecutorial work in the region, he had never witnessed anything that came close to the kind of moral outrage expressed in the Samson case. In an interview, he explained:

> We had a case very close in time [to the Samson case], probably within a year or two, where a baby was left in a car and the mother forgot the baby was in the car. It was a hot day and the baby died. We had more calls and letters showing outrage and sympathy in the Samson case than we did in that case. We often commented about that around the table, you know, what and where are our real sentiments and priorities?

It was in this context of moral outrage and widespread indignation that Samson's Law was proposed and eventually accepted in the State of Colorado.

The Origins of Samson's Law

In interviews, many of those who led the charge for the enactment of a new law indicated that they did not want Samson's death to

158   ROBERT GRANFIELD & PAUL COLOMY

be in vain. Many residents were disappointed by the fact that, although initial discussion of the punishment for the poacher involved possible fines of up to $100,000 and a lengthy jail term, the final sentence was significantly less than their expectations. The poacher eventually plead guilty to a series of wildlife violations including hunting without a license and the willful destruction of wildlife and paid $6,000 in fines and spent ninety days in jail.

A number of memorials were erected to honor Samson. For example, visitors to Estes Park are now greeted by a larger-than-life bronze statue of the elk. In addition, each year Samson's head and antlers are displayed during the annual Elk Festival. Tourists may also purchase reproductions of his image on post cards, posters and tee shirts. Also, the Colorado Division of Wildlife adopted Samson's image for its official state logo. But perhaps the most significant tribute was the passage of Samson's Law.

Samson's Law, as it is widely known in Colorado, adds a surcharge for "illegally taking" (the legal phrase for "poaching") select, "trophy-sized" animals. The statute defines trophy status for each species included in the bill—bull elk, mule deer buck, whitetail deer buck, bull moose, bighorn sheep, mountain goat and pronghorn antelope. The definitions of trophy-class wildlife are based on the tenth edition of Boone and Crockett's *Records of North American Big Game* (1988) record book and use a minimum antler/horn standard. A trophy pronghorn antelope, for example, must have a horn length of fourteen inches or more; a trophy bull elk must have at least six points on one antler; and a horn length of one-half curl qualifies a bighorn sheep as a trophy. The surcharge for trophy poaching varies by species, and these variable rates are tied to the estimates of the "cost of replacement." Replacement costs, in turn, represent the average amount paid for guides, licenses, airfare/travel, skinning and other processing and taxidermy fees. In accord with these costs, the law stipulates that poaching a trophy-sized pronghorn antelope, for instance, will incur a surcharge of $4,000 (that is added to the existing fine of $700); illegally taking a trophy bull elk (like Samson) incurs a surcharge of $10,000 (on top of the existing fine of $1,000); and poaching a trophy bighorn sheep incurs a surcharge of $25,000 (added to an existing fine that ranges from $1,000 to $100,000). The revenue generated by the surcharge goes to the local town, city or county where the citation is issued.

State Senator Mark Udall, a Boulder-based Democrat whose family has long been involved with environmental and wildlife issues and whose district includes Estes Park, initially introduced the bill to the Colorado General Assembly in 1997.[4] Despite public support the bill was voted down, a victim of partisan politics according to its proponents. Udall was a Democrat and a freshman to boot, and his measure was killed quickly in the Republican-controlled legislature. The following year Udall enlisted a powerful Republican co-sponsor, Senator Tilman Bishop of Grand Junction, while also securing the support of other influential Republicans in both chambers. With key Republicans in tow and important alterations to the original measure, the bill was approved and signed into law in 1998.

In his introductory remarks to the Assembly, Udall initially attempted to distance the measure from Samson and what he termed "legislation by anecdote."[5] But by then Samson had become the state's most infamous instance of poaching and Udall's reticence notwithstanding, his colleagues repeatedly brought the bill back to the big bull elk, peppering Udall and the director of the Colorado Division of Wildlife (DOW), David Croonquist (who testified at length during the legislative hearings) with questions about Samson and the penalties imposed on the poacher. For legislators, and the public at large, Samson was the "poster animal" for trophy poaching, supplying not only a shared point of reference for discussion but a primary impetus for "doing something" about the problem.

Legislators were not alone in making Samson a touchstone for Udall's bill. Local papers, including the *Denver Post*, the *Rocky Mountain News*, the *Estes Park Trail Gazette*, the *Coloradoan* (in Fort Collins) and the *Reporter-Herald* (in Loveland), consistently referred to Samson's Law in their news stories and editorials. So did DOW which, in a 1998 release circulated to lawmakers and wildlife organizations during the legislative session, offered the following explanation of the measure's origins and purpose (Lewis and Smith 1998):

> The bill was written in response to the poaching of Samson, the spectacular bull elk which freely roamed the area around Estes Park. Randall Francis, the man who shot Samson, received a sentence of only three months in jail and a $6,000 fine for the wanton act. That sparked a storm of protest around Estes Park, as well it should have. It's more than appropriate to stiffen penalties for those who think nothing of slaughtering wildlife simply because they want a hunting trophy. That's why Mark Udall introduced a bill to establish harsher penalties for trophy poaching.

By the 1998 session, Udall's reservations about legislation by anecdote had dissipated, and both he and (co-sponsor) Bishop frequently
referred to Samson as the prototypical trophy the bill sought to protect from poachers.

According to the bill's proponents, the harm associated with trophy poaching is both symbolic and material. When testifying before
the House Committee on Agriculture, Livestock, and Natural Resources,
Udall characterized trophy wildlife as a "symbol of our way of life
here that's so special about Colorado."[6] Similarly, Jo Evans, a lob-
byist representing several hunting and conservation groups, described
trophy-class animals as "the largest, the best, and the most beautiful."[7] Poaching such animals constitutes "a crime against the people
of Colorado whose wildlife it is."[8] Diane Gansauer, Executive Director
of the Colorado Wildlife Federation, depicted these animals as "invalu-
able," portraying them as an essential part of America's "national
treasury" and as "crown jewels."[9]

In addition to their symbolic value, trophy wildlife was presented
as a significant economic asset, attracting tourists and hunters from
across the country. Focusing specifically on hunting, Udall and Bishop
noted that it represents a $1.6 billion industry in Colorado. And the
vast majority of those who testified at the legislative hearings represented organizations whose core constituency was hunters, and these
witnesses hammered home the point that poachers endanger this
industry by depriving legitimate sportsmen, who often pay significant
licensing fees, from the opportunity to legally hunt trophy animals.

The proponents of Samson's Law also wanted to ensure that penalties for poaching would be administered. Proponents sought to reduce
judicial discretion in cases where an individual had been found guilty
of poaching. The bill's proponents felt that some judges had not
taken wildlife crime seriously in the past and had used their discretion to impose minimal fines, if any at all. The language of Udall's
bill sought to remedy this perceived problem by effectively eliminating judicial discretion.

The Context of Legal Action

What explains the level of moral outrage about the loss of Samson
the elk to the point that a new law was enacted to honor his memory? Interestingly, the moral outrage over the case and the ensuing

law occurred at a time when wildlife violations were on the decline. According to DOW statistics, the number of violations associated with the illegal taking of big game (elk, mountain lions, big horn sheep, etc.) had been declining since the early 1990s. In 1991, the DOW reported a total of 669 big game violations while in 1995, the year of Samson's death, only 392 big game violations were assessed (Bredehoft 2001).

Movements to enact legislation often occur independent of statistical evidence of rising problems. For example, drug laws, including National Prohibition, have often symbolized and represented broad-based fear and anxiety associated with a changing society. Gusfield (1963), in his classic study of prohibition, maintained that the coercive reform movement to transform alcohol laws represented the social elite's fear of transition; they felt that their status was eroding within a rapidly changing social and cultural landscape. The point is that law emerges in a social and cultural context that is significantly broader than the problem or issue it is designed to address. As with other legislation geared toward affecting social control, the Colorado poaching law addressed a problem that was in reality on the decline.

So why was the law passed? In life and, particularly, in death Samson embodied a meaning that was beyond his own distinctive stature as a large bull elk. Residents and tourists who knew and visited Samson as well as the legislators who passed Samson's Law imbued him with a meaning that embodied the very essence of the wilderness. Although he was most certainly human-habituated and relatively tame, a fact that may have contributed to his demise, people envisaged in him their own projections of the wilderness. Animals frequently connote a sense of place for people. In their recent book on geographies of human and animal encounters, Philo and Wilbert (2000:11) comment that:

Zones of human settlement are envisaged as the province of pets or companion animals, zones of agriculture activity are envisaged as the province of livestock animals, and zones of unoccupied lands beyond the margins of settlement and agriculture are envisaged as the province of wild animals.

Thus, the human construction of animals is wrapped up with the human construction of place. As Scarce points out in this volume, communities are defined differently by different groups. In his study of the reintroduction of wolves into Yellowstone National Park, Scarce found that reactions to wolf reintroduction in the area depended on the relationship individuals had with the area itself. Long-term residents tended to see the reintroduction of wolves as a sign of uncertainty while the newcomers viewed wolves as a benefit for recreational purposes. In each case, the definition of the wolf was mediated by the individual's construction of place.

To the people of Estes Park as well as many legislators, gazing upon the elk is akin to gazing upon the wilderness itself. It is this wilderness aesthetic (Pickering, personal communication) that brings both residents and tourists to the Estes Park region. However, the landscape of the American wilderness has all but vanished from the scene. In towns across the West, growth and development have transformed wilderness into zoos without bars. In Estes Park growth and development have been so widespread that residents and tourists view elk, not from some remote area in a nearby forest, but from the green on one of the two championship-sized golf courses that have been recently constructed.

Game officers and residents complain about the increasing numbers of road kills of elk, elk-facilitated traffic jams and elk walking through the town with, as one game officer put it, "arrows in their butts." There has also been an increasing commercialization of hunting in the area where local ranchers will either herd elk onto their private land or raise them in order to sell private property hunting licenses. This has transformed hunting into what one interviewee described as a "slaughter." As this resident explained in an interview:

> January around here is a sad time. It's a mass slaughter of elk. It's gotten to the point where people shoot from the side of the road. Last year there was a guy who had killed an elk and was field dressing the critter right across the street from a school bus stop where children were waiting. I don't disapprove of hunting, but this isn't hunting. Things have really changed in this town.[10]

The wilderness is largely a myth within American society, although it continues to evoke powerful imagery (Cronon 1983). It is very likely that the wilderness image has become even more potent in the wake of increasing urban development and the resulting loss of the natural environment (Schmitt 1969). The Estes Park elk known as Samson was part of this wilderness narrative kept alive in order to maintain a kind of separation between the sacred and profane, between the wilderness and civilization. The killing of Samson and the passage of Samson's Law were played out on a field of a trans-forming social landscape. As one resident we interviewed insightfully commented, "the killing of Samson was the killing of an idea; an idea that brought people here. We thought we were immune to this sort of thing."

The residents of Estes Park and legislators who led the charge to pass Samson's Law and to memorialize him in other ways were, in addition to mourning a unique elk, responding to a felt crisis asso-ciated with the challenge to their ideology of the wilderness (Colomy and Granfield 2003). The effort to further criminalize poaching might actually be seen as an example of "governing through crime," a phrase that is used to describe crime rhetoric and increasing crimi-nalization as a response not to crime itself but rather to what Scheingold (1998) refers to as a general feeling of malaise and mar-ginalization associated with a sense of crisis in society.

In a related way, Boeckman and Tyler (1997) have argued that citizens who feel that the moral and social cohesion that holds soci-ety together is declining tend to be more supportive of punitive pub-lic policies. In their research on the public support for "three-strikes" legislation, the authors argue that rather than actually fearing crime, crime becomes a mobilizing theme for the public who feels a sense of foreboding—a feeling that social conditions and underlying social values have become too precarious and uncertain. In a similar way proponents of the Samson bill used law not only as a way of assert-ing a claim that the current criminal justice system is inadequate for not protecting them against poachers, but also as a way of reaffirming their own vision of the wilderness that is under attack on several fronts. The law was also a way to articulate its supporters' particu-lar vision of human-animal relationships. The killing of Samson not only became a mobilizing event for many of those who found the commercial poaching of these animals offensive, but also a symbol for the loss of the wilderness.

Discussion and Conclusion

This chapter offers insight into the degree to which nature and wildlife are socially constructed and act as powerful boundary mark-ers for certain groups. While framed as a problem-solving instru-ment, Samson's Law served as a boundary marker, establishing and

reaffirming several boundaries. First, it legally inscribed a hierarchical distinction between the more highly prized trophy-class animals
and their somewhat less valued, normal-sized brethren. Though this
dichotomy resonates in a very general way with many casual human
observers' appreciation for unusually large wildlife, the detailed
specifications of trophy-status incorporated in the bill clearly reflect
characteristics celebrated by the hunting community.

Second, affirming a particular iteration of the broader, longstanding
distinction between "good" and "bad" animals, the bill protected
"non-predator" trophy-sized wildlife while excluding equally spectacular (in size) "predators." The 1997 bill had sought to shield large
bears and mountain lions from poachers, but speaking on behalf of
ranchers and farmers, members of the House Committee on Agriculture
protested that these animals sometimes prey on livestock and occasionally threaten human life as well. Ranchers and farmers had a
right to protect their cattle and families from predators of whatever
size. Deferring to these interests, the 1998 bill deleted bears and
mountain lions from the list of protected wildlife.

Third and perhaps most significantly, the bill affirmed a bright
line between legitimate hunters and poachers. Pitched at a symbolic
level, legislators and those who testified on the bill's behalf reasserted
a radical moral contrast between these two groups. Within the legislative hearings, the hunter was characterized in an idealized, rev-
erential way, as a man (usually, though, lawmakers were well aware
that the number of women hunters is growing) who rigorously adheres
to both the formal (and often complicated) rules and regulations
established by the Division of Wildlife as well as the informal but
vitally-felt ethos of the hunting community. The hunter personified
values of restraint, conservation, safety, concern for others in the
field, respect for law and legal authorities, and a deeply-felt connection to animals. The hunter's project was lauded for its positive
contribution to wildlife management. By contrast, the poacher was
vilified, and he (no mention was made of female poachers) was vilified
most vociferously by those who testified on behalf of organizations
whose principal constituencies were hunters. During legislative hearings, poachers were portrayed as selfish and greedy, motivated either
by the prospect of large, illegitimate profits or unseemly ego enhancement. They had no respect for the law or legal authorities nor did
they exhibit much regard for hunters or their ethos. Poachers were
seen as exceedingly dangerous, posing a threat not only to wildlife

but, to (non-poaching) humans who might inadvertently encounter them in the wild. They were criminals with no respect for the law. Unlike hunters, poachers cared not at all for the animals they killed and were often satisfied with the rack alone, leaving the rest of the animal to rot on a secluded hillside.

No legislator (or testifying non-legislator) contested this idealized symbolic contrast. But after affirming this contrast, lawmakers (and others) reflected on more practical features of hunting and enforcing rules against poaching. This "practical rationality" parsed away (but did not challenge) the ideal-typical contrast between poachers and hunters. This leavening of symbolism with practicality was prompted both by a recognition of the difficulties even the well-intentioned confront in following the letter of the law (against poaching) and by a certain level of distrust some hunters harbor toward the Division of Wildlife. These concerns prompted legislators, particularly those who were hunters and/or whose constituencies included hunters, to advise DOW officials about using common sense in law enforcement.

Legislators and several witnesses held that not all poaching is equally deplorable. The target of the law was decidedly not subsistence poaching, the illegal taking of an animal for its meat. In this vein, a few legislators recollected their own dirt-poor youth when dire economic circumstances compelled them to poach for groceries. Mark Udall, the bill's principal sponsor, explicitly noted that the target of his bill was not "the man with the family back home in December driving a lonely county road to take a doe for some meat in the freezer for the rest of the winter."[11] Legislators also noted that accidents sometimes occur in the field, with an illegal take occurring when a bullet travels through an intended, legal target and inadvertently striking another animal for which the hunter has no license.

Also animating this practical rationality was a certain level of distrust some legislators expressed toward the DOW. Though the relationship between the Division and hunters is generally cooperative, with a sizeable portion of the Division's budget coming from the fees and licenses paid by hunters and anglers, the Division's law enforcement function introduces an inherent tension between its officers and hunters. Hunters complain that DOW managers sometimes enforce laws against poaching in an overly zealous way, and some legislators told the DOW representative testifying in support

of the bill about calls he had received from hunters complaining
about the officious way they had been treated by DOW officers.

Referring to past incidents where anti-poaching regulations had
been applied too rigidly, another legislator wanted assurance from
the DOW that the proposed bill would be enforced with common
sense and compassion. In this vein, the DOW official was reminded,
several times, about an infamous incident during the 1990s in the
San Luis Valley where an officer, working undercover, had befriended
a largely impoverished, immigrant community that partially relied
on poaching for subsistence. After the officer relayed these findings
to his superiors, DOW launched what many considered a SWAT-
like raid on the community. Though legally justifiable, this heavy-
handed approach provoked considerable resentment toward DOW,
not only in the Valley but throughout the State of Colorado. Legislators
wanted assurances from DOW that passage of the Samson bill would
not be taken as license for another San Luis Valley.

The elk of Estes Park have much more to fear than the occasional poacher. Development tracts that shrink corridors for elk to
move, ranchers who herd elk on their lands so they can be harvested and citizens who are increasingly unwilling to share their space
with these animals represent more urgent dangers. Samson's Law
constructs the threat to elk and wildlife in a traditional way, by
assigning blame to an old enemy, the poacher. Historically, this
enemy is well known: a lower class and commercially-motivated "outsider" and "non-hunter."[12] However, this law will do little to reduce
the modern threats that confront these animals and the wilderness
they represent.

Wildlife managers face an increasingly difficult and complex social
environment. While the Samson Law was initially cast as an attempt
to validate wildlife as a natural asset, interests and constituencies that
were removed from the original outcry concerning Samson's death
inevitably shaped the law. Initially pushed by constituencies who
viewed elk like Samson as valuable for their own sake as a part of
nature and wanted them protected, the Division of Wildlife officials
were eventually instructed by legislators and hunting groups to enforce
the Samson Law with commercial and recreational interests in mind.
The law erected symbolic boundaries in ways that meant that the
elk would not be made safe in their own right, but made safe for
hunters and other commercial interests to continue to kill elk legally.
Despite the fact that the initial impulse surrounding the death of

Samson involved a deeply-felt expression of community loss associated with the decline of nature due to growth and development, the law re-defined this sense of loss in a way that supported the interests and worldviews of the traditional communities associated with hunting and ranching.

While many community members in the town of Estes Park where Samson roamed may feel vindicated with the passage of the law, the law may do little to reduce the majority of poaching cases. Although the law has created new standards for poaching enforcement on the books, wildlife officials are still nevertheless faced with enforcing the law. Based on the evidence in this chapter, it is likely that wildlife enforcement officials will apply the law narrowly to cases of poaching that do not offend hunting or other commercial interests.

References

Asbury, Terry. 1995. "Famed Trophy-Sized Elk 1 of 4 Killed by Weekend Poachers." *Estes Park Trail Gazette*, November 15, p. 1.

Boeckmann, Robert and Tom Tyler. 1997. "Three Strikes and You Are Out, But Why? The Psychology of Public Support for Punishing Rule Breakers." *Law and Society Review* 31:337–365.

Boone and Crockett Club. 1988. *Records of North American Big Game: A Book of the Boone and Crockett Club*.

Bredehoft, John. 2001. *Colorado Division of Wildlife Annual Law Enforcement and Violation Report*. Denver, CO.

Chambliss, William. 1993. "The Creation of Criminal Law and Crime Control in Britain and America." Pp. 36–64 in *Making Law: The State, the Law, and Structural Contradictions*, edited by W. Chambliss and M. Zatz. Bloomington: Indiana University Press.

Colomy, Paul and Robert Granfield. 2003. "Memorializing Samson." Paper presented at the annual meeting of the American Sociological Association, Atlanta, Georgia. August.

Cronon, William. 1983. *Uncommon Ground: Rethinking the Human Place in Nature*. New York: W.W. Norton and Company.

Davis, Mike. 1999. *Ecology of Fear: Los Angeles and the Imagination of Disaster*. New York: Vintage.

Eliason, Stephen and Richard Dodder. 1999. "Techniques of Neutralization Used by Deer Poachers in the Western United States: A Research Note." *Deviant Behavior* 20:233–252.

Ewick, Patricia and Susan Silbey. 1998. *The Common Place of Law: Stories from Everyday Life*, Chicago: University of Chicago Press.

Gusfield, Joseph. 1963. *Symbolic Crusade: Status Politics and the American Temperance Movement*. Urbana: University of Illinois Press.

Herman, Daniel. 2001. *Hunting and the American Imagination*. Smithsonian Institution Press.

Hutchins, Judith. 1995. "Residents Share Outrage at Poaching: Samson's Slaying Spurs Call for Maximum Penalty." *Estes Park Trail Gazette*, November 22, p. 1.

Lee, Wes. 1997. "Samson's Legacy Will Endure." *Estes Park Trail Gazette*, September 17, p. 1.
Lewis, Cameron and Bud Smith. 1998 (February 6). "Make Poachers Pay." *Wildlife Report: News from the DOW's North Region*. Fort Collins: Colorado Division of Wildlife.
Martinez, Julia. 2002. "New Law Honors Feisty Cat. Penalties for Cruelty to Animals Increased." *The Denver Post*, June 9, pp. B-02.
Muth, Robert. 1998. "The Persistence of Poaching in Advanced Industrial Society: Meanings and Motivations—An Introductory Comment." *Society and Natural Resources* 11:5–7.
Philo, Chris and Chris Wilbert. 2000. "Animal Spaces, Beastly Places: An Introduction." In *Animal Spaces, Beastly Places: New Geographies of Human-Animal Relations*, edited by C. Philo and C. Wilbert. New York: Routledge.
Sampson, Robert and B. Groves. 1989. "Community Structure and Crime: Testing Social Disorganization Theory." *American Journal of Sociology* 94:774–802.
Scarce, Rik. [this volume]. "More Than Mere Wolves at the Door: Reconstructing Community Amidst a Wildlife Controversy." In *Mad About Wildlife: Looking at Social Conflict Over Wildlife*, edited by A. Herda-Rapp and T. Goedeke. Leiden, Netherlands: Brill Academic Publishers.
Scheingold, Stuart. 1998. "Constructing the New Political Criminology: Power, Authority, and the Post-Liberal State." *Law and Social Inquiry* 23:857–895.
Schmitt, Peter. 1969. *Back to Nature: The Arcadian Myth in Urban America*. Baltimore: Johns Hopkins University Press.
Scully, Matthew. 2002. *Dominion: The Power of Man, the Suffering of Animals, and the Call to Mercy*. New York: St. Martin's Press.
Thompson, Edward, P. 1976. *Whigs and Hunters: The Origin of the Black Act*. London: Allen Lane.
Warren, Louis. 1997. *The Hunter's Game: Poachers and Conservationists in Twentieth-Century America*. New Haven: Yale University Press.

Notes

[1] Funding for this research was provided through a Faculty Research Grant from the University of Denver. The authors would like to thank Lindsay Redd and Doug VanBibber for their assistance on this project.
[2] Colorado *Boulder Revised Code*, Secs. 6–1–11, 6–1–12.
[3] According to standard hunting guides, an elk with a 6 × 6 rack, that is six antler points on each side, is considered a trophy animal.
[4] Though Udall was the bill's principal author and sponsor, he relied heavily on expertise provided by Colorado Division of Wildlife (DOW) officials, especially David Croonquist, the Division's Assistant Chief of Law Enforcement. Udall also consulted with state hunting and conservation groups and with several Estes Park residents.
[5] *House Committee on Agriculture, Natural Resources, and Energy*, January 15, 1997.
[6] *House Committee on Agriculture, Livestock, and Natural Resources*, January 14, 1998.
[7] *House Committee on Finance*, January 28, 1998.
[8] *House Committee on Agriculture*, January 14, 1998.
[9] *House Committee on Agriculture*, January 14, 1998.
[10] Many people in the area did not necessarily oppose hunting. Rather, people generally constructed boundaries between legitimate hunting and non-legitimate hunting. For some, like this interviewee, the commercialization of hunting through

private hunts on ranches violates the sportsman's ethic of "fair chase" that is premised upon the animal having some, albeit limited ability to evade being killed.

[11] *House Committee on Agriculture*, January 14, 1998.

[12] The term "non-hunter" is by the hunting community to differentiate hunters who follow a sportsmen's ethic from "poachers" who are seen as wantonly violating this ethic thereby making them not real hunters. Many hunters we spoke to believe that hunting is not simply the act of stalking and killing animals but also represents a state of mind about wildlife and wildlife law.

THE HUNTERS AND THE HUNTED: CONTEXT AND EVOLUTION OF GAME MANAGEMENT IN GERMANIC COUNTRIES VERSUS THE UNITED STATES

RICHARD HUMMEL AND THERESA L. GOEDEKE

Introduction

Game management is the practice of manipulating the life circumstances of animals that are defined as game within a society (Munsche 1981:3–5). Management of these chosen animals is undertaken for aesthetic, economic and recreational reasons. Historically, humans undertook to control game populations either directly or indirectly because: 1) animals competed with people for domesticated food resources; 2) they wanted to tame them for domesticated sources of labor, food or fiber; and 3) they viewed them as objects of aesthetic appreciation.

The paramount goal in manipulating game species was and continues to be the improvement of the hunting experience for people. During the nineteenth century, hunting for sport continued in Europe and developed into a popular activity in North America. Hunters in Germany and Austria, described hereafter as the Germanic countries, make up .4 percent and 1.4 percent respectively, of the total population of these countries. Seven to eight million Europeans hunt each year for meat, skins or trophies (F.A.C.E. 1995:II, VII/1–2). This compares with states where hunters total five to six percent of the total population, or fourteen to fifteen million Americans per annum (NRAcentral.com 2004:1). Millions of hunters are affected by the game management practices discussed in this chapter.

The goals and experiences of hunters in the different countries are much different, however. This is a consequence of the way each society evolved in their relationship toward nature and, also, defined game and its importance to hunters. In this chapter we describe the historical development of current wildlife management systems in the Germanic countries and the United States. We explore how these two game management systems emerged from particular political structures, social forces and historical processes. We discuss how culture has helped shape the roles that hunters play in game management

and how, in turn, this influences what constitutes a desirable hunting experience. Finally, discussion is offered about how these different
views might impact conflict over wildlife issues.

Research Methods

To compare these two game management systems we relied on an
eclectic collection of primary documents and secondary materials.
The *Federation des Associations de Chasseurs de l'UE* (F.A.C.E.) handbook
was central to the analysis of Germanic game management. This
document, first published in 1995 by the Federation of Fieldsports
Association of the European Union and European Commission,
Brussels, Belgium, compiles data on hunting regulations, hunter participation censuses, and effects of hunting on animal populations for
all of Europe. It is published in four languages, including English.
To our knowledge, no other source of information on the broad
array of topics concerning hunting in Europe exists.

In addition to the F.A.C.E. handbook, the first author gathered
a number of documents about hunting and game management in
Germanic culture, about a third of them while on a sabbatical
research visit to Germany in 1999. In total, twenty-seven primary
sources were collected for analysis. Documents recorded solely in
German were not included in the study, which amounted to approximately eighteen sources. Also, the first author obtained anecdotal
information on modern Germanic hunting systems by interviewing
a professional forester during a second trip to Germany in 2003.

Finally, to examine the development of the game management
system in the United States, we relied on existing treatments of the
history of wildlife and its management laws.

The Social Context of Game Hunting in Germany

The F.A.C.E. handbook identifies Germanic hunting laws and wildlife
management practices as having provided the dominant management paradigm for European nations (F.A.C.E. 1995:VIII/2). This
is significant if one considers that the proportion of citizens engaging in sport hunting in Germanic countries is modest relative to the
proportion of sport hunters in other European nations. In Germanic
culture, and most of Europe, private landowners and hunting orga-

nizations handle game and wildlife management on a private basis, relying on what is called the revier system. This system evolved out of the complex social and cultural history of the continent.

Era of Feudal Stewardship

During the feudal/pre-revolutionary period in Europe (circa 800 A.D.–1789 A.D.), which we term the *Era of Feudal Stewardship*, royalty and nobility had exclusive rights to hunt while common people, meaning those who did not own land, were allowed virtually no access to game at all. Commoners typically could not own dogs or weapons that could be used to hunt the game animals. Farmers were even forbidden to protect their crops against wildlife designated as game.[1] There were severe penalties for harvesting or "poaching" game owned by the nobility.

Why did the nobility deny common people the right to harvest wild game? One answer is that the military and political elites considered hunting as useful training for warfare. This was because hunting provided military leaders with an opportunity to practice using weapons of war, such as horses, bows, crossbows, spears and guns. Because of the military association, the elite prohibited commoners' access to weapons and disallowed any opportunities for them to use such weaponry.

The goal was to keep the masses unarmed and at the mercy of the ruling classes, both for protection and a livelihood. It was a central governing principle meant to ensure the long-term stability of the feudal system by helping those in power to remain so. In short, the elites used their position to achieve social differentiation and subordination, and denying people access to game was an integral part of this process.

The tracts of land held by nobility were generally gifts by feudal rulers made in payment for political support and military services. The individual who owned the land owned and had responsibility for everything on that property. Most commonly, the landowners would employ foresters and gamekeepers to ensure sustainable yields of timber and game. These employees protected their employers' private sporting interests. Interestingly, these feudal controls on access to nature did much to guarantee the survival of many attractive and useful species by preventing unfettered use and access to them by growing human populations.

This system was also important in the development and maintenance of political alliances that helped the nobility gain and maintain power. Those parts of Europe where Germanic culture predominated, which included a region largest in both area and population, consisted of hundreds of political divisions of various sizes. In 1715 over three hundred political units existed in what later became Germany. Each unit had its own unique mix of cultural attributes, such as rulers, religions, laws, currency, courts and customs. These political units were too small to be serious players on the continental political stage. Consequently, their governing nobility secured status by forming connections and alliances among their neighbors. To do this they tried to impress each other with the magnificence of the entertainment they could offer, especially hunting parties.

Neighboring nobility invited each other to hunting parties as a major form of social networking, in a seemingly never-ending social system of give and take. To impress their guests, noblemen housed the hunting party in elaborate castles or lodges.[2] They demonstrated social status by controlling vast hunting grounds and by employing well-trained hunt servants who were skilled in finding game and adept at guiding guests to successful kills. They also employed arms smiths who crafted matched sets of weapons and loaned them to guests during the visit. Finally, the most prestigious accomplishment was to deliver an abundant array of game in a variety of interesting settings.

Hosts of these parties expected and received reciprocal invitations to attend other hunting parties. Each host attempted to impress others in their social class with the carefully staged extravagance of their hunting estates. Historians record that these petty princes risked bankruptcies as they vied for opportunities for the ever more lavish presentation of game.

The Reconstruction of Ownership: The Revier System

The sociopolitical revolutions beginning early in the nineteenth century brought about the downfall of the *Era of Feudal Stewardship* and jointly ushered in the *Era of Access by the Propertied Citizen*. New and reformulated national governments redressed the feudal hunting laws, the disparities from which topped the list of common citizen complaints. Shifting cultural views about individual rights and access to game led to changes in laws within new political regimes. Innovative social and political leaders did away with the exclusive access systems that previously reserved game for sportsmen of the upper classes.

These efforts resulted in what is called the revier system, which dates from roughly 1852 in what is now Germany. This system reflected emerging social values; people began to embrace the notion of private property rights. As in the feudal system, hunting rights again became enmeshed in the right to own property. The difference was, however, that now any person might own property and, consequently, game. The revier system gained dominance throughout Europe as capitalist ideas permeated the culture.

The modern revier system embodies the philosophy of private property ownership and, as when it originated, organizes all land deemed suitable for game hunting into formal hunting blocks. Moses (2001:2) provided a description of how these blocks are organized:

> Each of the hunting blocks has a minimum size determined by the number of licensed hunters who can gain access to the block by lease from a private owner or political entity. The revier system requires landowners with smallholdings of land to put their holdings together with other owners to form reviers of legal size.

Thus, the goal of the system is to create blocks of land that can adequately support game and hunters alike. Individuals can enter as leaseholders into a particular revier, which remains the property of the landowner.

In addition, there are different types of reviers, which relate to the type of game desired. Hunters holding a revier by lease are expected to continue the lease for nine years on small or "low" game reviers and twelve years on big or "high" game reviers. High game consists of red deer, wild boar and certain game birds, although other species might be considered so if present in harvestable numbers. Low game, then, are all other legally huntable species (Moses 2001:1–2). The mandatory lease period ensures that there is enough time invested in the lease to manage game effectively.

In theory all citizens have the opportunity to purchase access and, practically, many people gain access by exploiting networks and providing services to landowners. Although the system is based on property ownership, according to Woodward (1989:12–13), many blue-collar hunters pool their resources to rent what is called a syndicate revier. This is a shooting ground that is leased in common by as many as ten hunters. Hunters who cannot afford to lease these rights might trade labor for access by "constructing shooting seats, trapping vermin, and feeding game during the winter" (Woodward 1989:12–13). Nevertheless, because the system is based on property ownership the modern Germanic system is designed to provide access to only those who can pay for the privilege.

Management of the revier is explicitly dictated by law. Regulations specify how owners or lessors must manage reviers in order to achieve the legal objectives of the system, which are:

> ... maintaining varied and healthy game populations at levels compatible with landscape and agricultural conditions, ensuring requirements for game survival are met, and preventing game damage to crops, forestry, and fisheries (F.A.C.E. 1995: Vol. II, IX–1/14).

To meet these obligations, each revier employs a professional forester who serves as the overseer of hunting activities and habitat management. The forester is responsible for drafting a game plan each year that sets out the management strategy for particular species. This can be done only after he or she conducts a census of the animals typically hunted and, after, calculates the "huntable" surplus of animals living on each revier. In Germanic tradition, a surplus exists when the number of game animals exceeds the carrying capacity of the revier. The forester has the power to define what the carrying capacity is or should be.

When the forester develops and approves of this plan it then becomes the harvest objective for the next hunting season. Leaseholders are responsible for harvesting the surplus of animals as dictated in the plan. The forester might require hunters to target sick, deformed and old animals for removal. He or she continuously monitors and protects desirable trophy characteristics in the game populations on reviers.

An important component of the game plan is recordkeeping. The forester must maintain careful records on the numbers and kind of animals taken. This is done because taking too many of any particular species could harm future hunting prospects by depleting the population. On the other hand, taking too few animals might threaten the interests of various landowners by resulting in damage to habitat or agricultural crops. If leaseholders take too few animals, the professional forester may cull game populations to protect these interests. Leaseholders pay the expenses when a cull is necessary, as well as the cost of damage to agricultural fields through reimbursements.

Germanic hunting laws require winter feeding programs to sustain herds when forage is limiting, as well as to reduce damage in farm fields from browsing (Moses 2001). Leaseholders bear the expense of any feeding carried out by the landowner. However, to recapture some of these costs, the leaseholders can sell animals harvested from the revier in commercial game markets. This practice is legal and lucrative. Because the leaseholders are also responsible for animal damage to forests, they continually plant vegetation that is beneficial to game animals, while protecting trees and preserving thickets and hedgerows.

Members of each revier must participate in a regional game fair each year. At these game fairs, leaseholders have a legal obligation to transport and display the skull plates acquired from the red deer, roe deer, as well as the tusks of wild boar and other big game harvested on the revier. These mandatory show-and-tell sessions allow the foresters to monitor annually the physical trends in game population characteristics.

These game fairs serve hunters as well by giving them an opportunity to socialize young hunters into the community and to detect violations of game rules. For example, retired American army officer James McCoskey, a hunter with extensive German hunting experience, indicated in a personal interview that these gatherings allowed hunters to confront those who "cheated" by harvesting game animals (roebucks, in his experience) that were too healthy and too young. In other words, a hunter's status among his or her peers could suffer if the displayed trophies violate the revier's game plan.

The revier system motivates Germanic hunters to accept private responsibility for the operation and outcomes of wildlife management. Each hunter must undertake much study time to achieve the knowledge and skills that are legally required to earn a hunting license. Hunters participate in roughly one hundred hours of classroom work and complete three mandatory tests, including a written, an oral-practical and a target-shooting exam. These tests are used to evaluate whether aspiring hunters have acquired enough knowledge about:

> ... species, game biology and management, hunting management, game damage prevention, farming and forestry, firearms law and technique, gun dog handling, inspection and treatment of game meat for human consumption, welfare of game and wildlife, nature and landscape conservation law (F.A.C.E. 1995: Vol. II, IX-1/14).

Aspiring hunters who fail all or part of these tests may need to wait up to a year before the course is offered again. The average rate of failure for first time test-takers is thirty percent (Gottschalk 1972:112).

Hunter preparation courses also enable the formal socialization of novices into hunting traditions, customs and language. This corpus of language, lore and practice involves the following skills:

- proper hunting attire in the field and on formal occasions,
- conduct during various hunting activities (e.g., high-seat, drive and stalking),
- recognition of horn signals that communicate instructions during group events,
- signs conveyed by use of small tree branch configurations,
- proper handling, display and respect regarding harvested game,
- and the safe and effective use of firearms.

The revier system also requires that hunters have access to a trained hunting dog that can efficiently assist in locating and retrieving dead and, especially, wounded game.

As described by the Hunting Committee of the Heidelberg Rod and Gun Club in their volume, *Der Jungjaeger: A Handbook for the Young Hunter in Germany* (1989: unpaginated), the proper German hunter:

> ... honors the traditions and customs of hunting, spares animals any unnecessary pain or suffering, cares for his animals (non-game as well as game species), does not hunt without a trained dog, does not shoot an animal or anything else that he has not 100% correctly identified, and keeps himself informed on current happenings, changes in law, and the body of knowledge related to hunting.

According to written sources, in the Germanic game management system hunters must take their role as seriously as foresters do theirs. The system itself requires this high level of involvement.

Hunting in America: From Self-Provisions and Commerce to Sport only

In contrast to the Germanic experience, no feudal class established exclusive control over game animals in the New World. Wayne Regelin (1991) describes the history of wildlife management in the United States in four historical stages. He analyzes the growth of America's management system from its beginning to our current age of elaborate regulatory control. The first stage, termed the *Era of Abundance*, took place from the 1600s to the middle 1800s. This stage was marked by the arrival of European colonizers and immigrants who found unimagined numbers and diversity of wildlife resources. To the newcomers, these resources seemed inexhaustible (Tober 1981).

During this period there were few written laws governing wildlife harvest or protection of game animals. Hunters faced only scattered and seldom-enforced closed-season ordinances (Borland 1975; U.S. Department of Agriculture 1912). People viewed game as a resource of the commons, meaning that any and all could access and consume wildlife resources according to individual purposes (Warren 1997). Neither individuals nor political entities tried to lay claim to wildlife (Tober 1981).

Near the end of this era, Henry William Herbert, whose pen name was Frank Forester, brought a British value system regarding the conduct of hunters and the practice of hunting. In Herbert's philosophy:

> The gentleman hunts with restraint, seeking healthy recreation in the out-of-doors, harvesting only what he can personally use, using his weapons skillfully to ensure humane deaths to the game targeted, and achieving knowledge of the life habits of the game pursued (Reiger 1986:26).

According to Reiger (1986:26), "Herbert's model of the gentleman hunter had little to do, of course, with the hunter who only desired to feed his family or the gunner who sold his game harvest to others." He communicated these views to readers of his extensive writings on forest and field hunting topics in the 1830s and 1840s. Herbert is credited with socializing a generation of sportsmen who would go on to support the adoption of a conservation ethic for the United States in the late nineteenth century.

In the mid-nineteenth century the *Era of Exploitation* commenced. The promise of the California gold fields after 1849, offers of land with the Homestead Act of 1862, and the completion of the Transcontinental Railroad in 1869 set the stage for changes in American relationships to wild game. With westward expansion, people altered habitats at an accelerated rate and began to exploit wildlife on an unprecedented scale (Regelin 1991). Homesteaders and domesticated livestock supplanted the bison on the Great Plains as the latter fell victim to commercial hunters and those who sought to destroy the Indians.

Hunters, both individuals and companies, continued to turn America's game species into commercially harvested products, such as meat, furs and feathers, for income and barter. The results of commercial hunting, in association with other pressures from increasing urbanization, were broad and grave, especially as technology advanced in the new country. In addition to advancements in weapons technology, railroads, refrigeration and telegraph machines moved many species closer to extinction (Neuzil and Kovarik 1996). Wilcove (1999:30) explains that the passenger pigeon was snuffed out because "railroads enabled commercial hunters to reach even the most distant colonies and ship birds back to eastern markets; the telegraph ensured that hunters quickly learned about the locations of any new colonies." Virtually all game animals suffered under these same pressures and a number of them met the same fate.

As game animals were being slaughtered wholesale, many people began to speak out about havoc being wrought on the country's natural heritage. Citizen and budding conservation groups argued for controls on killing non-game birds for the feather industry (Borland 1975). Naturalist philosophers such as Ralph Waldo Emerson and Henry David Thoreau published their ideas about conservation and the intrinsic value of nature.

Naturalists were not the only persons dismayed at massacres taking place on America's plains and in her forests. Borland (1975:116) wrote that, sportsman, "had fought market hunting for years and had led the public campaign against it." Elite sportsmen lobbied in the United States for the end of market hunting and the observance of responsible hunting seasons (Dunlap 1988; Regelin 1991). Influenced by Herbert's ideas, hunters from the professional and upper classes sought to limit access to game to only sportsmen who endorsed the principle of "fair chase." Fair chase consists of pursuit of game according to socially constructed standards of behavior, which gives the game a good chance of eluding capture, thus rendering the sport difficult but not impossible.

Wealthy, eastern hunters expressed their views about proper hunting practices in articles and editorials published in outdoor sporting magazines throughout the late 1800s (Reiger 1986). Neuzil and Kovarik (1996:3) report that hunting and fishing magazines, most notably *Forest and Stream*, "focused on defining a new kind of hunting ethic at the expense of other types of relationships to wildlife, particularly market hunting." Naturally, such magazines nurtured the conservation movement and reported on the efforts of conservationists to lobby state governments around the country for more restrictive regulations (Reiger 1986).

Thus, the economic and political elite of the United States sought permanent conservation of America's sharply diminished game resources. Their cause was spearheaded by Teddy Roosevelt who, in 1887, formed the Boone and Crockett Club, a group that publicly endorsed the value system of the upper class sportsman. Once federal and state governments adopted a conservation ideology, American laws progressively eliminated market hunting, mainly an occupation of the lower classes, from the inventory of permissible behaviors (Dunlap 1988).

Although the conservation movement had been afoot for decades, Regelin indicates that the *Era of Conservation Awareness* officially opened with passage of the Lacey Act of 1900. This legislation ended the interstate shipment of illegally harvested wildlife and regulated the importation of foreign wildlife. Borland (1975:122) asserts, "the Lacey Act was one of the most important actions ever taken to preserve and protect American wildlife." Other federal laws regulated the harvest of migrating birds, such as waterfowl. Although enforcement was spotty, it is significant that some of the most skilled market hunters from the previous era became game wardens (Reiger 1986).

Teddy Roosevelt's administration (1901–1909) boosted conservation efforts mightily. The Roosevelt administration inserted large tracts of land held in the public domain into various public land systems. At this time, the executive branch created the U.S. Forest Service and increased the amount of land in the National Forests from thirty-two million acres to one hundred forty-eight million acres. Finally, Roosevelt's administration created over fifty wildlife refuges after establishing the National Wildlife Refuge System in 1907 and enthusiastically endorsed predator control programs to protect game animals (Borland 1975; Regelin 1991).

On the federal level, officials continued through the 1930s to create laws curtailing the ongoing decimation of game populations in the country. State governments, in many cases, followed the lead of the federal government by initiating bag limits and harvest restrictions of their own. These policies resulted in the widespread protection of, primarily, large game animals, such as deer and elk. Game officials reduced harvest levels, stymied poaching activity and fortified government-sponsored predator eradication programs.

The consequence of these protective policies was profound. "Ungulate populations erupted as a result of overprotection, overused their ranges, and subsequently crashed," while other game populations, "remained very low despite reductions in hunting and predation" (Regelin 1991:56). One of the most famous examples of this imbalance was in the Kaibab National Forest in Arizona where deer protected from hunters and natural predators starved by the thousands in the early 1920s (Borland 1975; Flader 1974).

When game conservationists, such as Aldo Leopold, noted the imbalance that these programs, coupled with the preceding overexploitation, had created efforts were redirected toward a more active management strategy, as opposed to simply protecting them. According to Flader (1974), Leopold urged the cause of science in the practice of managing wildlife in the early 1900s. "The new science, he believed, should be developed by foresters to make game a major forest product, just as foresters had developed the science of timber and range management" (Flader 1974:66). Gradually, "game" became "wildlife" and wildlife management became professional, as well as scientific (Flader 1974).

The *Era of Scientific Wildlife Management and Conservation* began around 1935 with the newly formulated American Game Policy of 1930. This policy was drafted by the American Game Protection Association, with Aldo Leopold as chair of the committee (Peek 1986:13). This policy recommendation, quoted in Regelin (1991:57), stated that wildlife agencies and managers must:

1. Train (people) for skillful game administration, management, and fact-finding, and make game management a profession.
2. Recognize the non-shooting protectionist and the scientist as sharing with the sportsman and landowners the responsibility for wildlife conservation and to insist on a joint conservation program, jointly formulated and jointly financed.
3. Provide funds, with public funds from general taxation to better wildlife as a whole, with sportsmen paying for all betterment serving game alone, and with private funds to help carry costs of education and research.
4. Remove state conservation agencies from the political process.

The effects of the application of these principles varied, but wildlife managers continue to be guided by them today in the United States.

An important effect of the American Game Policy was the professionalization of wildlife management. Leopold published the first textbook in the field, titled *Game Management*, in 1933. Subsequently, a number of academic programs to teach wildlife biology and management were established in universities throughout the United States (Regelin 1991:57). According to The Wildlife Society, today there are at least fifty universities in the U.S. offering named degrees in wildlife and another forty or so offering degrees in associated fields, such as forestry, range sciences or natural resources (The Wildlife Society 1996).

Another outcome of the implementation of these principles was the restoration of many game species that had nearly gone extinct prior to the advent of formal game management practices. Wildlife restoration and reintroduction programs have successfully reestablished viable populations of game species such as river otter, wild turkey, beaver and whitetail deer on their original ranges. Indeed, many of these species have gone from being rare to becoming nuisance species to people and management agencies. Whitetail deer, for example, are more numerous today than ever before in North American history, providing game for roughly ten million American hunters who harvest in excess of three million deer per year (Regelin 1991).

To continue restoration efforts, the 1937 Pittman-Robertson Federal Aid in Wildlife Restoration Act imposed an eleven percent excise tax on arms and ammunition sales. This tax had the support of recreational sportsmen. The U.S. Congress later added a ten percent excise tax to the sale of handguns. These taxes provided funding to state conservation agencies for habitat acquisition, population assessments and wildlife research (Regelin 1991:57). Since its inception, this law has collected in excess of one billion dollars (NRAcentral. com 2004:3).

Game Management in the United States

All the citizens of a state own wildlife in the United States until the animal is legally harvested, at which time it becomes the property of the hunter. Regulatory control over wildlife resources is vested in the state and federal governments almost exclusively. Individual states manage wildlife within their boundaries and, often, share management responsibilities with the federal government. Local governments can only affect hunting activities by restricting the use of firearms in specified areas.

States sell licenses to individual hunters, a practice Neuzil and Kovarik (1996) describe as "peculiarly American." Most states, at least forty-five, organize their fish and game conservation agencies according to the Model Game and Fish Administrative Policy (1930) (Regelin 1991). Generally, state agencies responsible for game management rely on an appointed board or commission to set seasons and harvest limits each year. Modern wildlife agencies almost always have professional wildlife biologists on staff. These scientists collect and analyze data, and are responsible for making recommendations to the board about wildlife regulation.

Frequently, state boards or commissions will actively solicit public input on proposed regulations, although participation may vary widely. In states where hunting is an important industry, state wildlife officials will regularly consult with wildlife interest groups and organizations. The primary management tools used by game managers are the establishment of harvest seasons, in terms of when the harvest will occur and how long hunters will have to hunt, as well as the setting of bag limits (meaning the number of animals that can be killed per day and/or per season) and the creation of guidelines for hunter licensing.

Although most authority for game management rests with the state, federal authorities have control in particular instances. For example, international treaties, such as the Migratory Bird Conservation Act of 1929, govern the hunting of a variety of animals, from birds to whales. Thus, the federal government takes responsibility for setting the overarching guidelines for state agencies that manage waterfowl and other migratory species. Also, there are a number of species in the United States that are presently protected because they are threatened or endangered. Species listed under the Endangered Species Act of 1973 are safeguarded from any form of "take," which includes harvest, although such protection could also be afforded by the state.

Finally, the federal government often imposes special restrictions on federal lands held in the public trust, which accounts for roughly thirty percent of the land surface within the United States. Most of this property is managed by either the Department of Interior or Agriculture. Within these departments, the U.S. Forest Service and Bureau of Land Management supervise lands following multiple use principles; this means that they allow commercial activities, consumptive recreation (including hunting and trapping) and non-consumptive recreation. The U.S. Forest Service and U.S. Fish and Wildlife Service dedicate portions of their holdings to the enhancement of wildlife populations. While the federal government allows hunting on most federal lands, hunting is prohibited within those areas designated National Parks.

The owners of private property can deny access to their land and bar hunting activities through trespass laws or they can permit uncompensated or fee access to their land. In the latter case, however, state and federal wildlife laws still apply. Hunting clubs, especially near cities, are becoming more popular in the United States. Typically, members of a hunting club will lease private lands on which they can hunt. Again, however, hunters taking advantage of such arrangements must comply with state and federal regulations.

Currently, many state governments require hunters to attend education classes before issuance of a first hunting license. These courses typically cover ethics, safety, and hunting regulations, along with the rudiments of game management and firearms ballistics. Further, some states have laws that require gun owners to take a formal course on gun safety prior to the licensing of a firearm, including weapons used in hunting. However, the overall time commitment for either type of course is minimal; a typical class requires only five to ten hours of participation. Unlike the rigorous qualifying activities of the Germanic system, in the United States mere attendance qualifies the participant for a hunting license.

American hunters purchase licenses in the state wherein they intend to hunt. Resident and non-resident licenses vary in cost; typically, an out-of-state hunter will pay much more for the privilege of hunting than will a resident. Additional "tags" are often purchased to hunt specific species or sexes of animals.

The American hunter is largely a solitary pursuer of game animals. Aside from the purchase of a hunting license, American hunters seldom work with professional wildlife managers. In many cases they do not even interact with each other. Often a hunter interacts only with the licensor, although licenses might be obtained via the Internet or mail, and the state officials operating post-harvest, wildlife check stations. At a check station a state official inspects and registers any animals killed by the hunter. Once a game animal is legally harvested it becomes the property of the hunter and is utilized as she or he sees fit, with the caveat that the commercial transfer of meat or products is unlawful.

History, Culture and Game Management

The Germanic game management system works in Germany because Europe has been long civilized and people came to view ideal nature as a pastoral landscape. There are few, if any, landscapes that are unaltered by people. Europeans worked industriously over the centuries to erase wilderness and replace it with a manicured, agricultural environment. Animal and plant species that were viewed as unnecessary, from a human perspective, were driven to extinction either intentionally or as an unintended consequence of progress. Only those species of value to people were protected and managed so that they might flourish.

Leopold, the architect of American conservation science and practice, toured Germany in 1935 for several months. During this trip he interviewed practitioners of forestry and game management. His conclusions about the Germanic game management system were summarized in a series of articles (Leopold 1936a, 1936b, 1936c, 1936d, 1936e). Leopold disliked Germanic management strategies because, in his view, the Germans over-managed the environment; they eradicated any element of "wildness" or "wilderness." They meticulously cultivated artificial habitats where game animals were not truly wild, meaning that they did not thrive by their own devices. Managers sculpted the structure of game herds and the environment to produce sport for people. Today foresters continue to ensure that game animals meet the standards of their customers through the use of culls and by undertaking feeding programs in the wintertime (Meine 1988:353–360).

The experience in the United States was somewhat different. Immigrants to the New World fled England and the political tyranny of the monarchy, which clung to a feudal system of political organization throughout the nineteenth century. Wildlife was established as a common resource and was exploited as such. Although wildlife was aggressively pursued to extirpation and extinction early in American history, a handful of people did work to place value on wildlife and, more significantly, wildlands (Wilcove 1999).

Views about what the human relationship to nature should be

became varied across culture. Granfield and Colomy (this volume) explain that some people began to identify hunting with adventure, manly strength and the American spirit. Such sentiments, however, were largely a characteristic of the political and economic elite. Scientists, naturalists and even some natural resource managers began to see the landscape from an ecological perspective, that is, they recognized that neither open hunting nor strict protection of game would be sufficient for maintaining future interests in game animals. More often the simplistic, one-species game management regimes gave way to more systemic, if not ecologically-enlightened planning. The management system eventually established by government agencies, which remains in place today, achieves this balance through the regulation of hunting, along with the manipulation of animals and habitat as dictated by science.

How the Germanic and American managerial systems have evolved is a product of and, in turn, has produced particular human perceptions about nature, hunting and game. In contrasting the two historical-political contexts of game management in Germanic countries versus the United States, the most important distinction is that in Europe the middle classes wrested exclusive hunting rights from the upper classes. When this occurred, the government redistributed access to game to all persons of property or those who had the means to lease property. In the United States, the opposite occurred. Elite sportsmen, government and scientists rescued game from the unsupervised predations of lower class market hunters. They enlisted the help of national and state regulators to set aside habitat and manage harvests.

Germanic hunting traditions exhibit continuity from their origins more than a millennium past. It is a highly managed and cultivated experience. The Germanic hunter is prepared and knowledgeable. However, this hunter does not seek a wilderness adventure of overcoming great physical odds to be close with and subdue the game species, which is a central goal of the American hunter. The Germanic hunter seeks, and has always sought, the "sure thing," meaning a predictable and controllable outcome. The hunter harvests a specific animal or specific types and sizes of animals that are often identified by the forester or leaders of group hunts.

The modern, Germanic hunter is a product of the system wherein he or she is socialized. The Germanic system creates a situation where hunters are, for the most part, self-directing, self-policing and

self-financing. The forester nurtures game stocks with careful population controls, maximizing numbers while monitoring habitat impacts.
He or she protects, enhances and conserves habitat of game animals
expressly to meet the interests of agricultural operators and hunters.

The act of harvesting an animal in this tradition will necessarily
comply with the game harvest plan of the hunting community who
manages the hunting grounds. There are no denotations or connotations of rugged individualism manifested in the hunting or harvesting acts. This is because the hunting tradition emerged from a
social context where people valued an orderly and well-managed
nature. Germans are taught that hunting is a privilege available to
those who carefully prepare themselves by study to assume the responsibilities of wildlife management.

Americans, on the other hand, are taught that hunting is a personal right, as opposed to a privilege that is earned. Regulation is
viewed as prohibitive to the individual, but necessary so that future
generations might have the ability to exercise their right to hunt.
They hunt for personal reasons, such as for meat, the thrill of the
chase or to test their wit against a prey animal (Miller, this volume).

This arrangement, however, limits the personal investment and
involvement of American hunters in wildlife management. The management of the habitat and game are the responsibility of government officials or, in the case of habitat, the owners of private property.
The hunter has only a nominal role in the management system, and
he or she is not obliged to be aware of or understand this role.
Hunters are only responsible for culling game populations annually,
while government managers and biologists are responsible for all
other management decisions and activities. American hunters undertake no management obligations that are comparable to their
Germanic-European counterparts, such as harvest of particular types
of animals or financial reimbursement for damage caused to agricultural operators. They consume the results of game management,
yet contribute little sweat equity to the system.

Germanic countries and the United States experienced different
social, cultural, economic and political circumstances throughout history. Consequently, people defined their relationship to game and
nature differently in Germanic areas as opposed to the budding
nation in North America. The formation of wildlife management in
a society is tied to the how people have perceived wild animals and
their own natural surroundings over time. More importantly, this

comparative study highlights the fact that these perceptions are ever-changing and subject to transformation with changes in economy, polity and culture.

Conclusion and Implications

Comparative studies across cultures are interesting from a theoretical standpoint because they highlight the fact that perceptions of nature are relative and, as evidenced in this chapter, influenced by history and culture. In other words, what we viewed as an acceptable hunting practice in 1893, like killing hundreds of birds in one outing, and what we perceived as an acceptable management strategy in 1924, namely eliminating hunting and predators from a game preserve, are not consistent with present-day values and perceptions. Similarly, what is acceptable hunting etiquette in Germany, such as taking the weak-est or oldest deer, is culturally unacceptable to the American hunter.

This chapter also highlights the fact that there are multiple sys-tems in place that regulate human interactions with wildlife. Each of these systems, the Germanic and American, emphasize certain culturally important ideas about nature and wild animals. The Germanic system focuses on the importance of game production. The reviers are managed exclusively to maximize the experience of hunters who pay, personally, for the privilege. The American sys-tem, on the other hand, has burgeoned into a broader framework that envelops the explicit regulation and management of non-game species as well. From a social constructionist perspective, neither sys-tem is inherently right or wrong, good or bad. Instead, they are each a reflection of the social context wherein they developed and matured. They are the manifestation of different cultural values, pref-erences and experiences regarding wildlife.

The overarching conclusion from this chapter is that context, whether temporally, culturally or spatially, is a critical component when attempting to understand how people understand and relate to wildlife and nature. Conflict over wildlife and management poli-cies will undoubtedly be rooted in the differences among groups of people that stem from the context wherein their perceptions, values and beliefs were formed or changed. Thus, recognizing the impor-tance of context is a precursor to understanding and resolving conflict among those whose belief-systems clash over wildlife.

References

Borland, Hal. 1975. *The History of American Wildlife*. Washington, D.C.: National Wildlife Federation.

Dunlap, Thomas R. 1988. *Saving America's Wildlife: Ecology and the American Mind, 1850–1990*. Princeton: Princeton University.

F.A.C.E. 1995. *Handbook of Hunting in Europe*, Vol. II, VIII/1–2. Federation of Fieldsports Associations of the European Union. Brussels, Belgium: European Commission.

Flader, Susan L. 1974. *Thinking Like a Mountain: Aldo Leopold and the Evolution of an Ecological Attitude toward Deer, Wolves and Forests*. Lincoln: University of Nebraska.

Gottschalk, John S. 1972. "The German Hunting System, West Germany, 1968." *Journal of Wildlife Management* 36:110–118.

Granfield, Robert and Paul Colomy. [this volume]. "Paradise Lost: The Transformation of Wildlife Law in the Vanishing Wilderness." In *Mad About Wildlife: Looking at Social Conflict Over Wildlife*, edited by A. Herda-Rapp and T. Goedeke. Leiden, Netherlands: Brill Academic Publishers.

Hunting Committee. 1989. *Der Jungjaeger: A Handbook for the Young Hunter in Germany*. [unpaginated] U.S. Armed Forces: Heidelberg Rod and Gun Club.

Leopold, Aldo. 1936a. "Naturschutz in Germany." *Bird-Lore* 3:102–111.

———. 1936b. "Deer and Dauerwald in Germany: I. History." *Journal of Forestry* 34:366–75.

———. 1936c. "Deer and Dauerwald in Germany: II. Ecology and Policy." *Journal of Forestry* 34:460–66.

———. 1936d. "Farm Game Management in Silesia." *American Wildlife* 25:67–68, 74–76.

———. 1936e. "Notes on Game Administration in Germany." *American Wildlife* 25:85, 92–93.

Meine, Kurt. 1988. *Aldo Leopold, His Life and Work*. Madison: University of Wisconsin.

Miller, Carol. [this volume]. "Virtual Deer: Bagging the Mythical 'Big One' in Cyberspace." In *Mad About Wildlife: Looking at Social Conflict Over Wildlife*, edited by A. Herda-Rapp and T. Goedeke. Leiden, Netherlands: Brill Academic Publishers.

Moses, David. 2001. "Restriction without Prohibition: Shooting, Hunting and Gun Ownership in Germany." *Gunshop.com*. Retrieved June 30, 2004 (http://www.gun-shop.com/moses1.htm).

Munsche, P.B. 1981. *Gentlemen and Poachers: English Game Laws 1671–1831*. Cambridge: Cambridge University.

Neuzil, Mark and William Kovarik. 1996. *Mass Media and Environmental Conflict: America's Green Causes*. Thousand Oaks, CA: Sage.

NRAcentral.com 2004, "Pittman-Robertson Funds." Retrieved June 19, 2004 (http://www.nracentral.com/pittman-robertson-funds.php).

Peek, James M. 1986. *A Review of Wildlife Management*. Englewood Cliffs, NJ. Prentice Hall.

Regelin, Wayne L. 1991. "Wildlife Management in Canada and the United States." Pp. 55–63 in *Global Trends in Wildlife Management Transactions of the 18th IUGB Congress (1987)*, edited by S. Bobek, K. Perzanowski, and W. Regelin. Krakow-Warszawa, Poland: Swiat.

Reiger, John F. 1986. *American Sportsmen and the Origins of Conservation*. Norman, OK: University of Oklahoma.

Tober, James A. 1981. *Who Owns the Wildlife? The Political Economy of Conservation in Nineteenth-Century America*. Westport, CT: Greenwood.

U.S. Department of Agriculture. Biological Survey. 1912. *Chronology and Index of the More Important Events in American Game Protection, 1776 to 1911*, by T.S. Palmer. Washington, DC: GPO.

Warren, Louis S. 1997. *The Hunter's Game: Poachers and Conservationists in Twentieth Century America*. New Haven: Yale University.

Wilcove, David S. 1999. *The Condor's Shadow: The Loss and Recovery of Wildlife in America*. New York: Anchor Books.

Wildlife Society, The. 1996. *Universities and Colleges Offering Curricula in Wildlife Conservation*. Bethesda, MD: The Wildlife Society.

Woodward, William V. 1989. "Lease Hunting: How It Works In Germany." Pp. 12–13 in *Peterson's 1989 Hunting Annual*, edited by C. Boddington. Los Angeles: Peterson.

Notes

[1] "Big game" is a term coined long ago by political elites who used it to designate what large wildlife they wanted reserved for their own pleasure. Big game species demonstrated various traits, such as strength, beauty, cunning or swiftness, that, when captured, conferred honor on those who harvested them. It was a prideful thing to harvest big game because it proved valor on the part of the hunter.

[2] Grand, old homes or estates found in the rural, forested areas of Europe were used extensively for sport hunting purposes. In other words, a big house in open or wooded countryside in Europe today was probably originally a hunting lodge.

PART THREE

DECONSTRUCTING AND RECONSTRUCTING
WILDLIFE POLICY APPROACHES

OF TIME, SPACE AND BIRDS: CATTLE EGRETS AND THE PLACE OF THE WILD[1]

Stella Čapek

Introduction: What Can We Learn from Cattle Egrets?

In recent years, the "animal question" has surfaced as an important theme in sociological and anthropological theory (Mullin 1999; Wolch and Emel 1998). This theme has acquired urgency as human beings encroach upon wildlife habitats and produce socially and ecologically stressful encounters with animals. In this chapter I document an incident in which a local developer in Conway, Arkansas, bulldozed a cattle egret nesting colony while constructing a road for a new suburban subdivision. As thousands of birds died and injured survivors spilled into adjacent neighborhoods, community residents, city officials and wildlife management officials found themselves in a dialogue about causes of the incident and how it could have been avoided. Among other things, they had to consider the place of "the wild" in the midst of a growing suburban community. The Conway case is useful because it helps us to imagine what kind of a design needs to be in place for socially, ecologically and ethically acceptable human-wildlife interactions in rapidly developing areas. Cattle egrets offer an interesting example because of their constant successful expansion into new habitats.

I draw on two kinds of theories which, when combined, provide a helpful context for this discussion. Theories about the social construction of nature help us to see how human beings categorize and interpret nature, including living creatures. Theories about globalization and modernity suggest that human beings are having new experiences of time and space that, I argue, have an important impact on relationships with animals. Drawing on these theories and on my case study, I focus on what we can learn about categories of *space* (changing human-animal settlement patterns), *time* (human versus animal time schedules), and the *social construction of ideas about human relationships to the wild* from the perspective of various groups responding to the incident. I then consider how this knowledge can be used to produce better designs for human-animal interactions that include understandings of "bird time" and "bird space." My goal is to take a more bird-centered view of landscapes, a perspective lacking in most sociological writing.

Local and Global Connections: A "Cosmopolitan" Bird

Cattle egrets are classified as members of the heron family, but are less dependent on an aquatic habitat than other herons. Their range is therefore much wider and they have had great success in migrating and adapting to new habitats, including urban areas (Hancock and Elliott 1978). The birds are believed to have originated in Africa, and to have flown to other continents, aided by favorable winds. Currently they are found in North and South America, Southern Europe, China, Japan, Australia, and New Zealand. Since they were first spotted in South America in 1877, they have worked their way northward, reaching North America in 1953. The first confirmed nesting site in Faulkner County, where Conway is located, was identified in 1983 (Johnson 1998). Cattle egrets are present seasonally, between March and mid-November, when they migrate to the southern United States or as far as Central and South America for the winter.

Cattle egrets are attracted to the rural landscape around Conway for the same reasons that they have settled in pastureland environments worldwide. They appear to have evolved a "commensal" relationship with a variety of grazing animals who stir up bugs for the birds to eat. In many parts of the world cattle egrets can be seen walking alongside or even perching on much larger animals, such as cattle. Researchers characterize them as a cosmopolitan bird and an "astonishing avian success story" (Line 1995:54) with an "explosive" and "spectacular" spread over the globe (Meyerriecks 1960). Les Line (1995:48), who has observed cattle egrets on four continents, explains:

> In Cuba, cattle egrets throng behind workers cutting sugarcane, gleaning insects from the slashed fields. Bulldozers are surrogate cows at New Jersey garbage dumps, while in Florida the birds dash onto highways to snatch bugs knocked down by tourists' cars, a dangerous and sometimes fatal form of foraging . . . In New Zealand, the herons raid silos for barley, peas and hay . . . One bird collected in Saudi Arabia had gobbled 68 ticks that dropped from camels sleeping at an oasis.

I myself witnessed cattle egrets at an airport in Ecuador following mowing machines and in the Galapagos Islands eating insects swarming near the resting bodies of sea lions.

Although cattle egrets have successfully introduced themselves into these new habitats, their diffusion patterns are inseparably linked to human alterations of landscapes. They are also increasingly likely to have encounters with humans. Joanna Burger (cited in Line 1995) links their growing numbers to a major global expansion of cattle farming. Cattle farming in turn is related to the rise of meat-based diets. This is as true in South America, where large areas of tropical forests have been cut down to make way for cattle ranches (Line 1995), as in Conway, Arkansas, where local settlers filled in wetlands to create farmland.

In Conway, egrets have been attracted to a combination of human-influenced landscape features including pine plantations, farmland, the Arkansas River, and some nearby lakes, including the artificially created Lake Conway. On the other hand, as farmland in the United States is converted to housing, suburban sprawl patterns are cutting into egret habitats. For example, Faulkner County grew by forty-three percent between 1990 and 2000, according to most recent census figures. The suburban sprawl pattern emerging there puts the birds on a crash course with human expansion.

For this reason, cattle egrets are increasingly perceived by some as a nuisance species. Due to their dense nesting pattern, they favor places like pine plantations in Conway where trees grow close together and where they can build many nests per tree. Typically they fly out in the morning to forage and return to roost in the evening. The inside world of an egret rookery is full of feathers, noise and intensely acrid odors, particularly in the hot and humid climate of the South. Over time, the egrets' excrement will acidify the ground and kill off the vegetation in the rookery; the birds will then move on. Although the landscape recovers, conflict with close human neighbors can be more of a problem, both for the birds and for the people.

Research Methods

In this chapter, I discuss some of the social constructions of cattle egrets and of the Conway incident from the perspective of various

groups in the community. Examining these constructions provides
insight into community conflict over wildlife issues and permits us
to consider some better solutions. To examine this conflict, I gathered data using personal interviews and documentary sources. Interviews
took place between August 2000 and March 2002. Although this
project was designed to be exploratory rather than a systematic representation of the entire community, I selected interviewees who represented a range of groups and perspectives in the community. These
included neighborhood residents and outside volunteers who helped
to save the birds, wildlife rehabilitators, federal wildlife officials, elected
officials in Conway, and some members of organized groups with
an interest in the incident, such as the Faulkner County Humane
Society and the local Audubon Society.

I constructed my sample in a snowball fashion, beginning with a
few names from the newspaper or personal recommendations, and
broadening it as the project unfolded. My objective was to explore
people's value constructions in this local environmental controversy
while not losing sight of the more global story of people and birds,
so that my findings could prove useful beyond the local setting. In
total, I interviewed twenty people for this research.

The documentary sources I used included newspaper articles, letters to the editor in the Conway-based *Log Cabin Democrat* and the
Little Rock-based *Arkansas Democrat Gazette*, photographs and video
footage, correspondence and miscellaneous documents from official
sources as well as residents' files. I initially collected all articles and
letters to the editor from July through October 1998 when there
was heavy local media coverage, although I have included updates
as recent as May 2003.

Constructing Meaning: "What Do We Do with the Cattle Egrets?"

The Egret Incident

On Friday, July 24, 1998, a crew of men hired to clear land for a
developer in Conway bulldozed a large portion of a cattle egret nesting colony. The men claimed that they did not know the birds were
there. They were preparing for the third phase of a project called
the Victoria Park subdivision, located in a rapidly developing area
of the city. Close to 5,000 birds were killed or seriously injured
according to a U.S. Fish and Wildlife Service estimate. The surviv-

ing birds wandered dazed through surrounding neighborhoods, seeking water and shelter from the heat. Videotapes and newspaper photographs showed images of birds inundating local streets and yards, struggling to survive. Some of the birds huddled around air conditioner condensers, and mothers tried to shelter their chicks. Passing cars killed some of the egrets, and curious onlookers aggravated the problem.

Some residents organized efforts to try to save the birds, working with a local wildlife rehabilitator and a veterinarian who volunteered their time and facilities. Others saw the cattle egrets purely as a nuisance or a health hazard, and wanted the city to remove them. Conway's elected officials found themselves face to face with some ugly consequences of rapid development and economic growth, and hoped that the incident would blow over quietly. This did not happen, as local media outlets seized upon the story. Local and regional branches of a number of organizations became involved, including the Audubon Society, the Sierra Club, and the Humane Society of the United States.

To the surprise of many residents, there were legal implications to the incident. Although egrets are not an endangered species, their nests and eggs are protected by the federal Migratory Bird Treaty Act, an international document dating back to 1916.[2] Under pressure from a variety of citizen complaints both from individuals and groups, the U.S. Fish and Wildlife Service and the Arkansas Game and Fish Commission conducted an investigation. Two developers were tried in federal court and assessed the maximum financial penalty, in this case $44,000, for destruction of the cattle egret rookery and violation of the Migratory Bird Treaty Act. This locally unprecedented situation led to broad debate in the community about the right thing to do about the egrets, then and in the future.

The Role of Social Constructions and Naturework

In her novel *In Country*, Bobbie Ann Mason (1986:36) writes of a Vietnam War veteran whose only good memory of the war was the beauty of flocks of egrets in flight, a bird "just going about its business with all that crazy stuff going on around it." As sociologists Rik Scarce (2000), Valerie Kuletz (1998) and others have pointed out, human beings constantly engage in the task of symbolically constructing nature as meaningful in particular ways.

Gary Alan Fine (1998) refers to these constructions as "nature-work," a process through which individuals draw on cultural resources to attribute meaning to nature and to define their relationship to the environment. This symbolic work, Fine (1998:2) points out, begins in childhood and "transforms nature into culture, while channeling and organizing our cultural choices. Naturework involves interpretations of the wild, justified through moral purpose and ratified in emotional response." Because of this emotional and moral component, social constructions exert a strong influence on people's imaginations and behaviors.

I draw on the concept of naturework to shed light on the social constructions of cattle egrets and of human-animal relations in the Conway incident. Although meaning construction is an ongoing process, it is especially evident in situations that sociologist Edward Walsh (1981) refers to as a suddenly imposed grievance. The spillover of wild egrets into the supposedly tamed spaces of suburbia was sudden and shocking, as neighborhood resident Pam Bugh remarked:

> It traumatized them (the neighbors). They went from a neighborhood of people who had swimming pools [to people] who could not swim in their pools, because there were dead egrets every day. They were afraid of disease, they were afraid to let their children play in the area ... We were prisoners in our home. For three months straight... Some people just locked their doors, went to work, came home, locked the doors, kept their kids inside, playing Nintendo.

Jay McDaniel, religion professor and rescue volunteer, described the situation this way:

> They (the birds) were very beautiful, and very vulnerable. There was a snow of beautiful white feathers, but a feeling of blood. The *numbers*. Everywhere you look there is a vulnerable life trying to survive, and dying.

Under such conditions, the usual taken for granted rules of life are disturbed and people are actively seeking to make sense of things. They are also less likely to censor their responses, which makes social constructions more visible.

In a previous paper, I explored value constructions that emerged in response to the egret incident in more detail (Čapek 2001). Here, I summarize the main themes and provide a few illustrations. The negative view of cattle egrets focused on the following: the nuisance element of the birds' nesting patterns, including odor and noise; a view of the birds as competitors with humans for scarce space in the city; a fear that the birds carry the disease histoplasmosis;[3] a view of the birds as useless; and a view of the birds as unremarkable and aesthetically unattractive. As one resident put it, "It's just an old cowbird."[4] While some of these individuals felt sorry for the birds, they saw them as standing in the way of progress, symbolized by the construction of new housing in west Conway.

More positive constructions of the egrets defined them as aesthetically beautiful, particularly when seen in flight and visually remarkable and objects of wonder, as in the Edenic image of very small creatures coexisting with much larger ones. People also described them as innocent creatures, like children, unable to defend themselves and in need of protection.[5] They were described as being useful because they ate insects, ridding the larger creatures of parasites and balancing the ecosystem. They were valuable because of their intrinsic wildness or, simply, worthy of love and protection because they were "God's creatures."[6] A Conway resident remarked, "They were beautiful. It sort of suggests a harmony or synergistic relationship. I had it in my head that they were helpful to cattle."

There was a noticeable contrast between views of residents who organized rescue efforts and those of wildlife officials. The rescue volunteers typically focused on the individual value of each creature's life, while wildlife officials used a discourse focused on preserving the birds at a population level. As wildlife official Allan Mueller noted:

> The whole issue of wildlife rehabilitation is an interesting one, and that came up here. And this is another case where the conservation community is really split . . . it comes back to this ecosystem perspective . . . They're (wildlife rehabilitators) really seriously committed, so you can't question their motives . . . Their concern is strictly for the individual animal. 'I want to help this cattle egret.' Now, my perspective is totally different. I'm really not that interested in one cattle egret, but I'm very interested in the population level, the big picture. Cattle egrets are doing very well. So we kill 2000 cattle egrets out there. That's not a good thing, that's not something I want to happen, the man deserved a fine . . . But in terms of damaging cattle egrets, it's an undetectable difference, you wouldn't be able to measure it.

This population-level approach contrasted with the experiences of those residents—both adults and children—who directly interacted with the cattle egrets as volunteers in the rescue efforts. Their naturework involved maintaining a delicate balance between affirming empathy for the birds as individual suffering creatures and having to take an emergency "triage" approach due to sheer numbers. Against their inclinations, rescuers were forced to concentrate their attention on helping only the most likely survivors. As volunteer Jay McDaniel observed, "The 'eachness' mattered. But to have to blatantly decide that whole masses can't be protected, when each one wants to live no less than you . . . it takes a kind of courageous defiance."

This was difficult and often personally transformative work. McDaniel, for example, came to see the egrets as "an icon or a spiritual lesson in impermanence." As volunteers, he and his children confronted the "beauty, horror, and futility" of the situation by learning to accept their limited efficacy even as they participated in individual ethical actions to reduce suffering. Like the wildlife officials, they knew they could not save every bird. Unlike the wildlife officials, however, they wanted to affirm the value of individual lives. Both groups saw themselves as ethical actors, but their discourse and naturework separated them from each other.

In line with what Fine suggests about naturework, people were not only constructing birds in a particular way, but also views of themselves, other human beings, and human-animal relationships more generally. The naturework done to construct the cattle egrets was almost always embedded in guilt/innocence narratives about humans, and these constructions carried a high emotional charge. Looking at some examples of these constructions can help us see some of the fault lines in the community, not only between human beings and the wild, but between (and sometimes within) human beings. These examples in turn have a relationship to people's ideas about possible solutions, since, as Fine (1998:2) points out, naturework performs the task of "channeling and organizing our cultural choices."

A useful illustration of guilt/innocence narratives was the community's response to the actions of Hal Crafton, a wealthy local developer who was fined in the egret incident. Accustomed to being a respected, major player in the community, he became a kind of villain to a significant number of residents after being linked to vivid images of wounded and dying birds. In statements to the *Log Cabin Democrat*, Crafton presented himself as naïve, innocent and a person with the community's interests at heart. He told a reporter:

We just thought there were some white birds flying around like you normally see in a cow pasture. We didn't have any idea there were that many birds there. We didn't have any idea what we were getting into (Meisel 1998).

He pleaded guilty in court, but insisted that his actions were inadvertent.

Crafton's critics were skeptical about his claims, and indeed, there is evidence to support that view (see below). Many who were most critical of Crafton and sympathetic toward the birds had become critics of growth and development in Conway. They saw the cattle egrets as innocent victims not only of this one dramatic incident, but of a larger pattern of environmental destruction in west Conway that benefited wealthy homeowners and greedy developers.[7] Conway resident Warfield Teague put it this way: "The old families get rich. They ran roughshod over the birds, not just people this time." He went on to remark that what sells people on west Conway is "pure snobbery." He noted that while there were typically three-car garages, there were "no baseball fields, no soccer fields, no community space at Centennial Valley."

The Centennial Valley development, which contains the Victoria Park subdivision, is built around a golf course and country club, and faces inward, with all of the trappings of a gated community. Teague's moral critique saw the birds as victims of a larger process that produces a lifestyle that not only separates humans from nature, but the wealthy and privileged from the poor. Many shared this view, as expressed in a letter to the editor:

> Once again the shortsighted greed of mankind has left me dumbfounded . . . These birds were "protected"? What would have happened to them if they were not "protected"? Do we really need another golf course? Will this developer decide to call his community Egret Estates and his golf course Hatchling Hill? . . . Will we ever evolve into a resource-preserving, care-taking species so that the Earth might stand a chance of sustaining life into the 21st century? (Fletcher 1998).

Another resident asked, "Are we tearing down fields just to show off our wealth? I hope not" (Amoakohene 1998).

Naturework here is permeated with judgments about human lifestyles and their implications for human-animal relationships. Constructions of cattle egrets are also ethical critiques of human behavior. This helps to explain the social tensions around wildlife issues in the community. As Ron Parker, a federal wildlife enforcement official, noted:

The birds aren't really the issue here. It's the expansion of Conway. They're pissed about it, and this brings all their emotions to a head, and then they use the birds to actually vent a lot of hostility and their feelings. Which I understand fully. I mean, I go around and look at places and I go, "God, what are we doing?" But—that's America. And that's how things are right now. It's progress, it's good for the economy, it's a lot of other things. I don't necessarily *agree* with everything *about* that, but there again, I'm part of this expansion. I am. And I don't *feel* bad about it. There's plenty of habitat for these birds and other birds. And again, there will be new habitat created [even though] it may not be just like the old habitat.

Parker's version of naturework rejects the idea that any of us are innocent when it comes to ecological damage. At the same time, it invokes progress and American lifeways to deflect critiques of suburban growth patterns, which his lifestyle supports. This reading of the situation permits what I will refer to later as "maps of innocence" to flourish. These maps are seductive because one is following the usual script or doing what is considered normal and right as part of the American Dream of homeownership. In Parker's case, this view also rests on the conviction that cattle egrets are in no danger at the population level.

Community supporters of Hal Crafton tended to affirm this American Dream of constant human expansion into the landscape, which depends on an aesthetic of separation from "wild" nature. City officials and many residents did not see themselves as bad actors whose city policies or lifestyles endangered the birds. They were likely to see the egret incident as exaggerated and overplayed by the media and other interested parties. They also saw the birds as secondary to the issue of progress and economic development. The birds' insignificance helped to make them truly invisible—egrets were killed in the road while huddling around puddles of water or trying to cross the street when passing cars did not slow down.

They were also morally invisible as creatures with rights in the community. The fact that some people perceived them as dangerous added to this moral separation. Roby Hayes of Conway Animal Control told the *Log Cabin Democrat*, "They basically want us to get rid of them . . . But it's not that easy. They're not going to go away, this is their habitat . . . A lot of people want to shoot the birds and we're telling them not to do that" (Bennett 1998).

We can see in the Conway case that the cultural experience and meaning-systems of individuals and groups in the community strongly influenced their perceptions of cattle egrets and of other people. We can understand these social constructions of guilt and innocence even better if we locate them in a broader cultural context. In the next section, I do this by drawing on some sociological theories about contemporary human experience and exploring their implications for human-animal relationships.

New Experiences of Time and Space

Literatures on globalization and modernity, particularly the work of theorists such as Anthony Giddens (1990) and George Ritzer (1999), point to a relatively recent shift in our experiences of time and space. Giddens (1990:14) points out that the social systems that we invent "bind time and space." In other words, our cultural beliefs and social experience cause our expectations of time and space to fall into certain patterns. While this is true of every society, Giddens claims that a modern, globalized society "connects presence and absence" in a novel way. For example, although we all live in local places, a global economy and electronic communication networks pull us into relationships with people that are geographically remote from us.

At the same time we often know less about what is immediately around us, including nature. Giddens argues that modern technologies and global processes "disembed" us from local environments.[8] The technologies that we create, such as air-conditioning, cars, and computers often separate us from the outdoors and from direct, on-the-spot interactions with others. We thus are present and absent in space in new ways that are likely to have an impact on how we see nature.

According to theorists like Giddens and Ritzer, both modernity and capitalism are major forces shaping our experience. As a profit-oriented system that makes money by turning things into items that can be sold, capitalism can both destroy and create connections between people, nature, community and local natural environments. Its global expansion depends on finding new ways to turn things into saleable commodities, including land and nature. In the process, it breaks down familiar boundaries of time and space. Ritzer (1999) gives the example of 24-hour home shopping networks, where times and spaces that used to be separate now collapse or "implode" into one another. Implosions affect the economics of building construction, as we will see in the Conway case.

Capitalism is also a fast-moving, highly competitive structure. Allan Schnaiberg (1980) has likened this process to a kind of treadmill of production and consumption that moves faster and faster as consumers compete with one another to have the latest goods, while producers try to elbow their competitors aside. The pace of life speeds up in general, and capitalism constantly generates new commodities like housing and consumer items that fill up space and keep people busy in new ways (Schnaiberg 1980). Even though human beings are the ones playing the game, as Redclift and Benton (1994) point out, the process pulls in animals, physical objects and spatial surroundings.

Against this backdrop, urban and suburban developments come to be a kind of "borderland" where human-animal interactions take place in an uneasy way, since the time/space configurations of suburbia are built around an exclusion of the wild (Michel 1998; Wolch, Pincetl and Pulido 2001). What happens to nature, to people's social constructions of nature and themselves, and especially, to the category of the wild under these new conditions of time and space?

Of Time and Birds

What can cattle egrets teach us about time? "Rhythmicity," writes Barbara Adam (1994:95), "forms nature's silent pulse." Adam is among those who have written about how human time ("artefactual" time) has come to be out of step with "organic" time. Some of our inventions, such as nuclear power and certain toxic chemicals, for example, have impacts on the environment that extend long into a future whose time-scale we cannot possibly comprehend. Commodified time, as in Schnaiberg's treadmill (1980), speeds everything up and does not give us the time to comprehend things around us, or their relationships to us and to each other. As Adam (1994:101) points out, "in societies with commodified time, speed becomes an economic value: the faster goods move through the economy the better."

In contrast, David Orr (2001) writes of more ecologically beneficial slow "flows" of time, resources, and money that linger in and enrich local communities, as in the Amish tradition. At an international level, as societies are drawn into the global economic system their time scale shifts accordingly. This produces new types of landscapes. The cutting down of trees for agricultural land, for example, so that "cash crops" can be grown quickly for an international market. Egrets fly across these transformed landscapes and are both drawn to and imperiled by the new configurations.

A certain notion of time superimposed on the particular local landscape of west Conway set the conditions for the egret disaster. A theme that surfaced frequently in letters to the local newspaper was that the tragedy was easily preventable. Cattle egrets nest for a specified period, and anyone who has knowledge of this natural cycle can predict when the nesting will be over. In fact, had the bulldozing of the pine grove been delayed for one month, there would have been only abandoned nests in the rookery and the birds would not have been killed. In other words, taking the time to understand bird time, including cycles of migration, could have led to a very different outcome.

The federal Migratory Bird Treaty Act (MBTA) was originally created in the early part of the twentieth century to deal with precisely this kind of problem. Certain bird populations, such as egrets, were being hunted for their plumage. Because there was such a large demand for feathers in the women's fashion industry, and because the plumage is especially colorful during the breeding season, bird populations were being decimated. Ignorance about the migratory and reproductive cycles of the birds did great damage since killing birds as they were nesting did not permit the population to replenish itself.

While it contained loopholes, the MBTA successfully called attention to the need for human beings to know about natural cycles such as bird migration and breeding patterns, and injected a vision of ecosystem balance into the public dialogue. At least at some level it encouraged people to be on bird time. Interestingly, this was only possible because local knowledge was connected across international borders (the U.S. and Canada, for example), so that the migration trajectories became clear. This serves as a reminder that ultimately the kinds of maps we need to produce must include global ecosystems.

In Conway, very few people gave much thought to cattle egrets prior to July 1998. The sociology of visibility and invisibility points to the conclusion that we learn to "see" those things that have some kind of value for us. Developer Hal Crafton, in a statement to the *Log Cabin Democrat*, claimed that he did not know about the birds in advance: "Honestly, everything I know about a cattle egret, I've learned in the past few days" (Gaughan 1998). While quite a few readers were skeptical about this statement, what was indisputable was that the birds were not important enough to be on Crafton's mental map. As resident Debbie Gaj commented:

> What I felt was absolute outrage that they would purposely destroy them without finding anything out about them. "Oh, that's just an old cowbird" ... And maybe he (Crafton) really didn't know—but he should have taken the time to find out ... I think they knew it, but I think they didn't think about it. "Oh, the birds will just fly off, it's okay." They didn't bother to find out that these were migratory birds.

A major reason for the birds' invisibility was the commodified time that governs the financing and construction of suburban sub-divisions. The developers could not afford to put off construction, so they literally could not afford to see the birds because of the accumulation of interest/debt on the money that they borrowed to finance the construction. The production of large amounts of standardized housing units, or what Ritzer (1999) would call the McDonaldization of production, is built on an enormous structure of debt. Thus, there is an implosion of past and future time, in which the present time is permeated by the notion of debt in an imagined future. This means, simply, that the clock is ticking on loans that must be paid off by the developer. U.S. Fish and Wildlife official Allan Mueller connected this to the egret incident:

> This was, from what I understood, pretty egregious. These people knew what they were doing, and they also knew they weren't supposed to do it. Now, whether they knew it was the Migratory Bird Treaty Act and all the details of it, *they knew this wasn't the right way to behave*, and they decided the development schedule was important enough that they had to go ahead and do it anyway.

The homeowners living next to the rookery were themselves caught up in a pattern of commodified time that kept them busy going to work or maintaining daily schedules that did not leave time for noticing cattle egrets or even being very familiar with their natural environment. Allan Mueller remarked:

> You listen to what people say about the birds and it's things like, "Yeah, I knew there were some birds over there ... Yeah, I knew there was something over there, but I never realized what was going on." And I'm thinking, "You had 8,000 pairs of birds nesting a half mile from your house, and you didn't know anything about it." It *really* gives you a perspective on what people are paying attention to.

Time speeded up is linked to commodified space, including the American Dream of suburban homeownership. These social structures helped to produce the situation described above. They also present it as normal even as ecosystems are fragmented and human beings know less and less about their relationship to those ecosystems. Many people in Conway literally did not have time for the egrets and the birds did not count as creatures to whom one should extend compassion, or about whom one needs to have knowledge. Letters of protest written to the *Log Cabin Democrat* and observations by wildlife officials suggest that the pro-growth climate in Conway and the timeframe in which it was embedded functioned as a direct incentive for killing birds and for the destruction of the egret rookery in 1998.

Of Space and Birds

Long before human beings knew how to fly up into the sky or to circumnavigate the globe, they observed that birds performed these spatial feats with ease. Birds were often honored in myths and stories for this power to connect earth and sky in their trajectories, and they were constructed as wise beings, tricksters and teachers for human beings. In a society that took the technological knowledge of the mechanics of flying from birds, but devalued nature at the same time, what do birds—in this case cattle egrets—have to teach us about space?

One way to pose this question is to push our imaginations to ask, What would a birds-eye view of Conway and its surroundings teach humans that they cannot see on the ground? First, they would see from above the land in terms of habitat—not for human settlement, but for the needs of birds. This land would look quite different. It would be mapped in terms of trees and water, fields with cattle and other natural features. Space as bird habitat would be at the center of the experience. This is in contrast to how many human beings see bird habitat, particularly those with power to "develop" land. For them, the uncommodified landscape yields an image of empty space that does not yet have value (Davies 2000; Giddens 1990; Kuletz 1998; Wolch 1998). This cultural practice of thinking of space as empty is associated not only with capitalist economies but with colonialism and an imposed hierarchy of values that renders indigenous inhabitants, for example, invisible.

Secondly, a birds-eye view would show a larger pattern of landscape that the individual developer, homeowner or renter could not
or does not want to see from the ground. Mapped over time, in
Conway and elsewhere, this kind of spatial view would reveal expansion of suburbs and a steady destruction of wildlife habitat. It would
also make more visible the ecological footprint that humans and their
constructions leave on the environment.[9] Of course, humans can
make these kinds of maps from the ground if they are paying attention to ecological interrelatedness and developing the appropriate
tools to study it.[10] However, in pro-growth cities like Conway, and
in most cities in the U.S., this does not happen. In Arkansas, for
example there is no provision requiring environmental impact studies for new development.

The cultural habit of seeing land as empty or of looking for nature
only in parks rather than in the city or in one's backyard, produces
specific ecological consequences. As Wolch and Emel (1998) note in
their book *Animal Geographies*, economic development is frequently
synonymous with habitat loss. This means not only the destruction
and endangerment of many animal species, but also the overflow of
wild creatures into spaces that have been appropriated by humans.

Wolch et al. (2001:397) point out that just as we learn to "denat-
uralize" private property, or to see it as empty of nature, we "nat-
uralize" processes like urbanization and suburbanization by seeing
them as natural processes that should not be questioned. Both of
these ideas are social constructions that go hand in hand with capitalist production and have a vast impact on how we see wildlife.
Wolch and Emel (1998:xiv) remind us that "space is never simply a
stage for human action, and never 'innocent' in terms of its role in
shaping human affairs." In other words, space is never just a neutral container or backdrop; it is shaped by the hierarchical power
of certain groups and their social constructions. From an ecological
perspective, each space is already full of many lives, and not at all
empty. To map it as empty is at best a naïve and rather innocent
cultural construction.

Yet these "innocent maps" are precisely what are pitched to
prospective homeowners who dream of filling up bits of empty space
with creations that signal their social identity. This identity is embodied in the form of a house and an artificially constructed, de-natured
and re-natured landscape defined as their private accomplishment.
The bulldozer converts land into a stripped down, flattened patch

of dirt that is then packaged and sold to homeowners as a space that belongs entirely to them. In effect, nature is erased and returns only in the form of a tamed, suburban-style landscaping aesthetic.

Among other things, wildness is excluded from this space whose boundaries are assumed to be firmly in place. "Wildlife" is assumed to be appropriately located elsewhere, and wildlife management policies are seen as applicable only to the "nature" that is outside of these spaces. Any scenario that challenges these beliefs is likely to mobilize intense emotions. Challenging these constructions is likely to be the key, however, to designing solutions that work for both human beings and wildlife as their habitats converge.

On the hot, humid July morning in 1998 when hundreds of wounded cattle egrets began spilling into a suburban neighborhood, the innocent dream of homeowners who saw themselves as creatively filling empty space clashed with the image of innocent creatures (birds) who were victims of construction and development. When the egrets arrived in such large numbers, they disturbed the cultural habits and fragmented maps of suburban homeowners, developers and city officials. Their arrival and bodily presence implicated human beings in the destruction and death of vulnerable creatures.

In response, some of Conway's residents began to raise specifically ethical questions about the rights of nature and animals to exist free of human interference (Bell 1998). Although migratory birds are not endangered, the broader question is whether wild creatures have a right to carry on their lives undisturbed. As resident Debbie Gaj remarked, "My father always taught us that you leave wild things alone." But how can wild creatures be left alone as humans move into their spaces? And how can the needs of humans be accommodated at the same time? The unnatural deaths of the cattle egrets in Conway prompted those with ethical concerns to look for a connection between the design of human communities and the welfare of wild creatures that are increasingly trapped in these spaces. Likewise we might ask: can human beings and social policy instruments afford to support an innocent and naïve view of space, or do we need to incorporate bird time and bird space into our designs and imaginations?

Finding a Place for the Wild: A Search for Solutions

Postscript: Cattle Egrets in Conway

While the egret incident in Conway did not have a major impact on future development, it did bring people uncomfortably close to seeing what was previously not evident—the consequences of *not* knowing about their impact on the environment. As mayor Tab Townsell remarked in an interview, "What we have to realize is that there are rules, and we have to live by those rules, period. And we just can't go thumbing our nose at nature, or God, and particularly the Federal Migratory Bird Act to solve our problems. We have to pay attention and to do things at *its time*, not *our time*."

Despite the mayor's acknowledgement of bird time, however, the city of Conway does not presently allow for much space for the wild. Conway is located in a politically conservative area of the country where planning is resisted and the "growth machine" prevails (Čapek 2001; Molotch 1975). In an interview, Conway resident Warfield Teague wondered out loud, "Why did we not know the egrets were there? Is anyone looking for the *next* ones [animals that could be harmed by development]?" He answered his own question by noting that there was virtually no planning being done in the city by anyone except a well-known developer. While Conway has an excellent city planner, the planning office has a tiny staff and exists only in an advisory capacity. Under these circumstances, the unregulated suburban sprawl for the affluent continues to constitute a threat to wild creatures such as egrets.

After the egret "massacre," the birds did return in future years and attempted to nest in a nearby area. Because there were few trees left, the birds were very close to some new apartments, and their odor and noise disturbed apartment residents. City officials received many complaints from irate citizens. Their solution, working in concert with the U.S. Fish and Wildlife Service, was to make noise to scare away the birds before they laid eggs. This practice is legal prior to nesting. The March 26, 2002 headline in the *Log Cabin Democrat* read, "City girding to battle egrets once again: noisemakers readied in case birds appear." Mayor Townsell advised citizens, "If we see them gathering up we can go out with air guns and scare them and drive them away from the city . . . .They are a protected animal, but they are a nuisance. Our only hope is to get them before they have a rookery established" (Wright 2002).

This remains Conway's only strategy for coping with the egrets. In May 2003, the *Log Cabin Democrat* reported that cattle egrets had returned to the area, and citizens were advised to call a 24-hour hotline to report clusters of the birds (Mosby 2003). The Conway Fire Department was ready with noisemakers to drive the birds away from areas that are close to residents. Under the circumstances, city and wildlife officials felt that this was the best way to protect both the birds and the people from problematic encounters.

As a result of the city's experience with the MBTA, egrets and their migratory cycles became more visible in the city, but only in a rather instrumental way. The new awareness is not used to examine nature-human interactions more holistically, or to question the suburban growth model. Moreover, none of the wildlife officials whom I interviewed saw the egrets as being in any danger, given their successful adaptation to new environments and their large numbers. The city of Conway now sees egrets coming from a distance, but virtually no one is addressing the difficult issue of habitat destruction.

Few are addressing the ethical question of the rights of wild creatures to have a prior or co-equal claim to some spaces. There is less and less space for the wild in and around the city, and there are an increasing number of unwanted human encounters not only with egrets, but with deer and other creatures that are losing the spaces in which they can survive. Under such circumstances, naturework transforms the wild into "nuisance," and the nature/culture divide widens.

Finding a Place for the Wild: Better Solutions

If communities decide for ethical, ecological or other reasons to create spaces where the wild can flourish close to human beings, they need to understand how time and space works for animals. They also need to understand how naturework and social constructions divide people or bring them together around questions relating to the wild. The value of a social constructionist perspective is that it helps us identify deeply held symbolic beliefs that lie behind wildlife controversies. More than that, it reveals cultural blind spots and points to possibilities for social change.

Naturework is at one level an individual process of symbolic meaning construction. But the sociological truth of naturework is that it is also a community process, where social learning (Brulle 2000) takes place through interactions with others, including animals. The question is under what circumstances do human beings create environments that are inclusive of spaces for the wild? And what kinds of tools are useful in the process?

Even in Conway, where options are limited and where there is no critical mass supporting spaces for the wild, steps can be taken to better protect wildlife—in this case, migratory birds. The community can be better educated about the MBTA, which is already on the books. This law constructs migratory birds as valuable and is sensitive to time and space as it functions for animals. While the discourse of endangered species has become culturally familiar in the United States, the status of migratory birds and the need to protect them is not as well known. Raising the visibility of the law is therefore important.

Regardless of whether or not a community is unwilling to change its cultural habits drastically, knowledge of migration patterns and the species' natural history can minimize the harm done to migratory birds. Development projects are less likely to be based on an empty land model or to ignore bird time. While developers typically resist any regulations that prolong the construction process, the MBTA already has the force of law and thus can become a predictable element in the planning process. This is less likely to generate controversy than applying the law after the fact.

Just as importantly, all community members need to be educated more generally about bird time and bird space. Since Arkansas does not require environmental impact statements, homeowners, city officials and others need to know about the impacts of certain types of development. Also, learning about a birds-eye view of space allows residents have a more realistic understanding of what attracts the birds, how they make use of the landscape, when they are likely to be present and where their paths are likely to intersect with humans. People can better assess what it means to have the birds nearby. For example, Conway residents who understand the workings of a cattle egret rookery are less likely to panic due to a mistaken fear of histoplasmosis.

A birds-eye view of space is important for another reason. It reveals a fragmented habitat of vanishing farmlands and shrinking wetlands that is just as dangerous for people as it is for migratory birds. Hence there is a potential for naturework that creates common ground between people and animals. Through their flight patterns, birds stitch together our fragmented ecological landscapes and force us to think more holistically, just as the successful drafting of the MBTA depended on groups working across international borders to create a composite picture of bird space. By landing in particular communities like Conway, migratory birds help local residents to "connect the dots" of a global ecosystem. In this sense, "nature as teacher" (Oelschlager 2000; Orr 1994) allows people to see not only birds, but also themselves in relation to local community, region and global ecosystem.

Looking beyond the immediate situation of one community case study, what are some possible models that allow communities to build in a place for the wild? While the answer will vary depending on the type of animal under consideration, ideally it would take into account different levels of social organization—the individual, the community, the region, the nation and even the global system. At an individual level, communities need to produce people who can "see" nature. This means creating time and space for naturework that overcomes separations between people and animals and between people and other people.

Communities also need to put policies in place that protect wildlife and support designs that allow both humans and wildlife to meet their needs. Because ecosystems are much larger integrated units, and because animals move around in order to survive, some of the policies need to operate at a regional level while others—as the example of migratory birds and the MBTA shows so clearly—need to extend beyond regions and even to cross international borders.

What are some actual examples of such practices that can serve as models? This is a relatively new area of experience. As Jennifer Wolch (1998:131) notes in her discussion of the concept of "zoöpolis":

> A nascent trans-species urban practice, as yet poorly documented and undertheorized, has appeared in many US cities. This practice involves numerous actors, including a variety of federal, state, and local bureaucracies, planners, and managers, and urban grassroots animal/environmental activists. In varying measure, the goals of such practice include altering the nature of interactions between people and animals in the city, creating minimum-impact urban environmental designs, changing everyday practices of the local state (wildlife managers and urban planners), and more forcefully defending the interests of urban animal life.

Concrete examples include an entire range of available policy instruments that affect the design of communities and landscapes. Wolch's list (1998:132) of relevant urban planning tools at the local level includes:

> . . . zoning (including urban limit lines and wildlife overlay zones), pub-
> lic/nonprofit land acquisition, transfer of development rights (TDR),
> environmental impact statements (EIS), and wildlife impact/habitat
> conservation linkage fees.

She also includes regional-level planning efforts known as habitat
conservation plans (HCPs), an approach that preserves wildlife corridors. Publicizing this range of policy options would offer communities a choice of models that most are presently unaware of.

Yet, Wolch (1998:132) points out that despite the gradual incorporation of such practices in certain regions of the country, "minimum impact planning for urban wildlife has not been a priority for
either architects or urban planners." This is largely due to resistance
from powerful political and economic actors involved in land investment and development in the United States. Moreover, scenarios of
minimum impact are still a far cry from Wolch's zoöpolis, a situation in which our everyday practices would invite and even "enrich
or facilitate" interactions between people and animals (Wolch 1998:132).
A design of this sort would require some degree of community consensus on the positive value of animals, particularly wildlife, in human
communities.

How would a community move in this direction? While policy
design is essential for revisioning community spaces, the conflictual
nature of land-use decision-making in the United States has led some
to focus more on community environmental education. Separating
politics and policy-making from wildlife education is in any case a
conceptual mistake, argues Suzanne Michel (1998), since wildlife education lays the groundwork for political and social activism through
an "ethics of care" that is learned at the community and household
level. The policy instruments mentioned by Wolch, and legislation
such as the MBTA, are usually the result of pressures created by
social movements whose naturework challenges established practices.
These innovations then make their way into mainstream discourse
and wildlife policy.

Ideally, wildlife policy and community design are supported by
naturework at the individual level and vice versa. At the individual
and community level, Michel emphasizes the powerful transformative impact of direct encounters with wildlife through education
efforts. She draws on her study of golden eagle rehabilitation in
California to suggest that these activities allow "local communities
and individuals to become experientially and emotionally connected

with the plight of disappearing wildlife" (Michel 1998:174). This is often where an ethical connection is born, as human beings learn about the beauty, intricacies and vulnerability of ecosystems.

Environmental education can take place in a variety of ways. It can be built into community programs, as it is in northwest Arkansas, for example, where there is a higher degree of environmental activism than in Conway. The Fayetteville school district budget supports the Lake Fayetteville Environmental Center, which means that every student in the school system visits the center and learns about nature awareness, water quality and species identification.[11] Building environmental education into the structure of the community raises the likelihood that individuals will not grow up separated from their natural environments.

Environmental education also takes place on a more individual basis, as individuals seek out experiences with nature for reasons of aesthetic beauty or ecological interest. An interest in beauty for its own sake can be a strong motivator for ecological preservation. As wildlife official Allan Mueller remarked:

> It translates into things like, "Do you like to see the cattle egrets flying up and down the valley every morning and evening?" Yeah, I like that a whole lot, and I'll bet I'm not the only person that enjoys seeing that everyday. And that's important stuff.

Sociologist Michael Bell likewise emphasizes the role of beauty in connection with the development of an ecological sensibility and an ethical claim for the rights of nature to exist undisturbed (Bell 1998). Beauty is always to some degree a social construct, but, because it takes us by surprise, it is probably more than that. The Conway resident who loved to see the cattle egrets because "They look like little pterodactyls in flight" was connecting with a sense of wonder or fascination that has the potential to change the contents of people's naturework. An important element of community design is making sure that there is space for such encounters, whether through wildlife sanctuaries, ecological restoration projects (Jordan 2000; McCloskey 1996) or other means.

Regardless of their specific form or content, what all environmental education experiences share in common is that they counteract social constructions that rely on "hyperseparation" between humans and animals. Instead they cultivate "trans-species respect" along with the development of a more ecologically "relational self" (Plumwood, cited in Michel 1998). An expanded relational self is also more likely to inquire, as do Gullo, Lassiter and Wolch (1998:142) in their study of human-cougar coexistence, "how do animals learn to see us, over time?" The answer to this important question provides essential information for wildlife managers and community residents alike.

A relational self is also more likely to see human beings and animals as "networked in never-ending relations" (Adam 1994:110). This opens up the possibility that the wild might be found in places where we are not trained to look for it, such as in our own backyards, and in our bodies that have a kinship with other animals. Wolch et al. (2001:396) remind us that nature is found "within every human and throughout every city, however thoroughly manipulated and reordered, as well as far beyond the city." Understandings like these have the power to radically reshape our naturework.

Ideally, then, individual naturework complements specific policy instruments that carry legal force to protect wildlife at the community, regional, and perhaps even global level—but only if our naturework can resist the standard social script that rests on commodified time and space. That social script is powerful, as the American Dream of homeownership and suburban development exercises a strong hold on the cultural imagination. On the other hand, increasing numbers of people understand the need to rewrite the rules of human-animal interactions as our habitats converge. Even in the relatively conservative setting of Conway there was enough of a public outcry about the egret deaths to lead to sanctions of the developers.

Finally, the effort to create the knowledge that we need is necessarily interdisciplinary. For example, landscape ecologists who study how animals interact with landscapes at the micro-level are influencing our thinking about how to design protected spaces for animals (Johnston and Naiman 1987; Verboom and Huitema 1997; Wiens and Milne 1989). Social science helps uncover social constructions of nature that have particular impacts on ecosystems and makes visible the political and economic relationships that provide constraints as well as possibilities for social change. In this sense, social policy is naturework writ large. The point of this knowledge is not to blame people for their choices, but to offer them alternative models and a more ecologically conscious way to evaluate costs and benefits of their actions (Teague 1999).

As a variety of formerly separated fields begin to interpenetrate each other we are better able to gauge our place in a complex, mutually contingent ecosystem that includes animals (Freudenburg 1999; Love 1996; Norgaard 1997). Somewhat like a birds-eye view, this vantage point carries us above and beyond our limited versions of naturework to a viewpoint from which we can locate new strategies using policy and educational tools to rethink our practices. This will by no means be a simple process because there is still much that we do not know and because the competing ethical claims relating to human-animal relations are not always easy to sort out. But by now we have an array of tools to assist us in the task of creating good designs that respect the needs of people and make room for the presence of the wild.

References

Adam, Barbara. 1994. "Running Out of Time: Global Crisis and Human Engagement." Pp. 92–112 in *Social Theory and the Global Environment*, edited by M. Redclift and T. Benton. London and New York: Routledge.

Amoakohene, Bernice. 1998. Letter to the Editor, *Log Cabin Democrat*, July 27.

Bell, Michael Mayerfeld. 1998. *An Invitation To Environmental Sociology*. Thousand Oaks, CA: Pine Forge Press.

Bennett, David. 1998. "Volunteers Work to Rescue Egrets Displaced from Nest." *Log Cabin Democrat*, July 26.

Brulle, Robert J. 2000. *Agency, Democracy, and Nature: The U.S. Environmental Movement from a Critical Theory Perspective*. Cambridge, MA: MIT Press.

Čapek, Stella M. 2001. "'For The Birds': Cattle Egrets, Suburban Lawns, and the Federal Migratory Bird Treaty Act." Paper presented at the Annual Meetings of the Society for the Study of Social Problems, August 17, Anaheim, California.

Davies, Bronwyn. 2000. *(In)scribing Body/Landscape Relations*. New York: Altamira Press.

Fine, Gary Alan. 1998. *Morel Tales: The Culture of Mushrooming*. Cambridge, MA: Harvard University Press.

Fletcher, Susan. 1998. Letter to the Editor, *Arkansas Democrat Gazette*, July 31.

Freudenburg, William. 1999. "Counterpoint" (Point-Counterpoint Discussion, "Dancing With The Devil: Sociology and the Physical-Organic World"). *Newsletter of the Section on Environment and Technology*, American Sociological Association. Spring (no. 93).

Gaughan, Jan. 1998. "Birds Have Developer, Others Wondering What They Can Do." *Log Cabin Democrat*, July 26.

Giddens, Anthony. 1990. *The Consequences of Modernity*. Stanford, CA: Stanford University.

Gullo, Andrea, Unna Lassiter, and Jennifer Wolch. 1998. "The Cougar's Tale." Pp. 139–161 in *Animal Geographies: Place, Politics, and Identity in the Nature-Culture Borderlands*, edited by J. Wolch and J. Emel. London and New York: Verso.

Hancock, J. and H. Elliot. 1978. *The Herons of the World*. New York: Harper and Row.

Johnson, Martha. 1998. "Cattle Egrets in Central Arkansas." *Petit Jean Audubon Society Newsletter* XV, 3 (Summer):1,4.

Johnston, Carol A. and Robert J. Naiman. 1987. "Boundary Dynamics at the

Aquatic-Terrestrial Interface: The Influence of Beaver and Geomorphology."
  Landscape Ecology 1(1):47–57.
Jordan, William R. III. 2000. "Restoration, Community, and Wilderness." Pp. 23–36
  in *Restoring Nature: Perspectives from the Social Sciences and Humanities*, edited by
  P. Gobster and R.B. Hull. Washington, D.C.: Island Press
Kuletz, Valerie L. 1998. *The Tainted Desert: Environmental and Social Ruin in the American
  West*. New York: Routledge.
Line, Les. 1995. "African Egrets? Holy Cow!: How a Cattle-Chasing Bird Came
  to America." *International Wildlife* Nov./Dec.: 45–54.
Love, Ruth. 1996. "The Sound of Crashing Timber: Moving to an Ecological
  Sociology." *Society & Natural Resources* 10:211–222.
Mason, Bobbie Ann. 1986. *In Country*. New York: Harper and Row.
McCloskey, David D. 1996. "Ecology, Community and Culture: Toward Community-
  Based Restoration." Pp. 23–29 in *The Role of Restoration in Ecosystem Management*,
  edited by D. Peterson and C. Klimas. Madison, WI: Parks Canada and The
  Society for Ecological Restoration.
Meisel, Jay. 1998. "Bulldozed Egrets Receiving a Helping Hand." *Arkansas Democrat
  Gazette*, July 29.
Meyerriecks, Andrew J. 1960. "Success Story of a Pioneering Bird." *Natural History*
  69(7):45–67.
Michel, Suzanne M. 1998. "Golden Eagles and the Environmental Politics of Care."
  Pp. 162–187 in *Animal Geographies: Place, Politics, and Identity in the Nature-Culture
  Borderlands*, edited by J. Wolch and J. Emel. London and New York: Verso.
Molotch, Harvey. 1975. "The City as Growth Machine: Toward a Political Economy
  of Place." *American Journal of Sociology* 82(2):309–32.
Mosby, Joe. 2003. "We Egret to Inform You . . . The Birds Have Come Back." *Log
  Cabin Democrat*, May 5.
Mullin, Molly. 1999. "Mirrors and Windows: Sociocultural Studies of Human-Animal
  Relationships." *Annual Review of Anthropology* 28:201–24.
Norgaard, Richard B. 1997. "A Coevolutionary Environmental Sociology." Pp.
  158–168 in *International Handbook of Environmental Sociology*, edited by M. Redclift
  and G. Woodgate. Northampton, MA: Edward Elgar.
Oelschlager, Max. 2000. "Why Wilderness Matters in the New Millenium." Pp.
  3–5 in *Horizons*, Sigurd Olson Environmental Institute. Ashland, WI: Northland
  College.
Orr, David W. 1994. *Earth in Mind: On Education, Environment, and the Human Prospect*.
  Washington, D.C.: Island Press.
———. 2001. "The Nature of Speed." *Earthlight* 41 (Spring):16–19.
Redclift, Michael and Ted Benton. 1994. *Social Theory and the Global Environment*.
  London and New York: Routledge.
Ritzer, George. 1999. *Enchanting a Disenchanted World: Revolutionizing the Means of
  Consumption*. Thousand Oaks, CA: Pine Forge.
Scarce, Rik. 2000. *Fishy Business: Salmon, Biology, and the Social Construction of Nature*.
  Philadelphia: Temple University Press.
Schnaiberg, Allan. 1980. *The Environment, from Surplus to Scarcity*. New York and
  Oxford: Oxford University Press.
Teague, David W. 1999. "Central High and the Suburban Landscape: The Ecology
  of White Flight." Pp. 157–168 in *The Nature of Cities: Ecocriticism and Urban
  Environments*, edited by M. Bennett and D.W. Teague. Tucson: University of
  Arizona.
U.S. Fish and Wildlife Service. 2004. "Migratory Bird Treaty Act." Retrieved
  September 25, 2004 (http://ipl.unm.edu/cwl/fedbook/mbta.html).
Verboom, B. and H. Huitema. 1997. "The Importance of Linear Landscape Elements
  for the Pipistrelle *Pipistrellus Pipistrellus* and the Serotine Bat *Eptesicus Serotinus*."
  Landscape Ecology 12(2):117–125.

Walsh, Edward. 1981. "Resource Mobilization and Citizen Protest in Communities around Three Mile Island." *Social Problems* 29:1–21.
Wiens, John A. and Brue Milne. 1989. "Scaling of 'Landscapes' in Landscape Ecology, or Landscape Ecology from a Beetle's Perspective." *Landscape Ecology* 3(2):87–96.
Wolch, Jennifer and Jody Emel. 1998. *Animal Geographies: Place, Politics, and Identity in the Nature-Culture Borderlands.* London and New York: Verso.
Wolch, Jennifer. 1998. "Zoöpolis." Pp. 119–138 in *Animal Geographies: Place, Politics, and Identity in the Nature-Culture Borderlands,* edited by J. Wolch and J. Emel. London and New York: Verso.
Wolch, Jennifer, Stephanie Pincetl, and Laura Pulido. 2001. "Urban Nature and the Nature of Urbanism." Pp. 411–568 in *From Chicago to L.A.: Making Sense of Urban Theory,* edited by M.J. Dear and J.D. Dishman. Thousand Oaks, CA: Sage.
Wright, Sheila Doughty. 2002. "City Girding to Battle Egrets Once Again: Noisemakers Readied in Case Birds Appear." *Log Cabin Democrat,* March 26.
Zapparoni, Ceide. 1997. *International Environmental Law,* November 9 (electronic text).

Notes

[1] Acknowledgements: my thanks to student research assistant Sarah Hornstein for her work and shared ideas for the original version of this paper, and to Katie Falgoust, Amanda Moore, Linda McKenna, and Lauren Hollingsworth for library assistance. Many thanks to Pam Bugh for sharing her photographs and documentary materials.

[2] Origins of the federal Migratory Bird Treaty Act can be found in the 1916 Convention for the Protection of Migratory Birds, a treaty made between Great Britain (then ruler of the dominion of Canada) and the United States in order to protect specifically listed endangered species of birds which migrated between the territories of the U.S. and Canada from "indiscriminate slaughter" and trade, by restricting hunting and trade practices (U.S. Fish and Wildlife Service 2004; Zapparoni 1997). The Convention was implemented in the United States by a statute enacted in 1918, the Migratory Bird Treaty Act. It remains in force today, although an amending Protocol was signed by both governments in December 1997 which addresses procedures for evaluation, monitoring, and amendment as well as addressing more comprehensively the issue of indigenous hunting rights.

[3] Histoplasmosis is a human respiratory disease that has been linked to certain bird populations, most notably blackbirds. It can arise from accumulated droppings of large groups of birds. Cattle egret rookeries have never been linked to the disease, probably because they are usually abandoned before significant accumulation takes place (Mosby 2003).

[4] Cattle egrets, however, are not the same thing as cowbirds, one more piece of evidence that cattle egrets were not very well known by residents in the community.

[5] John T. Holleman IV, an Audubon Society of Central Arkansas member, writes in a 1999 letter to U.S. Attorney General Janet Reno and Secretary of the Interior Bruce Babbit about the Conway egret incident: "Even worse was the indifference to poor creatures unable to defend themselves. I don't believe it too strong of an analogy to liken such conduct to child molestation or rape or other crimes of predatory behavior."

[6] Since Conway is located in the so-called Bible Belt, religious constructions often surfaced in letters to the editor of *Log Cabin Democrat.* These most commonly took the form of "dominion" versus "stewardship" claims. In the former, human beings

are seen as having the God-given right to rule over the animal kingdom and to subordinate it to their needs. In the latter, human beings have a responsibility to care for nature.

[7] According to Bill Polk, the Director of City Planning in Conway, virtually no affordable housing is being built in the city for moderate income groups.

[8] In fairness to Giddens, he also identifies modernity with the possibility of new connections. Disembedding creates possibilities for innovation, as people learn to see beyond traditional structures and belief systems. To Giddens this is the positive side of globalization.

[9] The ecological footprint concept measures the impact of human lifestyles on the ecosystem, including the use of natural resources such as water and land and the generation of waste. It is possible to measure the impact of individual people's practices as well as that of communities and entire nations.

[10] An interesting example of mapping is the use of Geographic Information System (GIS) technology to identify the location of toxic land uses in conjunction with minority residence patterns. This birds-eye view has been a significant tool for social change.

[11] I thank Michelle Viney, Public Education Coordinator for the Tri-County Solid Waste District in northwest Arkansas, for this example.

YOU CAN'T EAT "PAPER FISH": RECENT ATTEMPTS TO LINK LOCAL ECOLOGICAL KNOWLEDGE AND FISHERIES SCIENCE IN ATLANTIC CANADA

Lawrence F. Felt

Introduction

They were first observed on a cold, misty morning in early April 2003 floating belly up and staring eerily into a gray, overcast Newfoundland sky. Northern codfish (*Gadus morhua*), once the foundation of the North Atlantic fishery in Europe and North America and recently driven to the verge of extinction, suddenly appeared by the thousands in Smith Sound, a narrow, fijord-like indentation on the Canadian province of Newfoundland's Northeast coast. As many as half a million deceased fish mysteriously appeared on the ocean's choppy surface.[1] Fishers and other members of the numerous small communities quickly launched their boats for closer investigation. The mass of dead fish appeared to include a wide range of ages. No marks or indications of disease were visible. They appeared well fed and in generally excellent condition, except that they were all dead (see Figure 10.1).

This chapter utilizes the Smith Sound incident in Northeast Newfoundland to explore the issue of fishers' knowledge or, more specifically, what many have termed fishers' Local Ecological Knowledge or LEK (Berkes 1999; Davis and Wagner 2003; DeWalt 1999; Dyer and McGoodwin 1994; Felt 1994; Weeks 1995) and knowledge claims by fisheries scientists, particularly assessment scientists who try to estimate population numbers for fish. I highlight the critical differences and similarities in construction, objectives, data, interpretive rules and degree of privilege or legitimacy in fisheries management.

While a simmering skepticism continues to underlie much of the relationship between fishers and scientists, government managers as well as scientists increasingly acknowledge the importance and legitimacy, if not yet equality, of LEK for management. Compared to ten years ago, more participative, consultative processes and structures

Figure 10.1. Fileted cod. Remains of Smith Sound cod after flesh removal
for testing and later consumption following die off in 2003.
Reprinted with permission from The Telegram.

have been established. Fishers and scientists generally have a less
tense relationship and some amount of progress in mutual understanding and trust between them has occurred. Smith Sound is a
very useful vantage point from which to understand these larger institutional and cultural changes in the world of marine fisheries.

Methods

The evidence presented in this chapter results from an earlier, multidisciplinary investigation of Local Ecological Knowledge and marine

management undertaken between 1994 and 1998[1] supplemented by more recent follow-up interviews I conducted with fishers and scientists following the fish kill of 2003. Between 1994 and 1998 a team of marine scientists, sociologists and anthropologists conducted interviews and participant observations with fishers, scientists and government managers in the Bonavista area of Northeast Newfoundland of which Smith Sound is approximately in the middle.

Semi-structured interviews were completed with approximately seventy-five fishers and nine scientists. Interviews lasted between two and four hours and topics ranged from a historical reconstruction of personal fishing careers through detailed explorations of knowledge of fish and the wider marine ecosystem. All but six interviews were tape-recorded and later transcribed for analysis. Average transcription was 120 pages. In addition, nautical charts were used with each interview to collect geospatial and temporal information on fish distributions, behavior and relationships to marine oceanographic as well as birds and sea mammals.

Fishers were selected for interviews through several strategies. Lists of commercial fishers were obtained from all regional fishers' union committees. From these lists, inshore fishers, totaling approximately three hundred and fifty, were enumerated and fifty randomly selected. Forty-two were eventually interviewed (six no longer active, two had moved away) with careers extending from six to fifty-two years. The sample was augmented through a snowball sampling technique to locate nine retired fishers. The remaining twenty-four fishers were selected using snowball techniques from our original sample. This was done to ensure adequate coverage of fishers using a range of gear and targeting a variety of species. Most interviews, cleaned of specific name and community reference, are available at Memorial University's Folklore Archive. Interviews most frequently took place at the fisher's home, although several were done on boats en route to fishing grounds.

In addition to formal interviews, researchers had extensive discussions with fishers during numerous trips to fishing grounds. As well, less extensive interviews have been completed with over one hundred additional fishers on specific issues including the recent cod die off.

Interview information was augmented with the Department of Fisheries and Oceans, Canada (DFO) harvest records and, oftentimes, fisher logbooks of personal catch records. Many fishers shared their logbooks with us and several allowed us to make copies. Fishers

have become highly organized in recent years through the efforts of
a fishers' union. Researchers attended numerous meetings during this
period. At these meetings many of the issues discussed in this chapter were debated, often hotly. While most formal interviewing ended
in late 1998 and early 1999, ongoing communication has resulted
from the many relationships that emerged from the earlier research.
In my own personal work I have continued to communicate with
many of the fishers in the original sample as well as attend union
and other organizational meetings. Following the fish kill, I conducted follow up interviews with several fishers, both in person and
on the telephone, linking the fish kill to the larger issues of local
knowledge discussed in this chapter and earlier work.

Similar semi-structured interviews were also originally undertaken
with most of the government scientists undertaking assessment of
Northern cod on Newfoundland's Northeast coast. Nine interviews
were completed in total between 1994 and 1999. This component
built on earlier research on fisheries scientists (Finlayson 1994) and
focused on assessment models and the relationship between inshore
and offshore cod stocks. Since all of these scientists are based at a
large government research station near Memorial University and are
personally known to the author, it was easy to discuss the fish die
off and its relationship to the larger issues of Smith Sound cod with
them. While no formal interviews were undertaken, I held discussions ranging from fifteen minutes to over an hour with all of them
since the fish kill.

The Rise and Fall of King Cod

The Atlantic cod was once one of the most abundant and valuable
fish species inhabiting the North Atlantic ocean. Since the sixteenth
century, boats from Portugal, Spain, England, France and other
European countries have braved great distances and uncertain weather
to harvest seemingly inexhaustible numbers of this bottom dwelling,
firm white-fleshed fish. More Easterly provinces of Newfoundland
and Nova Scotia owe their very existence in large part to this fish
(Alexander 1977; Innis 1949). Dried, salted and, more recently, frozen
it has been the object of conflict more than once over the last six
centuries, and even war. In Northeastern Canada and large parts of
coastal New England, human settlement followed cod.

For management purposes, Atlantic cod has been divided into five separate though genetically identical stocks ranging from the Gulf of Maine through the Grand Banks of Nova Scotia, the Gulf of St. Lawrence to the largest stock off Northeastern Newfoundland and Labrador (Government of Canada 1977). The latter, generally referred to as "the northern cod stock," was the largest both numerically and territorially. At its peak it is estimated to have comprised as much as 3.5 million metric tonnes[2] or nearly 1.5 *billion* fish (Rose 2003). Struggling to avoid commercial extinction, total biomass estimates currently place the stock at 1/100th of that level (Fisheries Resource Conservation Council 2003).

Until the mid 1950s, most cod fishing was shore-based, occurring within ten to twelve miles of the coast. As can be seen from Map 10.1, this represented a fraction of the spatial expanse of cod territory. The map depicts management zones for major commercial species on Canada's East coast. Of the valuable Gadoid species, northern cod was the most extensive and economically important. For management purposes this cod stock was divided into three management zones, 2J, 3K and 3L. Each management zone extends far beyond the limits of Canada's 200 mile management zone and, in total, encompasses approximately seventy percent of the marine area between Canada and Greenland, an East/West expanse of over 1,200 miles.

During a short summer season of June to October, fish were either caught on long lines of baited hooks or collected from box-like nets called traps as they chased a small fish called a capelin from offshore waters into the many bays lining the East coast. Depending upon location, processing consisted of either drying or some level of brine or salt finishing in preparation for the long trip back to Europe, the Caribbean or South America. The major exception was the Grand Banks South of Newfoundland and East of Nova Scotia where an offshore, baited-line fishery using small, double bowed row boats called dories lowered from larger boats harvested fish. Originally, these fisheries were British and French, latter displaced by Portuguese and Spanish as permanent settlement proceeded on the coasts.

After World War II a fishery that had supported thousands of fishers and shore-based processors for several hundred years underwent unprecedented expansion. Beginning in the early 1950s technological changes brought larger fishing boats with more powerful engines and steel-reinforced hulls to withstand winter ice. Fishing

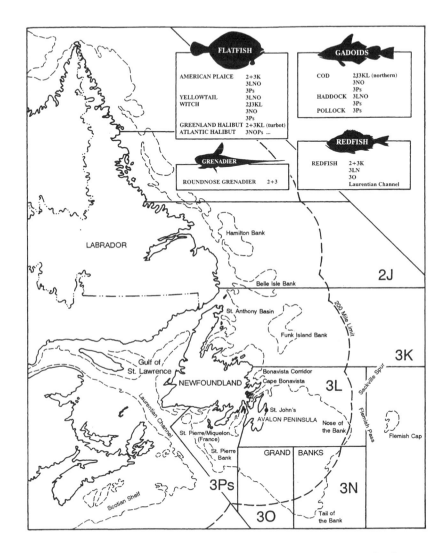

Map 10.1. Map of Eastern Canada showing management zones for important commercial species, including Northern cod. Source: Government of Canada, Fisheries and Oceans.

gear also became more advanced and expansive. These changes triggered massive increases in effort and a near geometric expansion in the size and catching capability of European fleets. The largest boats were essentially floating factories capable of staying on site for weeks while harvesting, processing and freezing a catch equivalent to that of several thousand fishers using more traditional gear. The former cod sanctuaries in off-shore banks (shallow underwater plateaus) such as Hamilton and Funk were now accessible (Harris 1998).

Not surprisingly, catches escalated dramatically. Between 1953 and 1968, annual catch went from approximately 250,000 metric tonnes to 680,000 (Storey 1993). These catches were "official reports" and did not include "highgrading," or throwing back, usually dead, smaller or blemished fish. Some have suggested actual harvests may have been twice the officially reported levels or 600 percent of historic levels (Harris 1998). From that point, catches declined steadily to 460,000 tonne in 1970 and 180,000 by 1975.

Cries of overexploitation rose as catches declined. Following Iceland's lead in 1975, the Canadian government declared a 200 mile EEZ or Exclusive Economic Zone. Unlike Iceland, which unilaterally declared total ownership within 200 miles, Canada eschewed ownership in favor of a first call on resource use and a primary, though not exclusive, role in management. An international organization called the Northwest Atlantic Fisheries Organization or NAFO was created in 1977 to provide advice on fishing levels and practices but lacked any enforcement capability. Enforcement was to be by gentlemen's agreement and administered by the particular national registry of a fishing vessel. This lack of enforcement continues to plague offshore management with several conspicuous European nations allegedly violating quotas and "non fishing" areas continuously.

Largely closed to foreign exploitation, domestic landings increased, reaching 270,000 tonnes in 1988 (Northwest Atlantic Fisheries Organization 1997:24). Landings precipitously declined thereafter and in 1992, the entire Northern cod fishery was shut down throwing approximately 40,000 Atlantic Canadians, the overwhelming majority in Newfoundland, out of work. Since 1992, little evidence of stock rebuilding has been detected.

An ecological, economic and social catastrophe of such magnitude led to numerous recriminations of fault and responsibility. Failure to prevent the Northern cod collapse was a result of several factors. Canadian leaders, fearing strong intervention might jeopardize more valuable trade in wheat, pulp and other resources with European nations, delayed intervention until it was too late. Many fishers continued to fish even when they recognized the impending consequences of their actions.

Perhaps the major brunt of the criticism was leveled at fisheries scientists who have been accused of using ineffective stock assessment methods as well as bowing to political pressure to understate risks and uncertainties (Finlayson 1994; Hutchings, Walters and Haedrich 1997). For their part, government scientists have responded by defending their science, suggesting that overfishing was but one factor, citing changing ocean temperatures and several other environmental factors as combining with fishing to limit both the number of fish capable of reproduction and the probability of survival for those young fish that were produced. In fisheries science language this led to a "recruitment failure" and, subsequently, a dramatic decline in the number of adult fish (B. Atkinson, personal communication).

Smith Sound plays an important and interesting role in post-collapse efforts to rebuild this once great fishery and create more participatory structures to prevent its reoccurrence. The Sound lies in the Southern third of the Northern cod's geographic range near the "bottom" of Trinity Bay, a large, deep, fertile bay on the East coast of the Canadian island province of Newfoundland and Labrador. Located near the foot of the Bonavista peninsula, it is a long, fijord-like indentation approximately a dozen nautical miles in length and nearly two miles across at its widest point. The sound is traversed with several trenches up to 350 metres[3] in depth and sill depths rising upwards to 150 metres (Rose 2003). Since 2001, it and a five nautical mile buffer zone around it have been closed to all recreational and commercial cod fishers except for less than a dozen fishers allowed to conduct, under strict government control, a "test" fishery to monitor any ongoing changes in cod abundance. This "sentinel fishery," as it is known, represents the only commercial fishery explicitly targeting Northern cod in the area since 1992.

The Sound is encircled with small fishing communities or outports that have fished the sound and adjacent waters for over 170 years using several types of fishing technology including trawls, traps and more recently gill nets. Up to the 1992 closure, the area was one of the more lucrative fishing areas in Trinity Bay with fixed-gear fishers often harvesting upwards of 400,000 pounds of cod per year.

As good a fishing area as the Sound has been, it is much more likely to be remembered for its contribution to transforming fisheries assessment science and in so doing promoting greater participation of fishers in cod management and a greater role for LEK in the underlying scientific assessment process. To understand that, we need to understand in greater detail the nature of fisheries science that arose with post war European expansion and how events at Smith Sound proved difficult to reconcile with that paradigm (Kuhn 1962).

Two Tales of a Fish: Contested Constructions of Northern Cod

This chapter utilizes what might be termed a "soft social construc-tionism" (Brown 2001; Hacking 2001; Harding 1991; Neis and Felt 2000) emphasizing the ways in which fishers' and scientists' respec-tive claims to knowledge are socially constructed, arising from the experiences, training and organizational constraints within which each group operates. Fishers as well as scientists construct their respective knowledge in quite different ways. Understanding the respective par-adigms[4] through which selected information becomes a particular knowledge is essential if meaningful collaboration is to occur in fisheries management.

While the two frameworks share certain features, they retain impor-tant differences. One critical difference is the privilege or legitimacy accorded each. Elsewhere I have argued that for fishers' knowledge to be highly valued, fishers themselves must also be accorded sufficient legitimacy in the management process itself (Neis and Felt 2000). While the quest for legitimacy is still very much a work in progress, notable advancement has been achieved. The Smith Sound occur-rence and its aftermath is a useful vantage point from which to view this larger process as well.

While claiming that Local Ecological Knowledge and fisheries sci-ence are social constructions, I wish to avoid dragging this discus-sion into the heated confrontations about the nature of science found in discussions of the "science wars" (Brown 2001) that have occu-pied much of the modern critique of natural science. This larger exchange on "objectivity," "positivism," "personal values" and "rel-ativism" within traditional science, while interesting, offers little res-olution and has served to entrench respective camps on a number of important issues (Hacking 2001).

To assert that both scientists' and fishers' claims to knowledge about Northern cod are socially constructed is a much more modest and perhaps less politicized avenue. It is an axiom of all social science research, particularly anthropology and sociology, that individuals form groups and that out of such groups emerge cultures and subcultures. Cultures and subcultures in turn provide normative guidance through symbols, artifacts (tools), values, norms and roles that allow interpretation and meaning to be constructed. In a very important sense, then, to claim something is socially constructed is nothing more than an obvious starting point for social analysis. In the sense it is used here, all social science description is about characterizing social constructions and analysis about deconstructing them to their underlying assumptions, rules, language and rules of integration. This is as true of both fisheries science and fishers' LEK as it is about any social phenomenon.

The Construction of Fisheries Assessment Knowledge

Until the last ten years, the form of Northern cod science was the result of a particular combination of biological, political, economic and technological factors. Biologically, cod science was based on a particular understanding of cod migratory behavior. Northern cod were presumed to reproduce and spend substantial portions of the winter months in offshore underwater plateaus or banks in the Labrador Sea between Labrador and Greenland. From February to April, depending upon latitude, water temperature, and several other factors, spawning occurred. Spent and famished, cod began an inshore migration in pursuit of capelin (Rose 1992). Following intense feeding, most cod settled in deeper inshore trenches where gillnets or other deeper water technology was required to catch them. As water temperatures cooled in later October and November the fish once again began to actively feed in preparation for their return migration to the offshore from which the cycle would begin anew the next early summer.

Technological innovations such as factory freezer trawlers quickly led to catching capacity several fold greater than historic levels. Within a decade concerns were raised from several quarters and even within government itself that catching capacity had exceeded sustainable levels. The most common initial response was to impose 200 mile ownership zones of varying levels of exclusivity. By and large, such actions simply reallocated effort and economic gains to the adjacent nation without leading to more sustainable fishing practices (Storey 1993).

As Wright (2001) and several others have argued, these events, in combination with a growth in preference within biology itself for highly quantifiable population estimation methodologies, led to a need to "count fish." Fisheries assessment or "assessment science" evolved as the foundation for fish management providing estimates of total population, spawning biomass and other parameters considered critical for establishing catch levels that could ensure profitability. Relegated to lesser importance were several other types of fisheries science including fish behavior, species interaction and emphases on relationships between fish and the marine environment more generally. Interestingly, one did not even need to be a fisheries biologist to do fisheries science. Mathematicians and statisticians with little actual knowledge of the fish themselves often played critical roles in the assessment. To meet this demand for a new type of fisheries science, the Canadian government established a new Ministry of Fisheries and Oceans in 1975 and created a strong departmental capability in this support activity.

To count fish sophisticated sampling methodologies and mathematical models were developed to guide research vessel trips. Using expensive, specially equipped research vessels, government scientists created elaborate protocols on site, gear effect, seasonality, water temperature and a number of other factors in an effort to ensure the entire range of a species was covered under all known situations. After a sample net was retrieved, scientists and technicians on board carefully enumerated number, size, condition, age and length of the fish. Using this information, scientists utilized complicated mathematical models to estimate spawning biomass as well as a range of recommended harvest levels for the coming year. Offshore commercial trawler landings were compared to research vessel numbers as an independent check for reliability.

Throughout the 1980s special "resource units" of quantitative modelers staffed with modeling specialists were created to advise and develop sampling grids and refine models from epidemiology, risk assessment and several other areas of quantitative emphasis for estimating fish populations. Each model made a number of assumptions and elevated certain variables as critical. The most prevalent model, and still in use with several refinements, was Virtual Population Analysis or VPA (Hilborn and Walters 1992).

VPA is an analysis of the catches in commercial fisheries typically obtained through fishing boat logbooks, combined with detailed data on the proportion of each age cohort in the catch to estimate total population. Distributions of age cohorts are usually gathered independently by government research vessels deploying elaborate sampling frames as well as through sampling of commercial catches. An estimate of the total population from which both data came is then "back calculated" using a complex equation and assumptions about natural and fishing mortality. The word virtual is drawn from an analogy with the "virtual image" in physics. The idea behind the method is to analyze that catch and age data in order to calculate the population that must have been in the water to produce this. In the words of a document of the Food and Agriculture Organization of the United Nations (1998, emphasis added) on the technique:

> The total landings from a cohort in its lifetime is the first estimate of the numbers of recruits from that cohort. It is however, an under-estimate because some fish must have died from natural causes. Given an estimate of M [overall estimate of mortality] we can do a backwards calculation and find out how many fish belonging to the cohort were alive year by year and ultimately, how many recruits there were. *At the same time we learn the values of the fishing mortality coefficient F, because we have calculated the numbers alive and know from the beginning how many of them were caught in any particular year.*

The fishing mortality coefficient or F is the critical factor in this technique. Allocations are recommended that keep F at a level of 2.0, approximately twenty percent of the adult fish population, or lower to ensure population stability or modest growth.

Several important critiques of VPA have been made by social scientists (see Finlayson 1994; Neis and Felt 2000) emphasizing "constructed" elements in the form of inaccurate assumptions, limiting parameters as well as poor quality data in the VPA models used up to the 1992 collapse. To cite just a few examples, commercial trawler catch data was a poor choice for reliability due to high grading or retaining only the largest fish. As well, more sophisticated electronic technology on board commercial trawlers more efficiently targeted fish as populations declined masking what would normally have been recorded as a dramatic decline in catch per unit of fishing effort.

In a similar vein issues with the research vessel sampling procedure as well as overly optimistic VPA assumptions relating to natural mortality are weaknesses in some writers' views (Finlayson 1994;

Harris 1998; Hutchings et al. 1997). Regarding the former, a rigid, complex sampling frame might have made it difficult to respond to any behavioral changes of cod resulting from population depletion or environmental triggers (Finlayson 1994; Neis and Felt 2000). Due, in part, to the back calculating nature of the VPA model, these limitations were not detected until it was too late since one never knew how many fish existed until after they had been caught. In the sense we use the term, VPA models are very much socially constructed strategies to see and interpret a particular facet of the natural world, in other words to estimate how many fish are out there.

Scientifically, the inshore, adjacent to the coast, remained largely a mystery. There were three primary reasons for this. First, prevailing scientific understanding of cod at the time suggested they were but temporary inshore residents during the brief summer season dwelling most of the year and reproducing in the offshore banks. Second, sampling technology in the form of larger sea going vessels hauling bottom nets was impossible in the narrow, shallow inshore areas with their uneven, rocky bottom. Third, irregular configuration of Newfoundland's coast made it difficult for scientists to lay out straight sampling grids from which to pick areas to sample.

Inshore commercial landing data was avoided as well due both to scientists' and managers' perceptions that it was inaccurate and as a result of the hundreds of landing sites, numerous buyers and lack of paper records in many cases. All of this was about to change dramatically as a result of an unanticipated event in Smith Sound in April 1995.

During a routine fisheries patrol to capture a small number of northern cod for tagging, government fisheries scientists "discovered," "an unusually large and dense aggregation of cod" (Rose 2003). This discovery was at considerable odds with conventional scientific wisdom of the time (Rose 1992; Scott and Scott 1967). While not unusual to find scattered groupings of cod "over wintering" and spawning in near shore bays and sounds, numbers were thought to be minimal and sparsely distributed. The initial scientific estimate of between 12,000 and 17,000 metric tonnes (or 4.5 to 6.2 million fish) in Smith Sound that April posed a significant challenge for conventional fisheries science.

The discovery reinvigorated long-standing discussions and disagreements within the fisheries science community as well as between commercial fishers and scientists regarding stock structure of Northern cod. For more than forty years, a few scientists argued that populations of northern cod were vastly more complex than official science portrayed. Northern cod populations, they suggested, consisted of a large, offshore migratory component and numerous, largely independent populations existing within suitable bays. Such "bay stocks" remained resident in an area though portions might migrate to nearby bays or even offshore. During summer inshore migrations, they would mix with considerably greater numbers of incoming fish and become nearly invisible as a result. Since little or no assessment was conducted in inshore waters, for all intents they did not officially exist. While several retired fisheries scientists have recounted to me frequent instances of vigorous debates occurring during preparation of annual assessment documents, no official record is to be found in stock overviews and status reports provided by government scientists.

Without unambiguous evidence for bay stocks such as distinctive DNA genetic markers or systematic inshore sampling that might reveal visible physical differences in shape, color or average size, discussions remained unofficial within a closed scientific review process. Several former government scientists have suggested that pressures from fisheries managers for specific quotas and a government clearly committed to expansion resulted in considerable pressure for scientists, who were after all government employees, to provide and defend scientific advice that was inconsistent with the caution and considerable uncertainty that both the data and analysis warranted (Finlayson 1994; Hutchings et al. 1997). This debate over whether unfettered science can co-exist in government bureaucracies continues to this day with proponents on all sides.

Interviews with present and former government scientists provide no clear resolution. There is agreement on several points worth mentioning, however, without exploring the issue in greater detail. First, there is no clear evidence that government scientists have been or are ordered to falsify evidence or conclusions. Whatever pressures might occur are more subtle. Second, there was and is a considerable gulf in language between managers who develop harvesting policy, politicians who approve it and scientists providing advice. In the words of a scientist:

> ... Managers want some numbers or maybe more accurately a number for their TACs. They don't want confidence limits around that number or any expression of uncertainty or confidence in that number. I guess it's hard to tell a trawler skipper there is a ninety-five per-

cent probability you can catch 8,000 tonne without doing any harm but there is still a fair bit of uncertainty even around that number because of a limited number of parameters we have good data on.

The entire process leads to varying degrees of homogeneity and uniformity in scientific advice that are inconsistent with the normal discourse of scientific analysis. Whether this could be reduced if scientific assessment were more independent, such as contracted out to third parties or undertaken by an independent research institute funded by government, is unclear; there are both advocates and opponents to the idea.

The Smith Sound cod discovery gave focus and impetus to discussions among scientists that additional methods for assessment were needed, particularly in the inshore. Since at least 1935 (Sund 1935), acoustic sonar in which highly controlled sound waves are bounced off fish has been used to identify species and provide population estimates. Through filtering the returning echoes through specifically developed algorithms or mathematical formulas, estimates of numbers and size of fish were made. In the last decade, government scientists utilized a variety of such technology to estimate populations of highly migratory, pelagic fish such as herring, mackerel and capelin. Smith Sound offered new opportunities to direct this technology to the inshore in hope of greater understanding of inshore dynamics.

In important respects, Smith Sound has been the development site for evaluating a number of echosounding methodologies for inshore cod detection (Foote et al. 1987; Robichaud and Rose 2002; Rose 2003). From 1995 to 1997 two echosounding systems were utilized: a BioSonics 38kHz single-beam DT system and a BioSonics 38kHz model 102 analogue, dual beam system. Beginning in 1998, a 38kHz EK500 split-beam system has been used. As well, extensive experimentation has occurred in season, hour (daylight and night time) and comparison with some trawl surveys (Rose 2003). In addition, more systematic sampling techniques have evolved from more or less haphazard transects across the entire length and width of the Sound to a more rigorous grid of seventeen three-dimensional blocks (Rose 2003). Acoustic techniques then use these blocks as the units of analysis for the population survey.

In acoustic-based surveying, returning sound beams are interpreted through computer software algorithms to allow three-dimensional mapping of ocean structure as well as identification of different fish species. More recent refinements allow identification of fish species, estimates of biomass from density and size estimates and even some aging based on known age/length/weight relationships. While acoustic-based assessment is still very much a work in progress, government managers feel that considerable progress has been achieved in the nine short years since scientists first noted the concentration. As with VPA, primary emphasis is upon estimating population numbers so that a range of harvesting levels may be undertaken without sub-jecting the population to significant reduction (G. Rose, personal communication).

Using acoustic technology, several conclusions about the Smith Sound aggregation have been made. The population is thought to have increased steadily until 2000 reaching somewhere between 20,000 to 23,000 tonnes with all age classes increasing. Since 2000 the stock has stabilized and may even have begun a slight decline. Of par-ticular concern in recent assessments is the decline in the commer-cially valuable eight to ten year old fish in the population. This decline is puzzling since there is limited commercial harvest. As a result scientists recommend a continuation of fishing prohibition except for "by catch" allocations (cod caught while fishing for other species) and the sentinel fishery.

While admitting that some details are unlikely to ever be confirmed, scientists are not particularly surprised by the fish kill of 2003. As one scientist told me:

> ... It seems like a lot of fish but it really only represents five percent or less of the fish that are there. I don't think there's any reason to worry about it since the total numbers are not that significant ... I do wish we had done some systematic aging of the fish, though, to see whether those eight and nine year olds were there in the numbers we think.

Given the absence of any predator tooth marks or indications of dis-ease, the exact cause of death is still not completely known. Scientists, however, are convinced that an unusual but not rare circumstance termed a "super chilling" effect was the immediate cause. Super chill-ing occurs when unusually cold water, typically about −1 to −3 degree Celsius, is swept into the path of fish such as Atlantic cod. Lacking sufficient anti-freeze proteins, ice crystals form in blood and organs with death resulting. Normally, however, fish such as cod are able to avoid super-chilled water. Why were they unable to this time? Most likely, in their view, was the extensive volume and depth of the super-chilled water. The result was a "wall of death" occupying the entire water column from which escape was impossible.

Very recently, DNA analysis has confirmed that Smith Sound cod, while related to their offshore brethren, possess distinct genetic markers separating them from their offshore relatives (Beacham et al. 2002; Ruzzante et al. 2001). As a result, there is grudging acknowledgement that some cod may, in fact, remain in inshore waters all year. The numbers of these fish, whether they constitute a different stock and what role, if any, they might play in rebuilding offshore cod populations remain hotly debated within the scientific community. Officially, Smith Sound cod remain the largest, genetically distinguishable, localized remnant of northern cod with some scientists describing them as a local bay stock and others as a localized remnant that may in the near future vacate the Sound for the offshore.

While local fishers generally feel vindicated by recent research, there is still considerable disagreement with scientists over the size, age distribution and relevance to offshore populations and, of course, whether numbers warrant a local commercial fishery. Most also feel that there are numerous Smith Sounds around the Newfoundland coast as well, waiting to be discovered by government researchers. Most, if not all, bay stocks are healthy and could easily sustain localized fisheries. To more fully understand this view, an examination of fishers' knowledge and the conclusions drawn from it are required.

The Construction of Local Ecological Knowledge

The mysterious death of cod in Smith Sound reinvigorated long-standing disagreements between fishers and government scientists. As one fisher remarked shortly after the event:

> ... Those fish sure aren't paper fish are they? It'll be interesting to see how the government explains this. We've been telling them for years these fish are healthy and growing but they keep telling us there aren't enough of them to re-open the fishery. Yet every year we exceed the cod by catch in our blackback flounder fishery (another bottom dwelling fish whose habitat overlaps cod). I wonder how they'll fit this into their calculations.

The term "paper fish" is a sarcastic reference used by many fishers to fish population estimates derived from scientific models such as those, discussed earlier, used by government scientists to estimate numbers of fish (Foote et al. 1987; Maclennan, Fernandes and Dalen

2002; Robichaud and Rose, 2002; Sparre and Venema 1998; Sund 1935).

The skepticism is not limited to the recent fish kill. Another fisher provided a second, earlier example from the scientific discovery in Smith Sound discussed earlier:

> . . . I remember in 1995 when they suddenly discovered all those fish in Smith Sound. We told them all about the fish for years but nobody paid much attention. They told us those fish were supposed to be on the Hamilton Banks a thousand miles from here but we told them they've always been here and spawn here. They did start researching them in 1998 or so but all they want to do is count them rather than understand why they're here and what it means to us.

For fishers, the two events represent undeniable affirmation of their views that local cod populations are successfully rebuilding. For several years fishers such as these have often caught nearly as many cod as blackback flounder in their flounder nets. Flounder are a bottom dwelling fish like cod. When a specified "by catch" level of unintended cod harvest is reached in the legal flounder fishery, the entire fishery is shut down. Fishers have frequently communicated their frustration with this and what they feel are the clear implications to government scientists and managers but without seeming effect. As a result, both comments were expressed in a tone of bemused yet smug satisfaction tinged with frustration.

In the twenty-five years since the path breaking work of Robert Johannes (1981, 1989) social scientists have documented the extensive traditional knowledge that resource users acquire through their daily, long-term interactions with marine resources. They have also highlighted how that local knowledge has been traditionally applied to marine and freshwater resource management (Berkes 1999; Ellen, Parkes and Bicker 2000; Higgins 1998). One stream of this investigation has compared local knowledge with resource management science (Davis and Wagner 2003; Neis and Felt 2000; Poizat and Baran 1977) in the hope that such integration might avert future resource collapses.

Earlier and ongoing research (Felt 1994; Neis et al. 1999) in the Smith Sound area has documented a rich knowledge held by fishers of the sound itself and species that inhabit it. To differentiate it from traditional knowledge held by first nations and other groups, with perhaps hundreds of years of history, we have termed this knowledge Local Ecological Knowledge or LEK. This terminology is used to emphasize both its spatial scale as well as the fact that it is seldom drawn from more than three generations of local harvesting experience (Neis and Felt 2000).

Smith Sound LEK, like most local marine knowledge, is fundamentally framed by the relationship between fisher and fish. It is a predator's knowledge evolving from the experiences of hunting fish for a livelihood. It shares many of the same characteristics of traditional knowledge in its vernacular construction, integration or holism, content, expression and spatial reach. Moreover, like traditional knowledge, it is inductive, cumulative and largely shared, drawing on collective experiences of fishers as they continuously strive to extract a living.

In contrast to assessment science, LEK is subject to ongoing reliability and validation. Its ultimate vindication is fish in the net. Over time it acquires an integrated, holistic quality from which specific, instrumental strategies may be drawn for specific ends. Because it is drawn from the lived experiences of its practitioners, it is typically expressed in non-numeric language and categories of the culture from which it arises. This makes it something of a difficult fit with a more universalistic assessment science. Such differences need not make it less comprehensive, valid or predictive, however.

In the case of Smith Sound, evidence from fishers in the surrounding communities suggests clearly that they possess a fairly integrated knowledge of not only local codfish but the larger local ecosystem. This knowledge is summarized in a range of colorful taxonomic categories for different fish species, tidal forms, water quality, weather, marine mammals and sea birds as well as how all fit together into a local ecosystem. Using this terminology, complex relationships are expressed linking each to the other with the ultimate objective of predicting where, when and how to catch cod successfully. To give but one simple example, "capelin cod" or cod satiated from eating small capelin who have moved to deeper water depths to digest, can only be successfully fished with gill nets in deeper water on a Southwesterly wind that keeps the nets spread out rather than entangled due to tidal movement. In a similar fashion, local or bay cod can be immediately differentiated from offshore fish by color, shape, when caught and, early in the season, by stomach contents.

The end result is a reasonably integrated understanding of living and physical elements that define the bay as a "living system." It would be an exaggeration to say that everyone possesses knowledge to the same extent and that there is no disagreement. Fishers harvesting specific fish species generally know more about those species than do fishers for whom it is an incidental by catch. Additionally, the type of gear and boat one uses mediates this knowledge to some extent. For example, "hook and line" (baited lines of hooks up to a mile long) and gillnet fishers possess more detailed knowledge of ocean bottom configurations than trap and seine fishers. Nevertheless, the interview evidence suggests a strong consensus on the broad features of the Smith Sound ecosystem.

As extensive and integrated as local knowledge is, much is shrouded in mystery and uncertainty. Many events occur for no apparent reason. In Smith Sound, as with most fishing areas, fish catches vary, in many instances, for no known reason. In some years, the fish do not arrive and catches are extremely low. In such instances, fishers and their families "hunker down" for a difficult year in that prospects will improve in the coming years. More often than not, the fish do return. In the relatively few instances that fish disappear for long periods of time, communities often simply moved to new fishing grounds. This uncertainty colors fishers' knowledge with a fair bit of fatalism and irony that is forcefully communicated in stories and sayings.

Knowledge is communicated through a wide variety of forms including stories, jokes, one or two sentence phrases or a simple term. The tone may be one of humor, understated sarcasm or even confessional piety to the uninitiated. Consider the seemingly disconnected comment I heard a fisherman make to his son and fishing partner in an enraged voice one evening: "Take the bloods of bitches to the gallows! We got to get the blueberries off the nets." The explanation was simple enough. The nets were to be taken to a three-pole tripod (gallows) to be dried in order to remove a parasite thought to infect codfish with bluish-black spots in their flesh (blueberries) and therefore fetch lower prices. To assemble such knowledge in a comprehensive and integrated fashion is no easy task given such subtlety and variety of expression. The difficulty should in no way lead one to underestimate its existence and its continual use in guiding people's livelihoods in the area.

Commercial fishers have long maintained that a large, local stock of Northern cod existed in Smith Sound. A 1995 interview (emphasis added) with another fisher shortly after the official discovery captures this:

... Those fish have been there as long as anybody here can remember. You can even tell them from the incoming fish. They're shorter and a bit fatter. They're also a bit browner unless they are real "motherfish" (very large, females). When anybody needed a meal of fish you could always go out and catch a few even in February ... Full of roe (eggs) they was too. Don't know why all *they* (scientists) want to do is count them, they could have asked anybody here about them and we would probably have told them.

Considerable knowledge exists regarding fish physiology, behavior and relationship to wider meteorological and oceanographic conditions. Cod fishers can easily draw cod migration routes, on charts or even paper bags, within the bay, to adjacent bays and to offshore sites according to season, tide, water temperature and prey species. Known deep holes within the underwater trenches are pinpointed, local names assigned and, all too often, stories told in remorseful detail of how they, themselves, contributed to the decimation of its population of large female fish in the late 1970s and early 1980s.

Fishers surrounding the Sound have followed the assessment process with great interest. Many have discussed the ongoing work with scientists and have been pleased with the confirmation of their knowledge. Varying levels of disagreement continue to exist, however, as indicated earlier. Of particular divergence is the conclusion that the reproductively and commercially valuable six to nine year old fish are declining. In conversations with several fishers, the mysterious die off of April 2003 reinforced the disagreement.

Many fishers feel that recent, acoustic-based estimates made by scientists have a number of shortcomings. These include 1) an incomplete understanding of the relationship of Smith Sound fish to those in nearby bays and sounds, 2) the role of marine predators such as seals, and 3) the seasonal movement within the bay and to adjacent areas such as the North West Arm of Trinity Bay that might account for fluctuations in the numbers of adult fish present during scientific assessment.

Many fishers have views about the possible role local fish have had or might have in repopulating offshore populations. For fishers, understanding seasonal movements within the Sound and between it and adjacent bays is critical to estimating the cod population. Depending upon a number of tidal, temperature and prey abundance conditions, significant numbers of Smith Sound cod move throughout the bay and to adjacent ones. Because assessments are done in January and February, many feel some years have produced lower estimates due to environmental conditions. Moreover, there is pervasive concern that seals, in particular, are preventing faster population recovery. Virtually every fisher voiced their frustration with the government for allowing seals to fish while they could not.

Several fishers expressed skepticism that these older fish were absent. They indicated that numerous examples of eight, ten and even older fish of twelve to fourteen years could be found among the dead fish. For them, this was evidence that even these large motherfish, that they admitted had become badly depleted through gillnet fishing in the 1970s and 1980s, were beginning to rebuild.

Another fisherman explained that even if these fish were down in numbers it was part of normal behavior. In his view:

> There's about as many fish here as there has ever been. Once they get to be so many some of them moves out into South West Arm or up the shore. You can see them passing through the Causeway coming onto Random Island . . . Probably because there's only so much food in the Sound.

Fishers also had explanations for the sudden die off itself. Marine predators, particularly seals, were the most frequently cited explanation. Without denying super-chilled water as the immediate cause of death, every fisher felt something must have prevented the cod from avoiding the lethal water. Seals were everyone's first choice. Several recounted similar die offs, though involving far fewer fish, resulting from seals chasing cod in the confined area and driving them into the lethal cold water. A few fishers offered entirely different explanations ranging from "toxic blooms" of lethal marine algae to illegal fishing.

All of this has created a certain frustration among fishers. Since 1992, most fishers have had limited opportunities to directly fish for cod. A January 2004 conversation with a fisherman continuing to fish species other than cod captured this frustration:

> Fishermen need to fish to know what's going on . . . It's not that I don't believe them (scientists) but the only way I can be convinced is to go and try and catch fish on my terms. Sometimes I feels like they've taken one arm away from me with all these restrictions.

This frustration has led some, though by no means all, area fishers to ask for a small allocation of cod in the Sound and adjacent areas on a trial basis. Several others would be satisfied to be more involved in the assessment surveys, in particular any trawl (bottom net) fishing done to verify acoustic methods. Fishers feel they might be able to help by identifying local fish from offshore ones and in directing research vessels where to fish. These possibilities are discussed frequently with all parties, including scientists, according to several fishers and serious consideration is being given to several. Despite progress along the above lines and generally amicable relations with scientists, virtually every fisher expressed some level of frustration at not being taken as seriously as they felt they deserved.

Bridging Troubled Waters: Linking Fishers and L.E.K. with Science and Management

The physical, social and symbolic distance separating fishers from government managers and scientists has shortened, though certainly not disappeared, since the collapse of 1992. The collapse was widely interpreted as a failure of science, management and government. Many fishers admit to illegal practices; some state that they might have caught too many fish. Overwhelmingly, however, blame is directed toward foreign trawlers, large offshore Canadian boats and badly flawed scientific support. Indeed, it has become something of a mantra to state that the inshore fishery, by itself, could never have created the collapse. Whether this is completely true is an interesting digression. The media, fishers' organizations, environmental groups as well as several government reports used the collapse to promote new strategies to increase the participation of fishers and other constituencies in both scientific review and management deliberation. A number of respected authors published books and articles concluding that government personnel had developed tunnel vision and needed to expand the consultative process if recovery was to succeed (Finlayson 1994; Harris 1998). Assessment science, in particular, received heavy criticism. Politicians, ever resourceful in distancing themselves from blame, joined the chorus and said, in effect, government bureaucrats should listen more to fishers.

The immediate result was that talking to fishers became official Canadian government policy. A former government scientist recounts the changing emphasis beginning in fall 1992:

> ... Most of us had always had pretty good relations with fishermen. We'd even used them to assist us with some of the research going back to the late 1970s. Most of them knew a lot about a lot of things

> I didn't. After '92 it became kind of official. We were supposed to consult and discuss even though most of us really didn't know what we should do differently.

The new policy was extremely general and offered few precise guidelines on what should be discussed or how it might affect scientific assessment. The most common accommodation seems to be using fishers as "research assistants" in carrying out research largely designed according to scientific rules. As such fishers might rent their boats for scientific, experimental fishing, record data and perhaps give advice on sampling strategies. The knowledge generated was still nearly exclusively defined by the assessment paradigm. Nonetheless, most fishers appear to have acquired new respect and a heightened sense of participation. As one fisher remarked:

> ... It still gets done mostly their way but they do listen a lot more to us. One of us always gets a call when one of them (scientists) is coming out to do something. They come visit and explain what they're going to do and ask what we think. I can remember a couple of times when they changed their plans as a result of what we told them.

Similarly, fisheries managers also expanded formal as well as informal discussions with fishers. While consultation committees had always existed to varying degrees, new ones grew up quickly for all commercial species. Between 1993 and 1995, a hierarchy of formal consultative structures arose for most commercially important species. Community level consultations fed into regional ones that in turn contributed to a top level one responsible for the particular species throughout its Canadian range.

The diffuse consultation system for managers and scientists was an interim response. Politicians had promised at the time of the 1992 closure that new, more transparent and inclusive decision-making processes would be created as one means to minimize a repeat of the Northern cod collapse. In late 1993, the Canadian government created an arms-length advisory organization called the Fisheries Resource Conservation Council (FRCC). The FRCC consists of twenty-six appointed representatives and two co-chairs drawn from government and industry. The Canadian Minister of Fisheries makes appointments for upwards of three years and reappointments are common. Representation is intended to reflect fishing industry constituencies as well as Canadian and provincial levels of government.

The Council exists independently of the fisheries bureaucracy and reports directly to the Canadian Minister of Fisheries. It receives separate funding for offices and full-time staff, along with operational funds for extensive traveling for consultation. While fisheries science continues to exist within the government bureaucracy, all research is vetted in the open environment of FRCC hearings. Where research gaps or inadequacies are perceived to exist, the FRCC directs government scientists to address them and report back to the Council. In preparation for the fishing season for each commercial species, the Council reviews all information, holds extensive consultations and makes specific recommendations jointly with fisheries managers directly to the Minister.

Most fishers enthusiastically endorse the FRCC and see it as very much theirs. There is a reasonable basis for such feelings of ownership. Fishers are exceedingly well represented through their unions as well as at-large appointments. Ordinarily, one of the co-chairs is a fisher or fisher union representative. The Fisheries Resource Conservation Council's independence and commitment to a more inclusive process for scientific assessment and management is forcefully captured in a January 1996 (R.2:17) report:

> We have heard a serious lack of confidence expressed by fishermen in the results of scientific surveys. Similarly, Fisheries and Oceans, Canada scientists have difficulty incorporating fishermen's information into their stock assessment methodology. This lack of confidence is an obstacle to the development of reliable, widely acceptable criteria for re-opening and conducting the fishery. The precision of scientific abundance surveys does not meet the expectations of fishermen. New and improved methods of fish counting, the use of traditional knowledge, the development of additional indices of stock abundance and new approaches to interpreting these data are needed.

Monthly committee and quarterly Council meetings are lively events replete with discussion and challenge to scientific results and potential management initiatives. Sentinel fisheries, such as the one in Smith Sound, are largely a result of FRCC insistence that alternative data sources and information are essential for successful management and provide a "reality check" on scientific research. In a number of instances, substantial criticism by fishers or divergence between official research assessments and local knowledge has resulted in significant modification and, occasionally, even outright rejection of scientific advice. In June 2004, for example, the Canadian government approved a small commercial, experimental fishery for cod as a result of FRCC recommendations in spite of scientific advice to the contrary. Before the FRCC this would have been unheard of.

The FRCC is still very much a work in progress. Scientific advice still largely prevails and the majority of management recommendations from government officials still find their way to the Minister for approval. Having said this, the legitimacy and power of fishers and their knowledge has significantly advanced. While still not equal, scientific research has lost much of its hegemony. Using Smith Sound as an example, scientists officially and unofficially show a heightened respect for fishers and their views though most still grapple with how to link LEK to their own work. For their part, fishers have become considerably more familiar with scientific assessment and most try to relate their own knowledge to it. Occasionally, fishers or scientists make specific connections as, for example, in the following comment from a fisher:

> ... I'd always wondered why capelin went clockwise in the lower part of the Bay and counterclockwise in the upper part ... I remember seeing a map of current and temperature from DFO and now I know why since the capelin follow both.

Epiphanies work both ways as well with several examples of scientists expanding their knowledge of fish behavior as a result of discussions with fishers. Less commonly, one type of knowledge requires rejection or reformulation in the other. Fishers, for example, have had to revise some of their understanding of cod diet from stomach samples collected by scientists. Scientists have also benefited from the exchanges. Most concede that much of their limited knowledge of local stocks is attributable to contributions from fishers. Scientists have also modified their sampling schemes on the basis of information supplied by fishers on cod behavior according to season, temperature, ocean currents and the presence or absence of certain microbial organisms.

Despite these very positive signs of bridging, the different knowledge and their respective proponents are still far from equal. Moreover, distance from FRCC involvement most likely increases the inequality. In light of this, the occasional, bemused skepticism so clearly communicated in several fishers' comments is not surprising.

Conclusion

Following a devastating collapse in one of the world's greatest and longest prosecuted fisheries in 1992, the Canadian government dramatically reorganized the consultation process in Eastern Canada. The resulting process, with the FRCC as the primary focus, explicitly attempted to elevate resource users and their knowledge in the assessment and management processes. Using Smith Sound, a small inlet on the Island province of Newfoundland and Labrador as a focus, this chapter has explored these changes, focusing particularly on the structure, content and discourse of fishers' knowledge and its relationship to assessment science in a revamped consultation process. Generally, I argue that this process is successful though still very much in a developmental stage. Significant challenges exist flowing from the differences in how scientists, managers and fishers construct their understandings and the objectives flowing from them.

In retrospect, several factors likely facilitated the progress that has been achieved. The collapse itself with its massive social and economic impact brought considerable media attention. Much of this attention pointed to inadequacies in science, management and government. The collapse, combined with similar fishery collapses in industrial fisheries around the world, gravely weakened the hegemony accorded assessment science. Fishers were also highly organized through a large and politically sophisticated union. The message that more meaningful involvement of fishers might have prevented the collapse got extensive and supportive media coverage. Combined with an emerging world-wide view that sustainable management necessitated meaningful involvement of all sectors of the fishing industry, politicians felt considerable pressure to make dramatic changes. The result was the FRCC. Intentionally or not, the Council provides a platform, distinct from government, where challenges to management and science are mounted and defended with some success.

A Newfoundland spring has just passed without another fish kill. While assessment results have not been officially released, informal discussions suggest not much has changed from the 2003 report. On the surface, relations between scientists and fishers are cordial and friendly. In fact, relations are arguably much better between fishers, scientists and managers than ten or twenty years ago. It is not difficult, however, to still find suspicion of motives and lack of understanding on all sides. Most of the improvement is a result of the FRCC.

Prior to it, fishers were formally powerless. They typically expressed frustration about fish management to their colleagues, or suffered indignant silence. There is now a legitimate forum, run in part by fishers, where fishers are encouraged to voice their concerns and scientists willingly listen and respond. Nonetheless, as the chapter has indicated, much of the suspicion and misunderstanding remains. This is likely to surface in 2005 when, several fishers have indicated, they will press for a small commercial fishery in the Sound based on their knowledge of the health of the local stock. Scientists are likely to continue to preach restraint. When the FRCC comes to meet in the area during March 2005, the issue will be reviewed, debated and recommendations made to the Canadian Minister of Fisheries. Ten years ago the outcome was a forgone conclusion but not today.

Relationships, while not yet equal, are considerably better than before the collapse. In most respects this holds throughout Eastern Canada. A bridge in the form of the FRCC now exists, connecting fishers and scientists and their distinct ways of understanding fish and the larger marine environment. Creaky, sometimes shaky and a far cry from modern, steel trestles, it is a bridge nonetheless. Any bridge is likely to be preferable to a chasm as Canada tries to rebuild her once seemingly inexhaustible marine resources and searches for more participatory regimes with which to understand and manage them.

References

Alexander, David. 1977. *The Decay of Trade*. St. John's: ISER Press.

Beacham, Thomas, Donald J. Brattey, Kenneth M. Miler, Desmond Le Khai, and Robert W. Withler. 2002. "Multiple Stock Structure of Atlantic Cod (Gadus morhua) off Newfoundland and Labrador Determined from Genetic Variation." *ICES Journal of Marine Science* 59:650–665.

Berkes, Fikret. 1999. *Sacred Ecology: Traditional Ecological Knowledge and Resource Management*. London: Belhaven Press.

Brown, James. 2001. *Who Rules in Science?* Cambridge: Harvard University Press.

Davis, Anthony and John Wagner. 2003. "Who Knows? On the Importance of Identifying 'Experts' When Researching Local Ecological Knowledge." *Human Ecology* 31(3):463–489.

DeWalt, Bruce R. 1999. "Using Indigenous Knowledge and Scientific Knowledge to Improve Agricultural Land and Natural Resource Management in Latin America." Pp. 101–124 in *Traditional and Modern Resource Management in Latin America*, edited by F.J. Pichon, J.E. Uquillas, and J. Frechione. Pittsburgh: University of Pittsburgh Press.

Dyer, Chris L. and James R. McGoodwin. 1994. *Folk Management of the World's*

Fisheries: Lessons for Modern Fisheries Management. Niwot, CO: University of Colorado Press.

Ellen, Robin, Paula Parkes, and Allan Bicker. 2000. *Indigenous Environmental Knowledge and its Transformations: Critical Anthropological Perspectives*. Amsterdam: Harwood Academic Publishers.

Felt, Lawrence F. 1994. "Two Tales of a Fish: The Social Construction of Indigenous Knowledge among Atlantic Canadian Salmon Fishers." Pp. 251–286 in *Folk Management of the World's Fisheries*, edited by C. Dyer and J. McGoodwin. Niwot, CO: University of Colorado Press.

Finlayson, Christopher. 1994. *Fishing for Truth*. St. John's: ISER Press.

Fisheries Resource Conservation Council (FRCC). 1996. *Conservation Come Aboard: 1995. Conservation Requirements for Atlantic Groundfish*. FRCC.95.R.2. November 1995.
———. 2003. *Stock Assessment for 2J, 3K and 3 L cod*. FRCC. June 2003. 57 pp.

Food and Agriculture Organization of the United Nations (FAO). 1998. Fisheries Technical Paper No. 300.1, Rev. 2. Rome: FAO.

Foote, Ken G., Henry P. Knudsen, David N. MacLennan, and Edward J. Simmonds. 1987. "Calibration of Acoustic Instruments for Fish Density Estimation: A Practical Guide." *ICES Cooperative Research Report, No. 144*.

Government of Canada. 1977. *Canada's Oceans: A Plan to Manage Canada's Renewable Marine Resources*. Ottawa: Queen's Printer for Canada.

Hacking, Ian. 2001. *The Social Construction of What*. Cambridge: Harvard University Press.

Harding, Sandra. 1991. *Whose Science? Whose Knowledge?: Thinking from Women's Lives*. Ithaca: Cornell University Press.

Harris, Michael. 1998. *Lament for an Ocean*. Toronto: McClelland and Stewart.

Higgins, Charles. 1998. "The Role of Traditional Ecological Knowledge in Managing for Biodiversity." *Forestry Chronicle* 74(3):323–326.

Hilborn, Ray and Carl J. Walters. 1992. *Quantitative Fisheries Stock Assessment: Choice, Dynamics and Uncertainty*. London and New York: Chapman and Hall, Inc.

Hutchings, Jeffrey, Carl Walters, and Richard Haedrich. 1997. "Is Scientific Inquiry Incompatible with Government Information Control?" *Canadian Journal of Fisheries and Aquatic Science* 51:2363–2378.

Innis, Harold. 1949. *The Cod Fisheries*. Toronto: University of Toronto Press.

Johannes, Robert. E. 1981. *Words of the Lagoon: Fishing and Marine Lore in Palau District of Micronesia*. Berkley: University of California Press.
———. 1989. "Introduction." Pp. 1–17 in *Traditional Ecological Knowledge: A Collection of Essays*, edited by R.E. Johannes. Cambridge: IUCN.

Kuhn, Thomas. 1962. *The Structure of Scientific Revolutions*. Chicago: University of Chicago Press.

MacLennan, David N., P.G. Fernandes, and J. Dalen. 2002. "A Consistent Approach To Definitions and Symbols in Fisheries Acoustics." *ICES Journal of Marine Science* 59:762–772.

Neis, Barbara and Lawrence F. Felt. 2000. *Finding Our Sea Legs: Linking Fishery People and Their Knowledge with Science and Management*. St. John's: ISER Press.

Neis, Barbara, David Schneider, Lawrence F. Felt, Richard Haedrich, Jeffrey Hutchings, and Johanne Fischer. 1999. "Northern Cod Stock Assessment: What Can Be Learned from Interviewing Resource Users?" *Canadian Journal of Fisheries and Aquatic Science* 56:1944–63.

Northwest Atlantic Fisheries Organization (NAFO). 1997. *Status of 2J3KL Cod in the Northwest Atlantic*. Dartmouth, Nova Scotia: NAFO.

Poizat, Gregor and E. Baran. 1977. "Fishermen's Knowledge as Background Information in Tropical Fish Ecology: A Quantitative Comparison with Fish Sampling Results." *Environmental Biology of Fishes* 50:435–449.

Robichaud, Donald R. and George A. Rose. 2002. "Assessing Evacuation Rates and Spawning Abundance of Marine Fishes Using Coupled Telemetric and Acoustic Surveys." *ICES Journal of Marine Science* 59:254–260.

Rose, George. A. 1992. "Cod Spawning on a Migration Highway in the North-West Atlantic." *Nature* 366:458–461.

———. 2003. "Monitoring Coastal Northern Cod: Towards an Optimal Survey of Smith Sound, Newfoundland." *ICES Journal of Marine Science* 60:1–10.

Ruzzante, Daniel E., Christopher T. Taggart, Robert W. Doyle, and David Cook. 2001. "Stability in the Historical Pattern of Genetic Structure of Newfoundland Cod (Gadus morhua) Despite the Catastrophic Decline in Population Size from 1964 to 1994." *Conservation Genetics* 2:257–269.

Scott, James and Laura Scott. 1967. *Fishes of the Northwest Atlantic*. Ottawa: Canadian Ministry of Fisheries and Oceans.

Sparre, Per and Siebren Venema. 1998. *Introduction to Tropical Fish Stock Assessment, Part 1: Manual.* "Chapter 5 – Virtual Population Methods." FAO Technical Paper No. 306.1. Rome: Food and Agriculture Organization of the United Nations. Retrieved September 22, 2004 (http://www.fao.org/docrep/W5449E/w5449e07.htm).

Storey, Keith. 1993. *The Newfoundland Groundfish Fisheries: Defining the Reality*. St. John's: ISER Press.

Sund, Otter. 1935. "Echo Sounding in Fishery Research." *Nature* 953.

Weeks, Priscilla. 1995. "Fisher Scientists: The Reconstruction of Scientific Discourse." *Human Organization* 54(4):429–436.

Wright, Miriam. 2001. *A Fishery for Modern Times*. Oxford: Oxford University Press.

Notes

[1] Department of Fisheries and Oceans, Canada estimated that as much as 1250 to 1400 metric tonnes of fish were killed. Since a single metric tonne equals 2200 pounds and an average fish weighs about six pounds, the total number of dead fish could be as high as 513,000 or half a million. Calculation is (1400 × 2200) / 6 = 513,333 fish.

[2] The 1994 multidisciplinary project was funded under a $1.4 million dollar Tri Council Green Program grant entitled *Sustainability in a Cold Ocean Environment*, Dr. Rosemary Ommer, Principal Investigator, Drs. Lawrence Felt, Barbara Neis, Peter Sinclair, David Schneider and Richard Haedrich, Co-investigators and a Social Science Research Council of Canada (SSHRC) Strategic Grant for $174,000 entitled *Fishers Local Ecological Knowledge and Sustainable Fisheries*. Grant No. 809–94–0004. Dr. Lawrence Felt, Principal Investigator. Drs. Barbara Neis, Richard Haedrich, Jeff Hutchings and David Schneider, Co-investigators. All team members were faculty in the departments of biology (Haedrich, Schneider and Hutchings) or Sociology/Anthropology (Felt and Neis). I am grateful to these colleagues and our research assistants Paul Ripley and Danny Ing, for completing the earlier interviews and making them available.

[3] A metric tonne is equal to 2200 pounds of fish. With an average weight per fish of six pounds, this represents (250,000 × 2200) / 6 = 91,666,666 fish.

[4] One metre equals thirty-seven inches.

[5] The term "paradigm" is used according to Kuhn in *The Structure of Scientific Revolution* (1962). A paradigm consists of the assumptions, critical terms, important questions, preferred sources of data, research designs and interpretive rules within which a specific body of research is undertaken.

WE ALL CAN JUST GET ALONG: THE SOCIAL CONSTRUCTIONS OF PRAIRIE DOG STAKEHOLDERS AND THE USE OF A TRANSACTIONAL MANAGEMENT APPROACH IN DEVISING A SPECIES CONSERVATION PLAN

Brett Zollinger and Steven E. Daniels

Introduction

Wildlife management faces ample challenges in dealing with biological, habitat, climatological and a host of other ecological conditions. Increasingly, wildlife management entities at both the state and federal levels are realizing the significance of incorporating sociological conditions into their management efforts. The Kansas Department of Wildlife and Parks (KDWP) has undertaken an initiative to formulate a conservation plan for a species that has long been considered a pest by the predominant socio-legal-economic structures in the western half of the state (and in the Great Plains, in general). In many places in the Great Plains, Kansas included, where agriculture is a primary economic activity, the systematic extermination of the prairie dog has been pursued since Euro-American settlement. Consequently, the prairie dog might now be considered by most in the area, and particularly by farmers, a species with whom settlers engaged in a "long hard war." The National Wildlife Federation, the Biodiversity Legal Foundation, the Predator Project, and Jon C. Sharps petitioned the United States Fish and Wildlife Service (USFWS) in 1998 to list the species as threatened. As a consequence, the KDWP's conservation plan endeavors to change the patterned actions of our socio-legal-economic structures toward the prairie dog in such a way as to reverse the population decline of the species. Such action would, potentially, prevent the USFWS's listing of the species. The KDWP is one of several state wildlife management agencies in the eleven-state Great Plains region that constitutes the prairie dog's historic habitat. It is this context in which the KDWP has formed a work group consisting of multiple stakeholders charged with assisting the department in authoring a conservation plan.

This chapter will explore how a transactional management approach and a social constructionist perspective were applied to facilitate the Kansas Prairie Dog work group. This chapter will enhance wildlife managers' skills so that they may more consciously and effectively identify and react to the ways in which various stakeholder groups define reality with regard to wildlife, as these skills are essential for enjoying the most successful transactional management approach possible.

The Intersections of a Transactional Management Approach and Social Constructionist Thought

Increasingly wildlife management agencies are engaging multiple stakeholders in the process of wildlife management. Chase, Schusler, and Decker (2000) argue that within the past ten years approaches that move beyond public opinion/attitudinal data gathering have emerged. In such approaches the representatives of various stakeholder backgrounds are actively sought out for their input into the management process. The transactional approach involves gathering a diverse group of people representing resource users, management agencies, and non-governmental organizations (Chase et al. 2000). Multiple stakeholders are brought together into task forces or work groups, where members have direct access to members from other organizations, and this promotes dialogue. This perspective assumes that a potential barrier to non-controversial implementation of a management program is the lack of understanding of the issue in all of its complexity. Through this dialogue with others, the complexities of the management process are conveyed to all involved. At its base, a transactional approach simply means that the management decisions result from structured interaction among a diverse set of stakeholders, working in concert with the official management agency.

The transactional approach assumes tenets of collaborative learning and interactive learning, where participants in the process are actively engaged in making decisions. Walker and Daniels (1994) argue that these learning techniques are based on research that shows more effective learning through engagement, rather than passive exposure. For example, hearing a lecture or listening to a lecture tends not to be as effective as a question-and-answer seminar setting where group members become actively engaged in the clarification, revision and processing of information. In addition, the different opinions or worldviews represented at the table may even enhance learning. Walker and Daniels (1994:7) assert, "Group members can learn well from conflict situations when controversies are clarified, different values are respected and constructive disagreements are accepted."

Some have argued that a "pluralist" decision-making perspective most aptly characterizes the type of social interaction that occurs in management processes involving diverse stakeholders (Daniels and Walker 2001). Stakeholders do not necessarily arrive at a consensus on all issues, nor can they be expected to, given the fundamentally different constructions of reality under which they operate. Thus, a transactional management approach more appropriately seeks to manage conflict rather than resolve conflict, in the sense of achieving consensus on all issues.

From a sociological viewpoint, the pluralist decision-making perspective and a transactional management approach assume that certain tenets of social constructionist theory (see Berger and Luckmann 1966) are operative. These tenets are crucial to acknowledge in wildlife management if progress toward finding policies/solutions to issues are to enjoy as much acceptance as possible given the various groups involved. Multiple socially constructed realities, or frames of understanding and belief, are assumed to exist among the multiple stakeholders interacting. Thus, a pluralist decision-making perspective is foundational to transactional management, as it accounts for the multiple views of reality among stakeholders.

A social constructionist perspective on wildlife issues would contend that there are three important levels at which attitudes and values toward wildlife emerge: the individual level, the intra-group level and the inter-group level. Some discussion of each is warranted because a conflict management approach that is grounded in social constructionism must be cognizant of each.

Certainly values and attitudes toward wildlife are held at the individual level. People have their own attitudes, which can vary within communities and even within families (one person in a family may choose vegetarianism for ethical reasons, while no one else does). Since our thought processes and experiences are unique, our individual perspectives toward wildlife are unique as well. As such, we each hold our own mix of fear, fascination, wonder and revulsion.

Even though individuals are the most disaggregated social unit, values and attitudes are not shaped solely at the individual level. In fact, much of the meaning that we attribute to wildlife is shaped by our interaction with people around us and by the values they hold. Social psychologists use a term—reference group—that is quite useful in discussing the social formation of values. A reference group is merely that group of people that a person turns to in order to validate a belief or idea. One's reference group is typically a group to which one feels a considerable degree of affiliation or membership; certainly as one is growing up, the family is the most important reference group. Our attitudes toward wildlife are, therefore, largely shaped by immediate family as we grow. If we are born into a family of hunters or fishers, then we may well have positive attitudes toward those activities or participate in them ourselves. As we mature, our reference groups broaden to include people beyond our immediate family, but even then one's reference group is likely to consist of like-minded people. This may be little more than a long-winded social psychological explanation of the far more elegant dictum "birds of a feather flock together." But the key point is to think of the social landscape as dotted with social networks of like-minded people who tend to reinforce each other's views.

Greider and Garkovich (1994) have elaborated the implications of a social constructionist perspective for the understanding of nature and the environment and attitudes toward anticipated changes in nature and the environment. Drawing on social constructionist theory about ways of knowing and symbolic interactionism, they argue that:

> Our understanding of nature and of human relationships with the environment are really cultural expressions used to define who we were, who we are, and who we hope to be at this place and in this space . . . Thus, when events or technological innovations challenge the meanings of these landscapes, it is our conceptions of ourselves that change through a process of negotiating new symbols of meaning (Greider and Garkovich 1994:2).

At an intra-group level, then, we conclude that shared understandings and beliefs among groups of people about that which is real, admirable, appropriate, etc., shape attitudes toward wildlife issues.

Many of the interesting insights about wildlife issues occur when we broaden our scale of analysis yet again, and now look at inter-group processes. At this level there are again three interesting perspectives to explore: when inter-group attitudes are largely aligned with one another, when they are fundamentally opposed and when the inter-group attitudes somehow merge or transform into altogether new values. When inter-group attitudes are similar regarding a particular issue, the groups may well become allies in promoting those attitudes. It is not necessary that this attitudinal similarity across groups lead to a conscious alliance, nor is it necessary that groups agree on all issues in order to work together. The second case— when inter-group issues are fundamentally opposed—leads quite logically to a political fisticuffs/interest group politics view of the world. In this case, groups with the most direct power or access to power carry the day and their values gradually become institutionalized into policy while less powerful viewpoints become increasingly marginalized. The third case—where inter-group attitudes interact so as to evolve into new perspectives—is perhaps the most intriguing. Stakeholder factions have differing views of reality or cultural expressions. The process of negotiating and renegotiating meaning can occur through the transactional approach to management as a work group setting allows those different realities to become known to and discussed among out-group members. It is this work group type interaction that brings diverse others together, and if facilitated carefully, the work group environment allows definitions of meaning to be aired and negotiated toward formulating an operative definition for purposes of the work group. Chase et al. (2000:211) argue the utility of such an approach:

> Agencies have experienced several positive outcomes because of the transactional approach, including greater public acceptance of controversial management decisions, improved agency image, and a better educated public.

Because so much controversy surrounds the issue of prairie dog conservation, the transactional approach is appropriate to achieve each of these three outcomes. In addition, a sense of "ownership" among task force/work group participants has been noted in other transactional management efforts (Chase et al. 2000; Endter-Wada et al. 1998), and this sense of ownership means that participants exert great effort to assure the plan is an acceptable one for all involved. This, of course, makes the plan easier to "sell" to the participants' respective in-groups. In addition, to the extent that people in key positions of leadership for the respective stakeholder groups are involved in the planning process, the plan becomes credible. As Heberlein (1976:207) asserts, "Opinion leaders are important in the transmission of information since people form their opinions more by what others say than through formal mechanisms."

History of Black Tailed Prairie Dogs: Why All the Fuss?

The catalyst of the social action described herein is a petition to the USFWS to list the Black Tailed Prairie Dogs as a Threatened or an Endangered species, due to large population declines in the area that many consider to be the historical range of the species. Its distribution encompasses primarily those portions of ten states (North Dakota, South Dakota, Montana, Wyoming, Nebraska, Colorado, Kansas Oklahoma, Texas and New Mexico) that lie within the eco-region known as the Great Plains, but it also extends into southeast Arizona (see Hall 1981:411–12, for a map).

The following description of black-tailed prairie dog's feeding habits and population trends is taken from the draft Kansas prairie dog work group conservation plan (Roy 2000:4):

> The first description of the prairie dog in Kansas occurred in 1806–07 by Pike and he designated it by its Native American name, Wishtonwish. In 1859, J.R. Mead indicated that prairie dogs were innumerable; the divide between the Saline and Solomon rivers in Ellsworth County (north-central Kansas) and west was continuous prairie dog towns for miles. Lantz reported that sixty-eight counties in Kansas were occupied with prairie dogs. Lantz used a landowner survey to approximate occupied acreage. Results indicated that 1,224,855 acres were occupied by prairie dogs, which he rounded off to two million acres to account for non-respondents in the survey questionnaire.

The decline of prairie dogs associated with human activity occurred primarily through a combination of concerted effort to rid land of prairie dogs and a reduction in habitat from the conversion of grassland to cropland.

> Legislative action directed at extermination of prairie dogs in Kansas was initiated in 1901. The decline of the black-tailed prairie dog was largely due to poisoning efforts. Changes in land use practices after settlement of western Kansas also contributed to abrupt declines in populations of the prairie dog. Nearly two-thirds of the 33 million acres of range and pasture land within the geographic ranges of the prairie dog in Kansas was converted to cropland and other uses after

settlement . . . The number of prairie dogs in Kansas declined following the onset of the extermination efforts but seemed to have remained
fairly stabled since the earliest known account by Smith. In 1956,
Smith indicated that there was a total of 57,045 acres of prairie dog
towns remaining in Kansas (Roy 2000:4–5).

A key question that had to be tackled by the conservation plan
work group is how to resolve conflicting opinion survey data (collected from residents of the region) on extent of prairie dog populations with aerial photography estimates of populations. The draft
plan continues (Roy 2000:5):

> The use of aerial photography was shown by 3 separate authors in
> Kansas to provide more reliable and accurate estimates than the opin-
> ion survey [conducted by] the Soil Conservation Service and Department
> of Wildlife Conservation Officers. The use of the Agricultural Stabilization
> and Conservation Service's slides was initiated in the early 1980's and
> would thus make it impossible to reevaluate the acreage of prairie dogs
> in 1956, 1973 and 1977. The population of prairie dogs in Kansas
> seemed to have oscillated slightly but remained relatively constant since
> the 1956 estimates. Other more accurate survey methods are now
> available to evaluate prairie dog distribution and abundance and will
> likely be used in future surveys.

In sum, while population estimates (extent of inhabited acreage)
vary, the data clearly point to large declines in prairie dog populations since white settlement. In addition, a casual drive through rural
highways and county roads in a large portion of western Kansas will
find the landscape nearly void of prairie dog colonies, a striking contrast to the descriptions of almost continuous prairie dog colonies
from Ellsworth County (center of state) westward through the remainder of Kansas recorded in the early period of white settlement in
the state (Roy 2000).

KDWP Planning Activities: Public Meetings and the Work Group

The KDWP sought to manage conflict surrounding the conservation
plan through public meetings and by establishing a work group consisting of stakeholders from a diverse set of backgrounds. The KDWP
held three public comment sessions as an initial step toward understanding landowners' attitudes toward the black-tailed prairie dog.
Sessions were held in the Kansas communities of Hutchinson, Garden
City and Colby. Each site experienced a strong showing, nearly filling

the rooms that were reserved for the sessions. About fifty people turned out at each of the three sites. In addition to the high turn-out, a diversity of groups were represented at each site, including such groups as landowners, environmental/wildlife societies (Nature Conservancy, Wildlife Management Institute, National Wildlife Federation), prairie dog control agents and representatives from the federal agencies of the Bureau of Land Management and the U.S. Forest Service (responsible for managing federal grasslands in south-west Kansas and southeast Colorado).

The sessions began with introductory statements by KDWP personnel, who informed the audience of the agency's goal to develop a conservation plan as a result of the petition to the USFWS for listing the species. A USFWS representative explained the process of petitioning and the agency's mandated response. When petitioning to list, it is the onus of the petitioning party to provide sufficient evidence that listing may be warranted (i.e., in the absence of such evidence, a simple letter requesting petitioning does not receive further attention by the agency). As a result of the petitioning request and accompanying evidence for alarm, the USFWS determined that there was sufficient information to suggest a serious threat to the species. At the time of the public sessions, the USFWS's official position on the petition to list was described in agency lingo as "listing consideration." Final introductory remarks involved a brief presentation on the best available estimates of historical and current prairie dog populations in the region, prime habitat conditions, prairie dog effects on range/competition with livestock and various types of control measures currently used. A Kansas State University Extension Service representative made this final short presentation. Following the presentations, the floor was opened for public comment, and representatives from Fort Hays State University's Docking Institute of Public Affairs[1] facilitated and recorded the public comment.

Comment largely centered on the negative influences of the prairie dog. Landowners tended to express alarm that an agency of the state would actually encourage the presence of prairie dogs. Comments from all three sites indicated that certain cultural beliefs and attitudes toward prairie dogs were shared among landowners. Prairie dogs were perceived as some of the most grievous pests for those who own livestock. A landowner maintained, "Prosperity is tied to the prairie dog and how many colonies are in my pastures; our livelihood depends on the quality of those pastures." In addition, landowners did not view the prairie dog as being as benign a species to their operations as another species, the swift fox, for which KDWP has formulated a conservation plan. One commented:

> There is a big difference between the fox and prairie dog. Prairie dogs are very destructive rodents! They travel two to six miles and infest an entire area. How do you protect neighbors [if one does have prairie dogs on his property]?

The older generation of landowners in the assembly remember long-fought efforts to exterminate prairie dogs from their land. Prairie dogs were perceived as competing directly with livestock for grazing, and posing serious danger to livestock that step in prairie dog burrows. Younger generations of landowners (many of whom have no direct experience with prairie dogs) expressed agreement with their elders' assertions about the harmful consequences of prairie dog colonies. Several members in the audience recalled their ancestors' efforts to rid their land of prairie dogs. One stated "Our land has been in the family over one hundred years. My granddad and his dad before that fought prairie dogs." These comments conveyed a certain collective self-definition, one in which landowners continue to define themselves as "settlers" of the Kansas Great Plains. Part of the collective self-definition today holds landowners as residents of a "wild" country, a country in need of "taming," a view widely articulated in historical documents among white settlers of the Kansas frontier (Fleharty 1994).

Landowners expressed disbelief in the introductory information that outlined the potential beneficial effects of prairie dog colonies under some conditions. Some research suggests that in areas where woody type forage and forbs exist, the prairie dog's grazing of this vegetation actually improves the growing conditions for grasses that livestock (primarily cattle) eat. In general, even those landowners who expressed some belief that this potential benefit is real, argued that overall costs of having prairie dogs would more than outweigh this possible benefit: "Even if they do make it better in some ways, it's not enough with the broken legs they cause [in livestock] and their big appetites." At one of the three sites, some emotionally charged dialogue did occur between landowners and members of environmental/wildlife organizations over the extent to which prairie dogs enhance/inhibit the grazing potential for. A wildlife preservationist maintained that, as the Extension Agent's presentation suggested,

there are some benefits for livestock grazing with prairie dog presence, to which several landowners responded that this benefit has
not been apparent on their land and that people who do not "run
cattle" should not jump to such conclusions. The Docking Institute
facilitator attempted to not invalidate either belief by insisting that
both viewpoints were important and would be carefully considered
by the KDWP.

Landowners also largely expressed disbelief in data that suggest
high levels of decline in prairie dog populations since the widespread
efforts in the late 1800s to reduce/exterminate prairie dogs in the
region. One landowner commented, "Tax dollars are being used for
research and to publicize this issue. Estimates should not be publi-
cized because they are just allegations. The decisions being made
are based on bad statistics." Some landowners argued that prairie
dog numbers and extent of spatial coverage of colonies was never
as high as estimated prior to white settlement of the area, and others
argued that the declines were not as serious as estimated.

Some landowners found the presentation on petitioning and listing status by the USFWS representative and the presentation by the
KDWP representative confusing, and thus, an attempt to "snow"
landowners with technical jargon. In a frustrated tone, a landowner
asked "What is extirpate? Just say exterminate if that's what you
mean!" A representative of the KDWP explained that extirpate means
that a population of a species no longer inhabits a region, but this
does not mean the species is entirely wiped out of existence. Some
frustration and/or distrust between stakeholder groups stemming from
the different languages used by the groups is not unusual. This is a
common finding in research on social response to expert presentations on locally unwanted land use issues in particular, as an organizational construction of reality with its accompanying symbols meets
and clashes with the social construction of reality held by individuals and groups who are not part of the organizational culture (see
Edelstein 1988 and Easterling and Kunreuther 1995).

Comments from wildlife preservationists were infrequent, and normally met, as noted above, with quick rebuttals from the landowner
faction. Nevertheless, it was apparent from the meetings that preservationists, to their dismay, perceived a continued decline of prairie
dogs. They voiced concern not only about prairie dog decline, but
also other species, particularly the burrowing owl and the black-
footed ferret; preservationists argued that loss of the prairie dogs

would result in harm to the "environment" and "ecosystem" in a ripple effect. A landowner's response at one of the meetings to the wildlife preservationists' appeals to protect the environment and ecosystem was telling in terms of the way landowners often define themselves when it is implied that any of their behavior may have some negative environmental influence. The landowner argued, "You need to understand, a rancher has to be an environmentalist and a conservationist . . . I'm an *active environmentalist*—not an *environmental activist!*"

During one meeting the facilitator pointed out to the audience, as a response to numerous assertions that a state agency (KDWP) should not be in the business of promoting a "pest," that the state is attempting to prevent the species listing by the USFWS, and thus, keep some control over the issue at a state level, an action which may be more beneficial to landowners' continued ability to use and experience the full potential of their property than federal control. At another meeting, it was a landowner who made the same point, stating "If we come up with a state plan now, we maintain more options for landowners." Audience members' responses to this point moved the crowd in a more productive direction, with respect to the KDWP's goal of formulating a conservation plan.

One landowner stressed that the prairie dog work group must involve members of the agricultural (landowner) interests in the state. Another pointed out the importance of considering the federal policy environment in which farmers make decisions. He asserted that farmers operate under an umbrella of federal policies and proclamations, mentioning the vacillating federal recommendations regarding farming practices. For example, in the late 1930s there was a strong push for land conservation, including re-grassing cropland. But in the 1970s, the federal government urged farmers to plant "fence row to fence row." Insofar as farmers act on these federal recommendations, it contributes to instability in prairie dog habitat. Another person noted that perhaps federal policies regarding the Conservation Reserve Program (CRP) should be reevaluated to allow landowners to plant short grasses, instead of the tall grasses that are currently promoted under this federal program. Finally, a member of the audience cautioned that the current publicity on the present meetings and the initiative to formulate a conservation plan in general, may be prompting a backlash effect on conservation of the species. "I have to decide whether I should keep five acres of prairie dogs on my land, given the possibility of them being Endangered someday." He believed that some landowners were already beginning to step up extermination efforts on their land in anticipation of a possible federal listing—if the species becomes listed and is present on one's land, he/she will be subject to federal Threatened or Endangered Species regulations! The individual urged that an education campaign begin immediately to preempt efforts at extermination.

Landowners perceived the species and its accompanying management as a direct threat to the "bottom line" of their operations. Several farmers expressed the belief that management should involve compensation to landowners for the perceived loss of productivity. One summarized the position when he argued, "We need to figure out who is going to pay [for the production losses]. Maybe it should be the Wildlife Federation (one of the petitioners advocating listing). We need to be compensated if we are going to be required to have them."

As noted above, an open invitation was extended at the public meetings, inviting any interested person to be a part of the prairie dog work group. In addition, the KDWP contacted identifiable formal stakeholder groups, requesting work group representation from each of their groups. The first meeting of the work group convened in May 2000 in an all day meeting. KDWP contracted the Docking Institute of Public Affairs as neutral party to facilitate the discussions.[2] The stakeholder groups represented in the working group include the Kansas Farm Bureau, Kansas Livestock Association, Kansas Grazing Land Coalition, Rangeland Association, Kansas Biological Survey, Kansas Chapter of the Wildlife Society, Kansas Wildlife Federation, Kansas Mammal Society, Kansas Audubon, Nature Conservancy, KDWP, US Forest Service, Kansas State University Extension Service, Kansas Department of Agriculture Pesticide Use Section and three non-organizational affiliated landowners.

The work group was charged with developing a conservation plan under a fairly ambitious timeline. With a fall 2001 deadline for submitting the conservation plan, the work group had slightly less than a year to author the plan. In the first meeting of the work group, the Docking Institute facilitators charged the group with working together in an open forum, where questions and concerns could be aired and discussed thoroughly. Facilitators introduced a structure to the process that is common in planning. Goal formation and specification of objectives was the first step. It was then the task of the group to devise strategies to meet the objectives.

Introductions and preliminary statements from each task force member on what he/she hoped the group would accomplish were first solicited. This type of communication allowed group members an initial glimpse at interests and concerns of others in the group, constructions of reality being used by others. Group members began to understand others' definitions of reality, and could begin to compare others' constructions with their own. A good deal of the first part of the day involved airing of concerns and initial responses from others.

At this point in the work group process, members constituted less of a group, than a congregation of people representing diverse stakeholder factions: the landowner faction, the wildlife preservation faction and management agency personnel. Facilitators attempted to engage all members of the group in discussion, and allow every individual adequate time to articulate concerns and assertions, pose questions and field responses. In this early stage of work group formation, facilitators attempted to create a working environment where each member felt his/her input was both necessary and valid, and its members were instructed to seriously consider others' viewpoints (i.e., definitions of reality). Facilitators recorded comments on flip charts, and strove to ensure that each person had equal time for comment by systematically inviting comment from every person in attendance.

Just as aboriginal people and park rangers in Australia attach different meanings to fire, owing to the cultural constructions of reality held by each group (Greider and Garkovich 1994), the landowner faction, wildlife preservation faction and the state wildlife management agency each attached different meanings to the prairie dog. Embedded in these various social constructions was each group's own collective self-definition in relation to the prairie dog. Each type of group member asserted perceived characteristics of the prairie dog and its relation to other animals and people. In addition, each type of group member aired concerns over the effects on prairie dogs and other animals and/or humans if prairie dog numbers were to decline or increase.

During the initial work group sessions, comment from the landowner faction echoed comment recorded in the public meetings, namely, that prairie dogs are competitors and hazards. In addition however, it was stressed by the landowner faction that perhaps the most difficult task in implementing a successful conservation plan would be achieving landowner "buy-in." It was stressed that landowners would essentially view attempts by state or federal management agencies at preserving prairie dogs as a potential "taking" of land (i.e., diminishing the use and monetary value of the land for agricultural purposes). One landowner commented, "A farmer reduces the value of his property when he consents to have a prairie dog colony on his land!" Thus, he noted, the plan should endeavor to acknowledge this, and consider remuneration for costs associated with prairie dog presence. Not all in the wildlife preservation faction agreed with the detrimental effects of prairie dogs on agricultural operation profitability. Some members of this faction cited the data presented by the Kansas State University Extension specialist at the public meetings that suggested potential grazing enhancement in the presence of prairie dog colonies under some conditions. However, in fairly short order the environmental faction seemed to conclude that it would be unrealistic to believe that landowners would incorporate this notion into their own view of reality any time soon, and thus, to achieve a management strategy that could be implemented, the landowner faction's insistence on the inclusion of incentives to allow prairie dogs would be a necessary component of the conservation plan.

The wildlife preservation faction highlighted the apparent declines in the species across its historical range, and they argued that loss of this species has important implications for other species. An ecosystem frame of reality was invoked by this faction, who defined the prairie dog as near to, if not clearly, a "keystone" species, that is, a species ". . . whose very presence contributes to a diversity of life and whose extinction would consequently lead to the extinction of other forms of life" (Save the Prairie Dogs 2003). According to this faction, species depending upon the prairie dog and its activities such as the black-footed ferret and the burrowing owl have also experienced declines. The former is currently listed as Endangered, and the latter has the real potential to become listed if the prairie dog is one day listed according to this faction. Also, members of this faction intimated concern over the unforeseeable additional effects that extermination of prairie dogs would have on the ecosystem. Landowners also indicated a concern that extermination and/or continued decline in the prairie dog population could potentially lead to a listing of associated species, and thus, constitute another threat to landowners' options. Thus, while the wildlife preservation and landowner factions both voiced concern about prairie dog decline, it was for very different reasons. Still, common ground in terms of management goals was apparent. At minimum, opposing factions within the work group found their own reasons for initially agreeing that prairie dog *extinction* is undesirable.

State management agency personnel cited the importance of both protecting wildlife and being responsive to socioeconomic structures that are affected by the prairie dog and policy to conserve the species. To the state management agency, the prairie dog represents another element of the ecosystem to be managed for the broader public good. The management agency and extension agent representatives highlighted the shortcomings of and controversy surrounding the extant methods used to estimate the population of the species. This faction strongly suggested that additional counting would have to take place in order to finalize the conservation plan that stands a real chance of acceptance by the USFWS as a serious attempt to conserve the species. At the federal level, the USFWS personnel re-iterated comments made during the public meetings, that is, agency mandate requires them to act to protect a species when sufficient evidence shows petitioner concern is warranted.

A crucial issue for determining appropriate action steps in the plan is the efficacy of prairie dog control methods. A member of the work group was a long time prairie dog exterminator for a western Kansas county. His experiences provided the group with grounded, working knowledge of the most effective and ineffective control methods. He, along with the extension agent, discussed the various methods of control, focusing on cost and efficacy of the methods. Toward formulating a management strategy, it was important for the group to develop this working definition of control and the various control options.

Another major area for exploration established by the work group was the legal context in which the species is located. The rights and responsibilities of private landowners with regard to prairie dog populations was a key issue among work group members in establishing the conservation plan. Discussion centered on the issue of protecting one property owner from prairie dogs on another's property. Realizing that prairie dogs do not recognize legal boundaries, and instead, tend to expand colonies where habitat is favorable, the group felt it imperative to protect the property owner who does not want prairie dogs, in addition to the property owner who wants prairie dogs. The group was cognizant of the high emotions that prevailed when asserting the right to have prairie dogs and when asserting the right to rid one's land of what state legislation, at least in spirit, considers an agricultural pest. Representatives of agricultural interests in the group strongly cautioned that perhaps the most crucial aspect of the conservation plan for increasing landowner buy-in was including assurances to landowners that the conservation plan would not preclude control of the prairie dog. However, this assurance alone, they cautioned, would probably not be sufficient. In addition, the offended landowner (the one who does not want prairie dogs, but onto whose land prairie dogs may spread) will not want to incur the cost of controlling the species. At present, Kansas statutes allow counties local control over prairie dogs. The legislation allows for "eradication" and some counties have used local taxes to support a part-time control agent. The KDWP classifies the species as "wildlife," and currently allows an open season for the species (meaning that they can be taken at any time of the year under specified means).

The group also determined the need for more solid data on a number of different questions that could influence the steps taken in the conservation plan. During the first meeting all factions concluded that more data on population and extent of colony coverage in its historical range (sixty-eight counties of western Kansas) needed to be collected. Discussion of aerial surveys, satellite imagery and ground truthing (visiting a site in-person) concluded that, at present, satellite imagery is not quite developed enough to be of use but soon will be, and a combination of aerial and ground truthing surveys should be used. During the first two work group meetings there was also a large push from all factions to further study the interaction of prairie dogs with livestock in terms of how the two together effect habitat. However, it was agreed by all groups that the most important data to collect was that necessary for answering key management questions about present location of colonies, size of colonies and overall presence of prairie dogs in the state.

The work group decided that sub group task forces could most effectively outline strategies for revision of legislation and data collection. Composition of the task forces was defined based on areas of expertise that members brought to the group, with members of each faction (landowner, wildlife preservation, and management agency members) represented on each task force. Dispersing faction members among smaller task forces appears to have had the effect of reducing in-group—out-group boundaries, as members of the landowner faction, for example, began to collaborate with diverse others on the respective task forces. These task forces were charged with immediately going to work on questions the entire group had formulated. While observation of all task force meetings was not possible, task forces reported back to the larger work group on recommendations without dissent from task force members.

The work group formulated a conservation plan goal, value statement and objectives through the first two meetings of the work group. Taken from the draft conservation plan (Roy 2000), these were articulated as follows:

Goal:
The Goal of the Plan is to maintain biologically viable populations of black-tailed prairie dogs across the historical range in Kansas. Seven objectives were determined to be necessary to achieve this goal.

Statement:
The [Kansas Prairie Dog Work Group] recognizes prairie dogs and their habitat as valuable, important, and desired components of the landscape, while also recognizing the economic and political realities that control of the species will be necessary in many instances. Possible eradication may also be necessary in some instances.

Objectives:
• Establish a Statewide Prairie Dog Working Group
• Determine and monitor species distribution and status
• Establish regulatory protection
• Identify, maintain, and promote existing and additional suitable prairie dog habitats
• Education and Outreach
• Identify, prioritize, and implement research needs

The entire work group has now met a total of four times since that initial meeting in May of 2000. The only meeting in which the first author was not present was the third. The conservation plan goal, value statement and objectives have not changed. The task forces seem to have worked well in accomplishing their individual goals. KDWP personnel present at the third meeting did mention heightened tensions at this meeting when it looked as though the USFWS was going to require a formula for number of inhabited acres that would have resulted in the requirement of 350,000 acres in colonies as part of the conservation goal for Kansas. However, a recent meeting of the Interstate Prairie Dog Work Group (which some Kansas working group members attended) established a different criterion for extent of prairie dog, with the "nod" of USFWS personnel in attendance. The ten-year conservation goals for the eleven-state range and each state would be as follows:

- Maintain current acreage in colonies as surveyed
- Manage for at least eleven complexes with greater than 5,000 acres range wide among the eleven states and have at least 15,000 acre colony per state
- Manage for ten percent of total acreage in complexes greater than 1,000 acres
- Eighty percent of historical counties need at least one colony
- Meet or exceed one percent actual acres and value added acres (resulting in a goal for Kansas of 105,000 acres in colonies)

This newly revised goal, with a bottom line of about 105,000 acres in colonies for Kansas, was presented at the opening of the fourth work group meeting. It proved much more palatable for the landowner faction, who had significant reservation about whether the previously discussed 350,000 could realistically (in the politico-legal context of Kansas) be reached. One hundred five thousand acres in colonies appeared even more acceptable, when the data task force revealed that recent aerial surveys suggested that the number of acres in occupied prairie dog colonies now may be close to 105,000 acres in Kansas. The greater acceptance among landowners of a targeted 105,000 acres of prairie dog colony occupation versus 350,000 acres is not surprising, given that this level of prairie dog colonization can more easily be incorporated into their cultural definition of nature—the prairie dogs can be "kept in check."

The KDWP coordinator of the work group and conservation plan effort believes that the presence of the interstate work group has actually been quite helpful in the relatively smooth flowing interaction and decision-making among the Kansas work group. She maintains that it has helped to have "the interstate group formulating proposals and making recommendations [as it] helps direct the group and shows how other states are also doing the same thing" (Roy, personal communication).

At the most recent meeting the group slightly revised and approved the legal task force's proposed revisions to Kansas statute regarding prairie dog control. The KDWP and the Kansas Department of Agriculture jointly sponsored a bill introduced in Agricultural Committee of the Kansas House of Representatives during the 2003 legislative session. The bill did not come out of committee this year, as the chair believed sufficient support among the legislature did not exist this year. However, the Chair of the Committee indicates that he will support the bill again next year, and believes its success is more likely with the additional time for educating the legislature on its importance (Johnson 2003). The bill amends Kansas statute to include provisions to protect both the person who wants prairie dogs on his/her land, and the person who experiences prairie dog colonization encroaching from adjacent land. The onus to pay for control of the offending prairie dogs will not be changed from its current status in Kansas, namely, counties still have the option to use tax fees to control the species on property where it is unwanted.

The Interstate prairie dog work group will be lobbying federal agencies to consider changing the federal Conservation Reserve Program, which has resulted in thousands of cultivated acres being turned back to grassland. At present, CRP requires tall grass varieties be planted on CRP enrolled land. Tall grass prairie is poor habitat for prairie dogs, and thus, changes in CRP policy to allow planting of short grass species, such as "Buffalo" grass and "Blue Grama" grass are being sought. In addition, discussion of providing direct monetary incentive to landowners for allowing a certain number of acres to be occupied by prairie dogs is ongoing. In a world of limited resources, such incentives might be targeted toward areas that are falling short on meeting one or more of the inhabitation objectives mentioned above.

Finally, the work group is now preparing strategies to convey the importance of accepting the conservation plan. Some of the strategies include informational articles in regular newsletters and at regular meetings of formal groups represented among both the wildlife preservation and the landowner factions. Landowner factions in the group are particularly aware of the difficulty in achieving massive buy-in from landowners in general. This is why this faction has so heavily promoted the idea of, at minimum, preventing any cost associated with the presence of prairie dogs from being incurred by those who do not want the species. This faction would like to see monetary incentives in place, as they believe the cultural attitudes are strongly unfavorable toward the prairie dog. A monetary incentive is, undoubtedly, the only way many would voluntarily consider allowing the species to exist on their land. The landowner faction developed a sense of ownership of the conservation plan. They feel that, owing to their efforts, the plan does adequately address these concerns, and that is why members of the landowner group are committed to using their respective landowner organizations to promote the conservation plan. The landowner faction, through two of its formal organizations (the Kansas Farm Bureau and the Kansas Livestock Association) held public information and comment sessions throughout the western part of the state in 2001, explaining the conservation plan and providing question and answer opportunities. This is particularly significant in light of the confrontational stance toward the Nebraska draft conservation plan taken by the Nebraska Farm Bureau and the Nebraska Cattlemen's Association as recently as August 2001, who argue that no plan should be implemented as "... scientific data needs to be gathered first to determine if black-tailed prairie dogs are indeed endangered in Nebraska" (Associated Press 2001).

Wildlife Conflict Management Tenets and Recommendations

Both conceptual discussion regarding the interplay between social constructions of reality on a controversial policy issue and use of a transactional management approach and the observations from the interaction processes in the prairie dog meetings and work group described above informs our formulation of some management observations and recommendations. We hope to clearly articulate some observations that may be thought of as preliminary tenets of a social constructionist perspective on wildlife management. These are discussed below. Further, recommendations for carrying out wildlife management given these social constructionist observations and the use of a transactional management approach are offered.

Conflict Management Tenets

Around any wildlife issue, there will be multiple viewpoints about what is important or what ought to be done, and each of these viewpoints will be valid in its own right. A pluralistic approach is often the best for achieving policy that works. This tenet is implied in a transactional management approach as the various stakeholders on an issue are actually involved in managing the issue. It is imperative that ways be found to honor the range of values and views represented among stakeholders.

People will hold to their attitudes and views toward wildlife quite strongly, and will be involved in social groups that tend to reinforce those beliefs. It was apparent from the beginning of the public meetings surrounding the prairie dog issue that different constructions of reality were being invoked, with at least three different constructions based along lines of landowners, wildlife management and wildlife preservation groups. In the work group setting, these opposing social groups were able to relate views (constructions) of the prairie dog to out-group members, and they were able to find enough agreement on central management issues that a new group reality was formed. A question that remains to be answered is whether members of the work group will retain and promote this new reality in interaction with the original social groups they represented at the planning process.

Some of the important social/ideological viewpoints will be organized into formal "interest groups," yet others may not. The most effective planning process cannot merely involve the formally designated groups (Friends of Wildlife, Livestock Association, etc.) because not all of the individuals of informal groups will necessarily feel that their interests are adequately represented by the formal policy players or feel that they are in some way bound to adhere to an agreement that a formal policy actor made in their absence. Unfortunately, there was relatively little participation in the work group by individuals representing only themselves or an informal group. While an open invitation was extended at the public meetings, there was no consistent participation by individuals not affiliated with formal groups. It is important to note, however, that landowners were represented at the table by members who themselves are agricultural producers, and thus, are not disconnected from the everyday work experiences of farmers and ranchers.

Science-based knowledge is not solely preferable, nor is length of tenure ("my family has been here four generations") the only route to wisdom. Different groups will invoke different standards of validity and notions of standing. It is not uncommon for the different groups to explicitly or implicitly assert in the work groups setting that their respective constructions are the truths. The facilitator can model for the work group a respect for the viewpoint, while remaining neutral with regard to its truth-value. One can employ phrases that indicate interest but neutrality, such as "that is interesting and there may be some other ways to look at it as well," "thank you for that viewpoint," or "that helps us all of us better understand your impressions." Faction members should feel as though they are being heard, and that their viewpoint will be given *equitable* weight in the work group's discussions. Toward the formulation of the management plan, the facilitator must impress upon the work group members that both scientific research is important and grounded knowledge is important. When participants perceive that the latter is not valued, full participation in the management of knotty issues is thwarted.

Conflict Management Recommendations

Focus on the emergence of new values, rather than a debate over which of the existing value sets is preferable. Focus on mutual learning among the various stakeholders about the different attitudes and beliefs. Emphasizing adequate dialogue before entering into deliberation offers to the various social groups involved an opportunity to be heard, and more importantly, an opportunity to more fully understand the constructions of others at the table. This dialogue should be facilitated in such a way as to allow equal time for articulation of views and systematic clarification of each group's respective language (symbols) for conceptualizing the issue. Indeed, much of the work group's first day was dedicated to presenting viewpoints and simply clarifying the meaning of terms and phrases used by the factions involved.

Do not debate the relative superiority of the stakeholders' current views, but do not merely try to blend attributes drawn from the existing values. To do so would be unlikely to produce satisfying results. Instead, use processes that emphasize creativity, innovation, and thinking outside of the box. This may require a switch in mind-set away from defining "the problem" and recognizing that this is a situation *with lots of different problematic aspects*, depending upon how one chooses to view it. Once faction members were exposed to dilemmas in resolving concerns that they raised, and once they realized that no faction involved in the work group held answers for all concerns and dilemmas regarding the prairie dog issue, it helped in convincing members that laying all possibilities on the table from each respective worldview provided the best array of information from which to draw toward formulating a conservation plan that was socially and ecologically efficacious.

Use a fractionation/partial solution approach. Move forward on those issues for which there is agreement on a course of action, while holding more long term/complex issues in abeyance. Do not hold the prospects for *any* progress hostage by longing for a more global agreement. It soon became apparent to the work group that each faction agreed on three issues: the need for more scientific data collection on prairie dog prevalence and its geospatial distribution, needed changes in state statute on the species and some sort of educational campaign to inform stakeholders of the management initiatives and their implications. The details in working through those issues, including understanding each faction's construction of reality occupied the majority of the work group's efforts. Issues that were raised but on which no consensus toward action looked hopeful, barring extensive effort and debate, were set aside. For example, the issue of landowners' right to have or not have prairie dogs and the issue of ecological rights of the species were both raised during a work group session. It was readily apparent that the various factions involved held values that precluded them from achieving some agreement on these issues. Instead, it was stressed that these issues need not be resolved in order to achieve a conservation plan for the species. Rather, more pertinent concerns related to these two intractable issues should be addressed in authoring the management plan such as preserving as much freedom of action as possible on the part of landowners (including as much protection from potentially negative prairie dog effects) and aspects of the USFWS federal mandates with regard to species protection that would influence the conservation plan, respectively.

Be cognizant of the potential reluctance of non-participants to accept an agreement. A working group that participates in a long negotiation or mediated decision process can develop some strong bonds and a shared construction of reality that non-participants do not experience. There have been numerous cases in environmental negotiation when the designated representatives came to an agreement that they could not then get their constituents to agree to; the wildlife preservations' representative was challenged for not being faithful to the cause while the commodity-producers' representative was criticized for being "too green." Time will tell how effectively members of the work group are able to convey the newly negotiated reality on prairie dog management to their respective social groups.

Conclusion

The Kansas prairie dog work group now represents an entity that feels ownership in the emerging conservation plan. The faction that represented the staunchest opposition to any protection of prairie dogs is now publicly endorsing strategies that were developed through collaboration with other factions in a work group setting and that will likely appear in the final conservation plan. As is the goal in strategic planning (Blakely 1989), the goal of bringing diverse, often opposing stakeholders together to formulate and pursue a strategy that represents a best case compromise seems to have been met. The learning of others' definitions of reality and the common pursuance of a goal in a forum where multiple stakeholders are present has also been referred to as social or collaborative learning (Endter-Wada et al. 1998). As individuals representing entities who often engage in what Sherif (1956) describes as in-group—out-group conflict begin to understand each other's definition of reality and work with each other toward a mutually desired solution, the individuals seem to have taken on a mutual in-group identity, as a group of people working on a very difficult ecological and social issue to maintain as much local control as possible. A new in-group created of people who were formerly members of out-groups in relation to each other has emerged. This in-group holds a view of reality unique and different than the constructions of reality initially brought to the table by members representing three groups often at odds with one another: landowners, wildlife management agencies and wildlife preservationists.

Furthermore, this transactional management approach has been inclusive of organizations that could have thwarted the success of the conservation plan had they not been included in authorship of the plan. Thus, a nontrivial outcome of the transactional management approach that has been employed in authoring the prairie dog conservation plan is, it is hoped, the avoidance of something similar to Habermas's (1987) concept of a "legitimation crisis," where the broader stakeholder populations lose confidence in the management agency. To the extent that work group members each feel a sense of ownership toward the conservation plan and feel a sense of commitment to diverse others in the work group, each member will be more likely to diligently sell the conservation plan to the constituency they represented in the Kansas prairie dog work group planning process.

References

Associated Press. 2001. "Prairie Dog Protection Under Attack." *Hays Daily News*, August 24, pp. A12.

Berger, Peter and Thomas Luckmann. 1966. *The Social Construction of Reality*. Garden City, New York: Doubleday.

Blakely, Edward. 1989. *Planning Local Economic Development: Theory and Practice*. Newbury Park, CA: Sage Publications.

Chase, Lisa C., Tania M. Schusler, and Daniel J. Decker. 2000. "Innovations in Stakeholder Involvement: What's the Next Step." *Wildlife Society Bulletin* 28(1):208–217.

Daniels, Steven E. and Gregg B. Walker. 2001. *Working Through Environmental Conflict: The Collaborative Learning Approach*. Westport, Connecticut: Praeger Publishers.

Easterling, Douglas and Howard Kunreuther. 1995. *The Dilemma of Siting a High-Level Nuclear Waste Repository*. Norwell, MA: Kluwer Academic Publishers.

Edelstein, Michael R. 1988. *Contaminated Communities: The Social and Psychological Impacts of Residential Toxic Exposure*. Boulder, Colorado: Westview Press.

Endter-Wada, Joanna, Dale Blahna, Richard Krannich, and Mark Brunson. 1998. "A Framework for Understanding Social Science Contributions to Ecosystem Management." *Ecological Applications* 8(3):891–904.

Fleharty, Eugene. 1994. *Wild Animals and Settlers on the Great Plains*. Norman, OK: University of Oklahoma Press.

Greider, Thomas and Lorraine Garkovich. 1994. "Landscapes: The Social Construction of Nature and the Environment." *Rural Sociology* 59(4):1–21.

Habermas, Jurgen. 1987. *The Theory of Communicative Action, Vol. 2. Lifeworld and System: A Critique of Functionalist Reason*. Trans. by Thomas McCarthy. Boston: Beacon Press.

Hall, E.R. 1981. *The Mammals of North America*, Vol. 1. New York: John Wiley & Sons.

Heberlein, Thomas A. 1976. "Some Observations on Alternative Mechanisms for Public Involvement: The Hearing, Public Opinion Poll, the Workshop and the Quasi-Experiment." *Natural Resources Journal* 16:197–214.

Johnson, Dan. 2003. Comments during legislator discussion forum hosted by author and broadcast on KOOD, Smoky Hills Public Television, April 11.

Roy, Christiane. 2000. *Kansas Prairie Dog Working Group Conservation Plan—Working Draft*. Emporia, KS: Kansas Department of Wildlife and Parks.

Save the Prairie Dogs. 2003. "Keystone Species: Why Prairie Dogs Are So Important." Retrieved June 15, 2003 (http://www.prairiedogs.org/keystone.html).

Sherif, Muzafer. 1956. "Experiments in Group Conflict." *Scientific American* 195:54–58.

Walker, Gregg B. and Steven E. Daniels. 1994. "Public Deliberation and Public Land Management: Collaborative Learning and the Oregon Dunes." Paper presented at the annual meetings of the Speech Communication Association, New Orleans, LA.

Notes

[1] The Docking Institute of Public Affairs is a Fort Hays State University based non-profit research and planning organization in Hays, Kansas. The first author is Director of the Institute.

[2] The first author was one of two Docking Institute of Public Affairs representatives who facilitated both the first and second meetings of the work group.

LIST OF CONTRIBUTORS

VÉRONIQUE CAMPION-VINCENT is a folklorist at the Maison des Sciences de l'Homme, Paris, France, and approaches rumors and contemporary legends as sociological and anthropological facts. On the subject of rumors of animal-release and social reactions to the return of predators, she has edited a collective book *Des fauves dans nos campagnes. Légendes, rumeurs et apparitions* [Beasts in our lands. Legends, rumors and apparitions] (1992), authored two research reports for the Environment Department (1990, 1994), co-directed a special issue of *Monde Alpin et Rhodanien* (2002) and published two English articles in *Fabula* (1990) and *Folklore* (1992). She has also studied organ theft narratives, rumors and contemporary legend, publishing three books and several articles and book chapters.

STELLA M. ČAPEK is Professor of Sociology in the Department of Sociology/Anthropology at Hendrix College. She has a B.A. from Boston University and an M.A. and Ph.D. in Sociology (1985) from the University of Texas at Austin. She teaches courses on environmental sociology, social change/social movements, medical sociology, urban/community sociology, images of the city, gender and family, and sociological theory. She is especially interested in interdisciplinary environmental studies and social justice issues, including community design. She has published articles on environmental justice, tenants' rights, urban/community issues and health social movements. She has co-authored two books, *Community Versus Commodity: Tenants and the American City* (SUNY Press, 1992) and *Come Lovely and Soothing Death: The Right To Die Movement in the United States* (Twayne, 1999).

PAUL COLOMY earned his Ph.D. in sociology from the University of California, Los Angeles in 1982. His research focuses on institutional change, juvenile justice, law and social theory. He has published in *Social Problems, Sociological Theory, Sociological Forum, Sociological Perspectives,* and *Symbolic Interaction.* He is currently Professor and Chair of Sociology and Criminology at the University of Denver.

STEVE DANIELS is the Director of the Western Rural Development Center (since 1999) at Utah State University and a professor in the

Department of Sociology, Social Work, and Anthropology and in the Department of Forest Resources. Prior to that he had been on the faculty of Oregon State University as a professor of forest policy and economics. Much of Dr. Daniels' professional interests focus on collaborative processes in natural resource management. He has been involved in a number of community-level collaborations, primarily in the Pacific Northwest. With Dr. Gregg Walker of OSU, he is a co-author of *Working Through Environmental Conflict: The Collaborative Learning Approach* (Praeger Publishers, 2001). Except for some years living in North Carolina while Steve earned his graduate degrees at Duke University (1986), he has always lived in the northern Rocky Mountains and the Pacific Northwest.

LAWRENCE FELT holds undergraduate degrees in biology and mathematics from Oberlin College as well as graduate degrees in fisheries ecology and sociology from Northwestern University (1971). He is the author of four books dealing with various aspects of community economic development and resource management including *Finding Our Sea Legs: Linking Fisheries People and Their Knowledge with Science and Management* (with B. Neis, ISER Press, 2000) and *The North Atlantic Fishery: Challenges and Opportunities* (with R. Arnason, Institute of Island Studies Press, 1995). In addition he is the author or co-author of over sixty professional articles and book chapters dealing with issues of resource management and economic development. He is currently Professor of Sociology at Memorial University in St. John's, Newfoundland, Canada.

THERESA L. GOEDEKE received her doctorate in May 2003 from the University of Missouri-Columbia, Department of Rural Sociology. She is presently a Research Associate at the Environmental Sciences Institute within the Florida A&M University. Her research focuses on social issues related to environmental science, policy and lawmaking, as well as the human dimensions of natural resources and wildlife. She has several publications to her credit including the book, *Anti-Environmentalism and Citizen Opposition to the Ozark Man and the Biosphere Reserve* (Edwin Mellen Press, 2000), which was co-authored with Dr. J. Sanford Rikoon of the University of Missouri-Columbia.

ROBERT GRANFIELD is currently associate professor of sociology at SUNY-Buffalo. He received his Ph.D. from Northeastern University in 1989, was a Keck post-doctoral fellow at Harvard Law School in 1993, and was a visiting scholar at Middlebury College in 1998. He is the author of over fifty scholarly articles and reviews and has published four books including *Making Elite Lawyers: Visions of Law at Harvard and Beyond* (Routledge Press, 1992) and *Coming Clean: Overcoming Addiction without Treatment* (New York University Press, 1999). In addition, Dr. Granfield was the 2001 recipient of the Distinguished Scholar Award at the University of Denver.

ANN HERDA-RAPP earned her Ph.D. in sociology from the University of Illinois at Urbana-Champaign in 1998 and joined the faculty at the University of Wisconsin-Marathon in Wausau that same year. Her research and teaching have focused on environmental sociology, gender, social problems and social movements. In addition to editing this book and contributing a co-authored chapter, her work has also been published in *Sociological Inquiry* (2003), *The Sociological Quarterly* (2000), and *Sociological Focus* (1998), and as a chapter in *Care Work: Gender, Labor and Welfare States* (Routledge Press, 2000).

RICHARD HUMMEL earned his Ph.D. in sociology at Indiana University in 1976. He has taught in the Department of Sociology and Anthropology at Eastern Illinois University, Charleston, Illinois since 1969. Dr. Hummel's research agenda has focused on the sociology of hunting and fishing as well as the target shooting sports in various cultures. He published a book resulting from his research in 1994 entitled *Hunting and Fishing for Sport: Commerce, Controversy, Popular Culture* (Popular Press, Bowling Green State University). His current research interests involved comparisons of Germanic and American systems of game wildlife management and their respective social constructions of sport hunting.

KAREN G. MAROTZ received her bachelor's degree from the University of Wisconsin, Madison in 2001, where she majored in Sociology and Scandinavian Studies. She is currently a graduate student in the sociology program at the State University of New York at Albany. Her specialties include race, ethnicity and demography. She is interested in the assimilation and incorporation of first and second generation immigrants in the United States.

CAROL D. MILLER grew up in Northern Wisconsin, where the deer population easily outnumbers people and where deer hunting is an integral part of social life. She received her B.S. from the University of Wisconsin-River Falls and M.A. and Ph.D. in sociology from the University of Arizona (1996). She is a member of the faculty at University of Wisconsin-La Crosse where she teaches Sociology of Gender, Rural and Urban Sociology and Comparative Sociology (Globalization) and conducts research on poverty patterns and globalization in Wisconsin and the cultural phenomenon of deer hunting.

RIK SCARCE earned his Ph.D. in sociology from Washington State University in 1995. Before joining the faculty at Skidmore College, he taught at Michigan State University and at Montana State University. Scarce is the author of *Fishy Business: Salmon, Biology, and the Social Construction of Nature* (Temple University Press, 2000) and *Eco-Warriors: Understanding the Radical Environmental Movement* (Noble Press, 1990). His latest book, *Outsider Looking Out: One View from America's Jails*, will be published by Alta Mira Press. Scarce has authored or co-authored papers and book chapters on the social construction of nature, the international environmental movement, environmental attitudes, environmental futures, teaching methods, electronic democracy, and research ethics.

BRETT ZOLLINGER is a faculty member in the Department of Sociology and Director of the Docking Institute of Public Affairs at Fort Hays State University. He teaches Sociological Theory, Applied Sociology, Methods of Social Research, Advanced Methods of Social Research, and Field and Survey. His primary research interests are in the areas of applied sociology, human dimensions of natural resources, and social change and rural development in the Great Plains. He has published in *Rural Sociology*, *Journal of the Community Development Society*, *Research in Community Sociology*, and *Economic Development Quarterly*. He received his bachelor's degree (1992) in sociology at Northwestern Oklahoma State University and both his Master's degree (1994) and doctorate (1998) in sociology at Utah State University.

INDEX